Journeys in Church History
Volume 2

Journeys in Church History

Essays from the *Catholic Historical Review*
Volume 2

Edited by Nelson H. Minnich

The Catholic University of America Press
Washington, DC

Introduction, essays, and selection Copyright © 2026
The Catholic University of America Press
All rights reserved

Cataloging-in-Publication Data is available from the Library of Congress

ISBN (paper): 978-0-8132-4011-4
ISBN (ebook): 978-0-8132-4012-1

Table of Contents

Introduction
    Nelson H. Minnich vii

An Accidental Scholar
    Averil Cameron 1

Recovering the Multiple Worlds of the Medieval Church:
    Thoughtful Lives, Inspired Critics, and Changing Narratives
    John Van Engen 29

On the Road to Italian Church History
    Paul F. Grendler 55

Reminiscences and Reflections
    Robert Bireley, SJ 77

Historian with a Double Major: The Church and Feminism
    Asunción Lavrin 101

Chalk and Cheese: Moving between Historical Cultures
    Hugh McLeod 123

A Story of Gifts: Becoming a Historian of American Catholicism
    Leslie Woodcock Tentler 147

Introduction

From its earliest days Christianity has been concerned with providing an account of the life of its founder and its providential growth: the synoptic Gospels, the Acts of the Apostles, the passions of the martyrs, the *Ecclesiastical History* of Eusebius Pamphilus of Caesaria (c. 260–339) all testify to this concern. In subsequent centuries the priest Paulus Orosius (c. 375–c. 420) wrote the *Seven Books of Histories* (c. 416) to demonstate that Christianity improved the human condition, while Bede the Venerable (c. 673–735), the patron saint of historians, traced the conversion of England to Roman Catholicism in his *Ecclesiastical History of the English Peoples* (c. 731). A collection of papal biographies from Peter to Stephan V (c. 885) known as the *Liber Pontificalis* (Pontifical Book), compiled to support papal claims to power, was brought up to date during the Renaissance by Bartolomeo Sacchi da Platina (1421–81) and revised by Onofrio Pavinio, OSA (1530–68). Hagiography has always been a popular form of history, whether the accounts of the matyrs, the lives of the fathers and mothers of the desert, or biographies of noted prelates. In the Middle Ages the Dominican Jacopo de Voragine (c. 1228–98) collected the lives of the major saints for his famous *Golden Legend of the Saints* (c. 1265), which was replete with stories of miracles. In the Renaissance humanist scholars such as Desiderius Erasmus of Rotterdam (ca. 1467–1536) strove to write histories based on facts. And in the early seventeenth century, the Jesuits Heribert Rosweyde (1569–1629) and Jean Bolland (1596–1665) began the scientific study of saints' lives with their *Acta sanctorum* (1643–), which is being carried on to this day by the Bollanist Society. During the Reformation, church history became a battleground, given the Catholic claim of the Holy Spirit preserving the institutional Church from error (Mt 16:18, 28:20; Jn 14:16–17, 16:13) and the Protestant assertion that there was always in the Church a group of true believers like themselves, even if very small. John Fox (1516–87) published in 1563 his *Actes and Monuments of these Latter and Perillous Days, Touching Matters of the Church*, in which he documented a series of martyrs from ancient times until his own who testified to the truth. In Germany the Centuriators of Magdaburg under the leadership of Mathias Vlasic (1520–74) argued the Protestant position in their *Ecclesiastica Historia, integram Ecclesiae Christi ideam congesta* (1559–74), which tried to show a continuity of Protestant teachings from the first to the thirteenth century. The Catholic Oratorian priest Cesare Baronio

(1538–1607) responded with his *Annales Ecclesisastici*, which debunked many legends while defending Catholic orthodoxy in twelve volumes full of documents and taking the story up to 1198. His fellow Oratorians Odorico Rinaldi (1594–1671), Giacomo Laderchi (1678–1738), and Augustin Theiner (1804–1874) brought the work up to their own times. A French Benedictine of the Congregation of St. Maur, Jean Mabillon (1632–1707), pioneered the field of diplomatics and produced nine volumes of lives of Benedictine saints (1668–1701). His Gallican contemporary Louis Ellies du Pin (1657–1719) beginning in 1686 published his fifty-eight volume *Nouvelle bibliothèque ecclésiastique*, in which he traced the development of church teachings. The scientific study of history in the nineteenth century produced on the Catholic side the *Geschichte der Päpste seit dem Ausgang des Mittelalters* (1886–1930) in sixteen volumes covering the years 1305–1799 by Ludwig von Pastor (1854–1928) and the collection of documents related to the Council of Trent, the *Concilium tridentinum* (1901–2001), in thirteen tomes edited by the Görres-Gesellschaft. Hubert Jedin (1900–80) provided a four-volume history of the council, *Geschichte des Konzils von Trient* (1949–75), that was devoid of the polemics of Paolo Sarpi (1552–1623) and Pietro Sforza Pallavicino (1607–67). Jedin left behind an autobiography that was edited by Konrad Repgen and published in 1985.[1]

The methodologies used in the study of the history of the Catholic Church have varied over time. Under the influence of theological concepts of the Church as a divinely instituted and providentially guided Bride of Christ, some historians sought to trace the mysterious action of God in the community of believers, preserving it from error, fostering its growth despite persecutions, and helping it create a better society. St. Augustine's *City of God* laid out a view of history as the unfolding of God's plan for humanity. Church history was thus seen as a theological discipline. While not denying a theological component in the discipline, scholars eventually saw the history of the Church as an independent branch of history to be practiced according to the scientific methods employed by secular historians—to recount "what actually happened" as stipulated by the father of modern professional history, Leopold von Ranke (1795–1886). To understand the past historians have used various tools borrowed from other disciplines: literature, law, political science, psychology, sociology, anthropology, geography, and so forth. Computers have allowed historians to

---

1. Hubert Jedin, *Lebensbericht: Mit einem Dokumentenanhang*, ed. Konrad Repgen, Veröffentlichungen der Kommission für Zeitgeschichte, Reihe A: Quellen, Bd. 35 (Matthias Grünewald-Verlag, 1985).

organize and analyze large bodies of data. The traditional hard work of sifting through masses of documents in archives to find the revealing text, to verify its authenticity, and to discern the presuppositions and multi-leveled message of its author still remains.

The following collection contains essays from contemporary scholars who study the Church across the centuries. Dame Avril Cameron focused her work on religion in the Byzantine Empire. John Van Engen has been interested in lay religion in the Middle Ages and has studied the rise of the Modern Devotion with its *Imitation of Christ* and experiments in communal religious life. Robert Bireley, SJ († 2018), specialized on Jesuit confessors to Catholic rulers during the Thirty Years War and laid out how both the Catholic and Protestant churches tried to adjust to a changing world in the early modern period. Asunción Lavrin has studied the role of women in the religious life of colonial Latin America. Hugh McLeod used sociological data to map how various Christian denominations fared in the industrialized world of modern Europe. And Leslie Tentler has traced the changes in American Catholicism, especially those related to the Second Vatican Council and the Church's teaching on women and sex. Each scholar shares the difficulties he or she encountered in doing their research and how their findings were initially received.

A previous collection of the intellectual autobiographies of six leading church historians published in 2015 was well received by seasoned scholars and those new to the field. Established historians enjoyed learning more about the people whose works they had read and whom they had seen at conferences over the years but never really gotten to know. Younger scholars learned how leaders in the field of church history got to be the way they were and why they investigated the problems they studied. May these beginners in the field draw inspiration from their elders' dedication to archival research, despite the difficulties they frequently encountered in doing this work.

Nelson H. Minnich

An Accidental Scholar

AVERIL CAMERON*

In this essay I reflect on my development as a scholar of late antiquity and Byzantium over many decades. I was a Classics undergraduate at Oxford in the late 1950s, and my subsequent history took me first to Glasgow, then to London as a professor and back to Oxford as the head of a college and a pro-vice-chancellor, with several stays in the United States along the way. I have been lucky enough to be able to follow my intellectual curiosity in numerous directions, but always as a historian, and especially as a historian curious about the history of religion.

Keywords: Oxford; late antiquity; Byzantium; orthodoxy; discourse

Our small terraced house in Leek, North Staffordshire, did not go in for books. We had a red one-volume encyclopaedia with a few color illustrations (I remember Raphael's Sistine Madonna), but the only history book I remember was *A Child's History of England* by Charles Dickens, a deeply Protestant narrative peopled by Good Queen Bess and Bloody Mary. I was sent by my parents to Sunday School at the local Church of England parish church, St Edward's, and later I used to play the piano there for hymns, and sometimes the organ at church. Like many of my generation I stopped going to church as a student, and it was the readings and music of the Christian year that stayed with me and left an abiding mark. But there was no church history in what we learned, and when much later I began to discover the actual history of early Christianity, it came as a revelation.

At my grammar school, a small local girls' high school with only three hundred pupils, I remember studying the Tudors, the French Revolution, and nineteenth-century British history, but history was not one of my choices for A levels, the final school examinations. Instead I took English literature, Latin, and Music, all three through the influence of their respective teachers. Music was taught as an academic subject, with set works that included Brahms' Fourth Symphony and *The Magic Flute*, and the teacher was also my piano teacher, and tried to persuade me to go to music college

---

* Averil Cameron retired in 2010 as Professor of Late Antique and Byzantine History and Warden of Keble College, University of Oxford.

1

like her. It was Muriel Telfer, the impressive head teacher, who came unannounced to our house and told my parents that I must go to university. My Latin teacher had been teaching me Greek during the lunch hour, and she also broadened my mind by lending me her own books; it was natural therefore to apply for Classics. No one from my family or my school had gone to Oxford, but the same teacher took me to a summer school in Greek led by John Pinsent of Liverpool University, and he told me I must go to Oxford and to Somerville College, so that is what I did. For all I knew about either, they might as well have been the moon.

In 1958 all Oxford colleges including Somerville were single sex, and women amounted only to a tiny proportion of the overall undergraduate body. The results of the entrance exam came by telegram, or rather, two telegrams, for I was offered a scholarship by Girton College, Cambridge as well as an exhibition by Somerville. An exhibition was less good than a scholarship, but influenced by John Pinsent's advice, I accepted it. I was entirely unaware of the uniqueness of the Oxford Classics course, officially called Literae Humaniores, but usually referred to as Greats. It was and is a four-year course, and it then consisted of five terms spent solely on classical languages and literature, followed by a tough set of exams known as Mods (Honour Moderations), after which ancient history and philosophy were studied together for seven more terms, with another tough set of examinations at the end. No concessions were made to those who like me had to catch up with the required standard of Greek. The male undergraduates who had come from public schools, that is, exclusive private boys' schools, were streaks ahead in their language skills and could often walk through Mods with virtually no extra work. Just as well I did not realise that at the time.

There were only four of us reading Classics at Somerville in my year, and the main mode of teaching was the weekly tutorial with two students and the tutor. We had to read all of Homer, all of Virgil, much of Cicero, and more, all in the original. Unseen translation was also important, and composition from English into Latin and Greek even more so. Literary critique of Latin and Greek texts played a far smaller part, and we were never given reading lists, as we were actively discouraged from reading secondary literature. Lectures (open to all students) were not compulsory and not always relevant; most assumed the high importance of textual criticism, and when they did cover our set texts, they were often peppered with disparaging references to earlier editors, or still worse, ignorant Byzantines. I was sent by my tutor to the seminar held by Eduard Fraenkel, the Professor of Latin, which was uncompromising in this regard and very frightening, but which I now see acted as a marriage bureau not only for myself and Alan

Averil Cameron
Malcolm Morgan Photographers, Hatch End, Middlesex.

Cameron but also for the classicists Martin and Stephanie West, and Jasper and Miriam Griffin. I recognised that Fraenkel was the real thing and spent much time poring over his commentary on the *Agamemnon* and his book on Horace. I also learned everything I knew about Greek metre from his metre class, during which he would give extraordinary one-man performances of choruses from *The Frogs* and other plays of Aristophanes. One of the reasons I became and have remained a fan of Horace's *Odes* was because of their use of the complex Greek lyric metres we learned from Fraenkel.

For examinations we had to dress in subfusc (academic gown, and for women, cap, black jacket and skirt, white blouse, black tie, and black stockings), and after Mods we divided our time between ancient history with Isobel Henderson and philosophy with Elizabeth Anscombe and Philippa Foot. Philosophy included large amounts of Plato and Aristotle in the original, but also moral philosophy and logic, or perhaps better, epistemology, including the later works of Wittgenstein (Elizabeth Anscombe had translated his *Philosophical Investigations* from the German and was also his literary executor). As before, the teaching consisted of weekly essays discussed in tutorials, now usually two a week. Ancient (i.e. Greek and Roman) history was divided into periods, with essays focusing on specific problems such as the nature of Athenian imperialism or the reforms of the Gracchi. No teaching was offered for the sole examination paper containing wider questions, and I never studied any Hellenistic history, or Roman history before the second century BC or after the reign of Nero. I had little conception of wider historical methodology as such. I could in theory have gone to the History lectures being given on other periods, but that was not presented as an option, and instead the lectures that I did attend and that made the biggest impact on me were those given by the art historian Edgar Wind in the Oxford Playhouse, in which he talked about Michelangelo's sculptures and Raphael's *School of Athens* (curiously a large copy of which hung in the upstairs drawing room in the Lodgings at Keble when I arrived there in 1994). But I became extremely good at the critical analysis of specific texts, including historical sources, and indeed at Greek and Latin.

There were few openings in ancient history in the UK the time, and for a woman in Oxford only if a fellow in ancient history in the few women's colleges were to retire. In any case I never imagined myself as an academic, and my impression is that many of my contemporaries at Somerville married after graduating and went into professions such as school teaching. I married Alan Cameron, a fellow Greats student and a very accomplished classicist, in the summer of 1962 after finals and went to live in Glasgow where he had taken up a lectureship in Latin (known there as Humanity). Somehow Glasgow University offered me a graduate scholarship of £400 a year to start a PhD, and I followed Alan in thinking that working on a later writer rather than a mainstream classical subject would be a good idea. Isobel Henderson suggested I consult the Byzantine historian Robert Browning, who was then a lecturer at University College London. He pointed me towards the late sixth-century Greek historian Agathias, and I started work on his *Histories*, drawing (in the then complete absence of any graduate classes or training) on my undergraduate experience of working on Thucydides and Herodotus. Henry Chalk was assigned to me as supervisor, as he had worked on the later Greek poet Nonnus, and he was kind, although we did not have a great deal to say to each other. Little had been written on Agathias's work, but Rudolf Keydell was working on the first critical edition, published in 1967, and I could find most of the relevant nineteenth-century dissertations in Glasgow's University library. Without distractions, I did much of the work within the first two years and finished it during 1964–65 in London when Alan moved to Bedford College in the University of London.

Being in Glasgow was a strong experience. Christian Fordyce, the Professor of Humanity, was a powerful figure in the University and lived with his wife in a large house with the address 2 The University, Glasgow. He had two collections, one of postmarks and the other of railway tickets, to which members of the department were expected to add when they could. As the wife of the newest lecturer I had a lowly status at Mrs Fordyce's tea parties and was positioned furthest from the fire, the only source of heating. Nor was Glasgow used to graduate students, especially female ones, as its best (male) classics graduates usually went on to Balliol with a Snell exhibition. But Classics at Glasgow was a lively environment, and there were visits to Edinburgh and meetings with classicists from other Scottish universities. We also got to know the Trossachs and the beautiful scenery near Glasgow, as well as the MacBrayne steamers that took us to the western isles and north to Oban and Fort William. I also had a role model close to home. Alan published his first articles in 1963, and the first of several major papers in the *Journal of Roman Studies* in the following year, when we also published our first joint article—an indication of the kind of conversations we were evidently having at home in our basement flat in Athole Gardens.[1] Agathias composed classicising Greek epigrams as well as history, and collected epigrams by his friends in his *Cycle*, which was later incorporated into the Greek Anthology; given the expertise in Greek verse which Alan had developed since his schooldays we wrote about this too.[2]

Places and people have been my greatest influences, and I was to spend more than thirty years in London, from 1964 until 1994. Once there I met Arnaldo Momigliano for the first time. Despite having given me a scholarship, Glasgow University declared that I could not submit my PhD in absentia, and I had to reregister as a student in London. Momigliano had already been in contact with Alan and now indicated that he would be interested in being my supervisor. My experience as a student of Momigliano was the same as that of Anthony Grafton and others; we did not talk much about Agathias, but I too came to share the loyalty of those

---

1. Alan Cameron, "The Roman Friends of Ammianus," *Journal of Roman Studies*, 54 (1964), 15–28; Alan and Averil Cameron, "Christianity and Tradition in the Historiography of the Late Empire," *Classical Quarterly*, 14 (1964), 316–28.
2. "The Cycle of Agathias," *Journal of Hellenic Studies*, 86 (1966), 6–25 (with Alan Cameron); "Further Thoughts on the Cycle of Agathias," *Journal of Hellenic Studies*, 87 (1967), 131 (with Alan Cameron); cf. also "Anth. Plan. 72: A Propaganda Poem from the Reign of Justin II," *Bulletin of the Institute of Classical Studies*, 13 (1966), 101–04 (with Alan Cameron); and Averil Cameron, "Erinna's Distaff," *Classical Quarterly*, n.s.19 (1969), 285–86. Alan's interest in the Greek Anthology and Greek epigrams (which also dated back to his schooldays) led to his books *Porphyrius the Charioteer* (Oxford, 1973) and *The Greek Anthology from Meleager to Planudes* (Oxford, 1993).

who attended the weekly seminars he gave at the Warburg Institute from 1967 onwards.[3] He and I would meet in the common room at University College, where he was always solicitous as to whether I was eating enough oranges or yoghourt. His conversation ranged from earlier scholarship unfamiliar to me to whatever historical problem he happened to be thinking about, and from there to personal impressions and observations. He was forthright in his opinions, and he wanted to know mine. Later there were regular letters from his London mansion flat in Hammersmith, where I visited him towards the end of his life, and blue airmail forms from Pisa or Chicago. He sent me to see Henry Chadwick in Oxford, though I was not sure at that stage what questions to ask him, and helped me to publish my two long articles on the Sasanians and the Merovingians and my first book with the Clarendon Press, as well as putting me in the way of an invitation to speak at the annual Byzantine symposium at Dumbarton Oaks in 1970, where I was the only woman and the youngest speaker by several decades.[4] I submitted the thesis in 1966, and my examiners were Momigliano himself and Peter Brown, who was then a fellow of All Souls, Oxford; this was my first meeting with him, in the year before the publication of his book on Augustine. The viva was held with just the three of us in a rather dismal classroom with old school desks and was more of a chat than an examination.

By then I had become an assistant lecturer in classics at King's College London, teaching classical languages and literature, but no ancient history and certainly nothing on the later Roman empire. In 1970, however, I was appointed as Reader in ancient history, succeeding the sole ancient historian, Howard Scullard, a gentle man who patiently endured the lack of appreciation for ancient history in the Classics Department. My teaching changed accordingly, and I now belonged to the History Department as well as Classics. I taught ancient history according to the University of London history syllabus, which meant long periods (until as late as AD 400 for Roman history, recently revised from AD 641) and lectures on political thought from Cicero to Augustine, with St. Paul and Eusebius

---

3. Anthony Grafton, "Arnaldo Momigliano: A Pupil's Notes," *The American Scholar*, 60.2 (1991), 235–41; and see Michael Crawford, "L'insegnamento di Arnaldo Momigliano in Gran Bretagna," in: Lellia Cracco Ruggini, ed., *Omaggio ad Arnaldo Momigliano. Storia e storiografia sul mondo antico* (Como, 1989), 27–41. See also Anthony Grafton, "Tell me a Story," *Tablet Magazine*, 1 September 2020; and Peter Brown's moving memoir, "Arnaldo Dante Momigliano, 1908–1987," *Proceedings of the British Academy*, 74 (1988), 405–42.

4. "Agathias on the Sassanians," *Dumbarton Oaks Papers*, 23–24 (1969), 1–150; "Agathias on the Early Merovingians," *Annali della Scuola Normale di Pisa*, II.37 (1968), 95–140; *Agathias* (Oxford, 1970).

1970 Byzantine Studies Symposium "Byzantium and Sasanian Iran" Group Photo: Back row (standing) from left to right: Professor Irfan Shahid, A.D.H. Bivar, Averil Cameron, Philip Grierson, Professor Andrew Alföldi, Richard Ettinghausen, Professor Elias J. Bickerman; Front center (seated): Professor Richard Frye. Dumbarton Oaks Research Library and Collection.

along the way. It was during the years that followed, and especially through having to teach the Roman empire, that I really developed into a historian.

Before this something had happened that seems extraordinary in retrospect. Both Alan and I were invited to spend a year teaching in graduate school at Columbia University, New York, while Gilbert Highet—as it happened, himself a Scot who had gone from Glasgow University to Balliol College on a Snell exhibition in the early thirties—was on sabbatical. Both our departments agreed, even though I had joined King's College only two years before. The invitation was for the academic year 1967 to 1968, which proved to be the year of student strikes and anti-Vietnam protests, and the shootings of Martin Luther King and Robert Kennedy. My first baby was also due just before we would need to travel and was late in coming. Gilbert Highet himself and the ultra-conservative William Calder III wrote to dissuade us from bringing him with us (Calder suggested leaving him with a "compliant aunt"), but I took him to New York at only four weeks old and began teaching very soon after. I taught graduate classes on Tacitus and Petronius, and one of my students was Froma Zeitlin, later of Princeton, who had returned to graduate school as her children started to grow up.[5] It was a momentous year. Anti-Vietnam War protests were going on, and the Students for a Democratic Society (SDS) were very active; Columbia students were protesting about the university's policies and blockading the main buildings, and we had to teach our graduate classes in our apartment. I also encountered the early stages of second-wave feminism at the annual meeting of the American Philological Society in Atlanta, at which women classicists were talking of forming a women's caucus to press for inclusion on speakers' panels. We returned to England in the summer of 1968, soon after the May events in Paris, and when the Women's Liberation Movement in the UK was beginning to take shape. Living in New York and being in the U.S. had been a mind-bending experience and a challenging introduction to teaching in a very different university system.

The 1970s were a crucial decade for me. Arnaldo Momigliano retired from University College and was succeeded by Fergus Millar in 1976, and Keith Hopkins was professor of sociology at Brunel University just outside London. The weekly ancient history seminar at the Institute of Classical Studies brought ancient historians together from across London and outside. It was a fixture every Thursday (and still is), and under Fergus Millar it included graduate students and anyone who happened to be visiting and interested, but interventions by Hopkins sometimes transformed it into a gladiatorial contest. I had become interested in the four books of Latin hexameters written in Constantinople by the North African poet Corippus in praise of the Emperor Justin II, justifying his succession to Justinian in 565, and was working on an edition, translation, and commentary.[6] This work had been neglected by historians and also turned out to be extremely important for Byzantine art historians, for example with its description of the triumphal ceiling decoration in the palace and that on Justinian's

---

5. This resulted in two articles by myself, "Petronius and Plato," *Classical Quarterly*, n.s. 19 (1969), 367–70; "Myth and Meaning in Petronius: Some Modern Comparisons," *Latomu,s* 29 (1970), 397–425; a paper by Froma Zeitlin followed: "Romanus Petronius: A Study of the *Troiae Halosis* and the *Bellum Civile*," *Latomus* 30 (1971), 56–82.

6. Corippus, *In laudem Iustini minoris libri quattuor* (London, 1976). I probably knew about Corippus because Frank Goodyear, of the Latin Department at Bedford College and known to me through Alan, and his friend David R. Shackleton Bailey were working on a critical edition of Corippus's other poem, the *Iohannis*; published in 1970, it approached the poem entirely as an opportunity for clever conjectures.

funeral pall; it is also central for understanding the working of late antique panegyric. Alan was then working on his book on circus factions, and Corippus' poem contains a long section on the four factions and the ceremonial of the hippodrome and the consulship. It also contains a lengthy prayer to the Virgin put into the mouth of the Empress Sophia, and this set me off exploring the cult of the Virgin in the sixth century and earlier.[7] However my teaching was focused on the Roman empire up to AD 400. A. H. M. Jones's *The Later Roman Empire* had come out in 1964, and the very different *The World of Late Antiquity* by Peter Brown in 1971. I reviewed *The World of Late Antiquity* and was not then sure about what was evidently a very original way of writing about the later Roman empire; I had not yet done enough wider historical reading to realise just how new it was, but I found it exhilarating.[8] The book almost completely bypassed the standard questions, demolished the issue of imperial decline by demonstrating the vibrancy of late antique culture, and introduced a far wider geographical perspective. It also drew on visual as well as textual evidence and invited readers to draw on their imagination to an extent that was completely unfamiliar.

I was by now reading major modern works including M. I. Rostovtzeff on the social and economic history of the Roman empire. Perry Anderson's Marxist *Passages from Antiquity to Feudalism* came out in 1974, and Keith Hopkins's insistence on the use of sociological and quantitative models and comparative history, especially the comparison between the Roman empire and Han China,[9] offered a further alternative to the standard interpretations. These differences led to culture wars between Keith Hopkins and Fergus Millar when Hopkins published a scathing review-article about Millar's large book, *The Emperor in the Roman World* (1977) in the *Journal of Roman Studies* for 1978, accusing it of piling up facts and lacking the kind of larger-scale sociological thinking he advocated himself. By then I

---

7. Alan Cameron, *Circus Factions: Blues and Greens at Rome and Byzantium* (Oxford, 1976); Averil Cameron, "Corippus's Poem on Justin II: A Terminus of Antique Art?," *Annali della Scuola Normale di Pisa*, III.5 (1975), 129–65; "The Empress Sophia," *Byzantion*, 45 (1975), 5–21; "The Early Religious Policies of Justin II," in: *The Orthodox Churches and the West*, ed. Derek Baker [Studies in Church History, 13] (Oxford, 1976), 51–68; "Early Byzantine Kaiserkritik: Two Case Histories," *Byzantine and Modern Greek Studies*, 3 (1977), 1–17; "The Theotokos in Sixth-century Constantinople," *Journal of Theological Studies*, n.s. 29 (1978), 79–108.

8. *English Historical Review*, 88 (1971), 116–17.

9. See his two books, *Conquerors and Slaves* (Cambridge, 1978) and *Death and Renewal* (Cambridge, 1983), especially the first. Hopkins had previously spent some time teaching at Hong Kong University.

was a member of the editorial committee for the *Journal of Roman Studies*, and Millar himself was the Editor; I did not think the review article should have been published, but Millar felt he ought not to intervene. He in turn had written an article in the *Times Literary Supplement* in 1977 which seemed to cast aspersions on the work of Momigliano, whom he had succeeded only months before, for which Momigliano never forgave him. All this was painful to watch and illustrated the deep differences that could exist between historians deeply committed to competing ways of doing history. Some years later I became the Editor of the *Journal of Roman Studies* myself, and my years of involvement with the *Journal* both as Editor and as a member of the committee were among the most educative of my life. My duties also extended to overseeing the Roman Society's new monograph series, including Charlotte Roueché's *Aphrodisias in Late Antiquity* (1989), which was followed a few years later by *Performers and Partisans at Aphrodisias* (1993). Between them they covered ground directly relevant to circus factions in late antiquity and to the wider issue of cities and the changing nature of urbanism which was central to the historical questions in which I was now engaged.

Late Roman archaeology had been developing since the 1970s, especially with the work of Italian archaeologists led by Andrea Carandini. John Hayes's *Late Roman Pottery*, published in 1972, now provided a secure dating system for the many thousands of pottery sherds found on Roman sites and made reliable stratigraphy possible. The UNESCO Save Carthage project of the 1970s brought seven teams of international archaeologists to the site of ancient Carthage, near the modern city of Tunis, among them one from the University of Michigan led by John Humphrey. He invited me, unusually, to visit while the excavations were going on with a view to writing about them from a historian's perspective at an early stage. This resulted in two visits to Tunisia during which I drove myself in the dig's old Peugeot to late Roman sites all over the country and got to know Edith Wightman and Colin Wells, who were leading the Canadian team. During my work on Agathias I had necessarily spent time on Procopius, whose history Agathias continued,[10] and as well as his account of the campaigns of Belisarius and his successors in the *Wars*, his *Buildings* has a detailed section on Carthage and the building activity that followed the Byzantine reconquest of North Africa from the Vandals in 534. I was able to explore the sites and the topography at first hand and could see for myself the signs of transition and remodelling in what had been typical Roman provincial cities

---

10. My first publication was an abridged translation of Procopius with introduction: Averil Cameron, *Procopius* (New York, 1967).

as public buildings and spaces were built over or turned into churches, or where small settlements were fortified against attack. It was also an important lesson in how far textual sources can and cannot be used by archaeologists, particularly when as here with the *Buildings* the main text in question is actually a panegyric. Corippus's other lengthy hexameter poem was on the campaigns in North Africa of the Byzantine general John Troglita in the late 540s, and while this is much less rich in detail than the panegyric on Justin II, it was also useful for its topographic indications. I was also struck by the way in which the Justinianic reconquest was followed by the introduction of the Greek language and the gradual arrival in North Africa of the cults of eastern saints. My direct experience of excavation had otherwise been limited to a very brief (and wet) spell at Verulamium (St. Albans) while still an undergraduate, and even though what I wrote at the time was necessarily provisional, these visits to Tunisia were important for me as well as memorable in themselves.[11] They stood me in very good stead later when I was involved, as I frequently was, as editor or author in dealing with urban change in the late antique period.

Hayden White's *Metahistory: The Historical Imagination in Nineteenth-Century Europe* was published in 1973, and unlike Momigliano I was drawn to the idea that history-writing was less a matter of finding objective truth about the past than of understanding the narratives created by historians themselves. By the time that White's collection, *The Content of the*

---

11. The immediate result was my article "Byzantine Africa: the Literary Evidence," in: *University of Michigan, Excavations at Carthage VII*, ed. John Humphrey (Michigan, 1982), 29–62, followed by "Corippus's *Johannis*: Epic of Byzantine Africa," *Papers of the Liverpool Latin Seminar*, 4 (1983), 167–80; "Gelimer's Laughter: the Case of Byzantine Africa," in: *Tradition and Innovation in Late Antiquity*, ed. Frank M. Clover and R. Stephen Humphreys (Madison, Wisc., 1989), 171–90; and "The Byzantine Reconquest of North Africa and the Impact of Greek Culture," *Graeco-Arabica*, V (1993), 153–65. John Humphrey's own book, *Roman Circuses. Arenas for Chariot Racing* (London), was published in 1986. I returned to some of the theoretical issues much later in "Ideologies and Agendas in Late Antique Studies," in: *Late Antique Archaeology 1: Theory and Practice in Late Antique Archaeology*, ed. Luke Lavan and William Bowden (Leiden, 2003), 3–21; to Vandal and Byzantine North Africa in: "Vandal and Byzantine Africa," in: *Cambridge Ancient History* XIV, ed. Averil Cameron, Bryan Ward-Perkins, and Peter Garnsey (Cambridge, 2000), 552–69; and to Procopius's *Buildings* in: "Conclusion, *De Aedificiis*: le texte de Procope et les réalités," *Antiquité tardive,e* 8 (2000), 177–80. Yvette Duval's *Loca sanctorum Africae. Le culte des martyrs en Afrique du IVe au VIIe siècle*, 2 vols. (Rome) also came out in 1982, and see Yves Modéran, *Les Maures et l'Afrique romaine, IVe–VIIe*, Bibliothèque des Ecoles françaises d'Athènes et de Rome, 314 (Rome, 2003). The discussion about the physical changes in late antique cities in North Africa and elsewhere has been ongoing: see Anna Leone, *Changing Townscapes in North Africa from Late Antiquity to the Arab Conquest* (Bari, 2007); *The End of the Pagan City. Religion, Economy and Urbanism in Late Antique North Africa* (Oxford, 2013).

Form: Narrative Discourse and Historical Representation, appeared in 1987, I had been further influenced by discussions with others in Princeton and by historical and anthropology seminars there, and by reading the earlier publications of Michel Foucault. Consciousness of the power of discourse and literary strategies to influence history lay behind my book on Procopius when it was published in 1985 and my Sather lectures in Berkeley in 1986. It has been an ongoing driver of much of my work since.

My interest in the role of the Virgin Mary in public and private piety in late antiquity led me to argue that this became more obvious during the later sixth century. Although Justinian's Hagia Sophia, finished in 537, had no figural mosaics, the importance of Mary in the sixth-century liturgical hymns of Romanos, her depiction in apse mosaics, and the stories that attached to her in relation to the siege of Constantinople in 626 pointed to my mind in the same direction as the early indications of devotion to icons.[12] It has been argued in the past that the Akathistos hymn addressed to Mary that is still sung today in the Orthodox church was composed by Romanos, and its present opening is connected with the siege of 626, but I was persuaded by the argument of Leena Mari Peltomaa that the hymn itself belongs to the aftermath of the Council of Chalcedon in 451,[13] and I was intrigued by the epithets for the Virgin so amply demonstrated there

---

12. "The Theotokos in Sixth-century Constantinople," *Journal of Theological Studies*, n.s. 29 (1978), 79–108; "A Nativity Poem from the Sixth century AD," *Classical Philology*, 79 (1979), 222–32; "The Virgin's Robe," *Byzantion*, 49 (1979), 42–56; these came together in "Images of Authority: Elites and Icons in Late Sixth-century Byzantium," *Past and Presen,t* 84 (1979), 3–35. Later I supervised the PhD thesis of Niki Tsironi dealing in particular with the ninth-century Marian homiletics of George of Nicomedia, on which see Niki Tsironi, "From Piety to Liturgy: the Cult of the Mother of God in the Middle Byzantine Era," in: *The Mother of God: Representations of the Virgin in Byzantine Art*, ed. Maria Vassilaki (Milan and Athens, 2000), 91–102, and I wrote more on Mary myself, especially in connection with conferences and exhibitions, where I became familiar with the important work of art historians including Maria Vassilaki and Annemarie Weyl Carr: see "The Early Cult of the Virgin," in: *The Mother of God*, 3–15; "The Cult of the Virgin in Late Antiquity: Religious Development and Myth-making," in: *The Church and Mary*, ed. Robert Swanson [Studies in Church History 39] (Woodbridge, 2004), 1–21; "Introduction," in: *Images of the Mother of God: Perceptions of the Theotokos in Byzantium*, ed. Maria Vassilaki (Aldershot, 2004), xxvii–xxxii; "The Mother of God in Byzantium: Relics, Icons, Texts," in: *The Cult of the Mother of God in Byzantium: Texts and Images*, ed. Leslie Brubaker and Mary Cunningham (Farnham, 2011), 1–5. On Romanos, see now Thomas Arentzen, *The Virgin in Song: Mary and the Poetry of Romanos the Melodist* (Philadelphia, 2017), and more widely *The Reception of the Virgin in Byzantium: Marian Narratives in Texts and Images*, ed. Thomas Arentzen and Mary B. Cunningham (Cambridge, 2019).

13. Leena Mari Peltomaa, *The Image of the Virgin Mary in the Akathistos Hymn* (Leiden, 2001).

and in other Greek texts from the fifth century onwards.[14] My arguments about a religious change in the late sixth century were taken further by Mischa Meier although countered by Cyril Mango. I continue to believe, against Leslie Brubaker, that it was from then onwards rather than a century later that icons became important.[15] The rise of icons also seemed to me to be intimately connected with language and with the expression of theology in contemporary texts; I did not see texts and images as contrasting with each other, still less in conflict, and for me they went together.[16] It was logical for me if perhaps surprising to others that when my attention was caught by Procopius's failure to mention a miraculous image at Edessa whose discovery during the siege of 544 was described by Evagrius, I should devote my inaugural lecture as professor of ancient history at King's in 1980 to arguing against the persistent attempts to identify this (lost) object with the Shroud of Turin.[17] I soon found out that nothing would persuade the true believers in the Shroud's authenticity.

When I had the chance of a year's stay as a Visitor at the Institute of Advanced Study in Princeton in 1977–78 I gave as my subject the book on Procopius that logically followed from the work I had done during my PhD,[18] but in practice I was thinking much more about the cult of the Virgin and gave the expected lecture on that subject instead. I had opted for the Institute over Dumbarton Oaks, with its wonderful library on Byzantium, because by now I was a single parent with two school-age children, and the Institute is ideal for visiting families.[19] It was an important

---

14. Stephen Shoemaker has taken me to task and argued for earlier devotion to the Virgin, but the apocryphal texts on which he relies are hard to date securely; see for instance Stephen Shoemaker, *Mary in Christian Faith and Devotion* (New Haven, 2016).

15. Mischa Meier, *Das andere Zeitalter Justinians: Kontingenzverfahrung und Kontingenzbewältigung im 6. Jahrhundert n. Chr.* (Göttingen, 2003); Cyril Mango, "Constantinople as Theotokoupolis," in: *Mother of God*, pp.17–25; Leslie Brubaker and John Haldon, *Byzantium in the Iconoclast Era, ca. 680–ca.850. A History* (Cambridge, 2011).

16. "The Language of Images: Icons and Christian Representation," in: *The Church and the Arts*, ed. Diana Wood [Studies in Church History 28] (Oxford, 1992), 1–42.

17. *The Sceptic and the Shroud* (King's College London, 1980); see "The History of the Image of Edessa: the Telling of a Story," *Okeanos. Festschrift I. Sevcenko* [Harvard Ukrainian Studies, 7] (1984), 80–94; and "The Mandylion and Byzantine Iconoclasm," in: *The Holy Face and the Paradox of Representation, Papers from a Colloquium held at the Bibliotheca Hertziana, Rome and the Villa Spelman, Florence*, ed. Herbert L. Kessler and Gerhard Wolf [Villa Spelman Colloquia, 6] (Bologna, 1998), 33–54.

18. As in: "The 'Scepticism' of Procopius," *Historia*, 15 (1966), 6–25.

19. As described recently by the French mathematician and winner of the Fields Medal Cédric Villani, in: *The Birth of a Theorem. A Mathematical Adventure* (Eng. trans. London, 2015). During their stay he and his family lived like us in Van Neumann Drive on the edge of the Institute housing complex.

stay. My horizons were broadened by Clifford Geertz's anthropology seminar and the Davis seminar in the History Department of the university, and I got to know and love the Firestone Library. It was to be the first of many later visits to Princeton. I also became aware of Michel Foucault and read *The Order of Things* as well as *Discipline and Punish*, though not yet the first volume of the *History of Sexuality*, published in French in 1976. In the end my book on Procopius was not published until 1985, and it was hard to finish as I was by then more interested in other issues.[20]

On my return I reviewed the two books on Constantine and his time by Timothy Barnes and wrote about Eusebius in a volume in honour of Arnaldo Momigliano.[21] Both Constantine and Eusebius proved to be continuing preoccupations: teaching Constantine as a special subject led to a long engagement with the subject and the period;[22] my later translation and commentary on Eusebius's *Life of Constantine* with Stuart G. Hall, my colleague in the Theology Department at King's College, took shape from an informal seminar with other London colleagues and was enriched by the experience of giving several lectures and other seminars in Berkeley and at the Collège de France in Paris during the 1980s.[23] I was also working with Judith Herrin on

---

20. *Procopius and the Sixth Century* (London, 1985). In some ways it certainly belongs to its time, for instance in its insistence on genre and as some might say its classicising approach, but the recent deluge of publications on Procopius has shown that the work I did in the main more than fifty years ago still remains basic: see "Writing about Procopius Then and Now," in: *Procopius of Caesarea: Literary and Historical Interpretations*, ed. Christopher Lillington-Martin and Elodie Turquois (Milton Park, 2017), 13–25.

21. Timothy D. Barnes, *Constantine and Eusebius* (Cambridge, MA, 1981); *The New Empire of Diocletian and Constantine* (Cambridge, MA, 1982); see "Constantinus christianius," *Journal of Roman Studies,* 73 (1983), 184–90; and "Eusebius of Caesarea and the Rethinking of History," in: *Tria Corda. Scritti in Onore di Arnaldo Momigliano*, ed. Emilio Gabba (Como, 1983), 71–88.

22. "Form and Meaning: the Vita Constantini and the Vita Antonii," in: *Greek Biography and Panegyric in Late Antiquity*, ed. Tomas Hägg and Philip Rousseau (Berkeley and Los Angeles, 2000), 72–88; "The Reign of Constantine, AD 306–337," in *Cambridge Ancient History* XII, ed. Alan Bowman, Averil Cameron, and Peter Garnsey (Cambridge, 2005). 90–109; "Constantine and the Peace of the Church," *Cambridge History of Christianity* I, ed. Margaret Mitchell and Frances Young (Cambridge, 2006), 538–51; "Constantius and Constantine: An Exercise in Publicity," in: *Constantine the Great: York's Roman Emperor*, ed. Elizabeth Hartley, Jane Hawkes and Martin Henig (York, 2006), 18–30; "Constantine and Christianity," ibid., 96–103; "Il potere di Costantino. Dimensioni e limiti del potere imperiale," in: *Costantino I. Enciclopedia Costantiniana sulla figura e l'immagine dell'imperatore del cosidetto Editto di Milano 313-2013* (Rome, 2013), I, 105–15.

23. "Eusebius's *Vita Constantini* and the Construction of Constantine," in: *Portraits: The Biographical in the Literature of the Empire*, ed. Simon Swain and Mark Edwards (Oxford, 1997), 245–74; *Eusebius, Life of Constantine* [Clarendon Ancient History Series] (Oxford, 1999) (with Stuart G. Hall).

a publication arising from another seminar held at King's with Alan Cameron in 1974–76, and this came out in 1984.[24] Though the seminar was held in the Classics Department, this was a more Byzantine project. The *Parastaseis* is a puzzling text, seemingly a collection of notes (*parastaseis*) on places and monuments in Constantinople including late antique statuary, which we dated to the eighth century and which became part of the later work known as the *Patria*. It reveals a world in which the historical Constantine had become the subject of legend, and when people could often provide only fanciful identifications of the late antique statuary that still stood in the city and which they invested with malignant powers. Our choice of subject fitted both the interest I had had in the city of Constantinople and Alan's work on chariot-racing and the hippodrome. He moved to a chair at Columbia University in New York in 1977, and the work on publication was undertaken by myself and Judith Herrin, but the idea that the *Parastaseis* was the work of a group of uneasy officials was his. We were insistent on the need to distinguish evidence from the *Parastaseis* from the later *Patria*, and our choice of text was prescient, in that Gilbert Dagron and Alexander Kazhdan each addressed the issue of the developing legends about Constantine in 1984 and 1987.[25] In the 1980s Alexander Kazhdan was grappling with the intellectual chasm between his previous academic life in Soviet Russia and the new conditions of Dumbarton Oaks and America.[26] He reviewed our book in detail in 1987;[27] subsequent publications have also moved the discussion on in various ways, but ours remains the only commentary on the *Parastaseis*.[28]

---

24. *Constantinople in the Eighth Century. The* Parastaseis Syntomoi Chronikai, ed. Averil Cameron and Judith Herrin, in conjunction with Alan Cameron, Robin Cormack, and Charlotte Roueché [Columbia Studies in the Classical Tradition, 10] (Leiden, 1984).

25. Gilbert Dagron, *Constantinople imaginaire* (Paris, 1984); Alexander P. Kazhdan, "'Constantin imaginaire': Byzantine Legends of the Ninth Century about Constantine the Great," *Byzantion*, 57 (1987), 196–250.

26. "In Search for the Heart of Byzantium," *Byzantion*, 51 (1981), 330–32; Alexander P. Kazhdan and Giles Constable, *People and Power in Byzantium: An Introduction to Modern Byzantine Studies* (Washington, DC, 1982); Alexander Kazhdan and Anthony Cutler, "Continuity and Discontinuity in Byzantine History," *Byzantion*, 52 (1982), 429–78. I was struck already by the aura of exoticism with which Byzantium was often surrounded: "Byzantium. The Exotic Mirage," *Times Higher Education Supplement*, 933, September 21, 1990, 13–15.

27. *Byzantinische Zeitschrift*, 40.2 (1987), 400–03.

28. Albrecht Berger, *Untersuchungen zu den Patria Konstantinupoleos* (Bonn, 1988); Liz James, "'Pray Not to Fall into Temptation and Be on Your Guard': Pagan Statues in Christian Constantinople," *Gesta*, 35, no. 1 (1996), 12–20; Benjamin Anderson, "Classified Knowledge: the Epistemology of Statuary in the *Parastaseis Syntomoi Chronikai*," *Byzantine and Modern Greek Studies*, 35 (2011), 1–19; Paolo Odorico, "Du recueil à l'invention du texte: le cas des *Parastaseis Syntomoi Chronikai*," *Byzantinische Zeitschrift*, 107.2 (2014), 755–84; Paroma Chatterjee, "Viewing the Unknown in Eighth-century Constantinople," *Gesta*, 56.2 (2017), 137–49.

At the same time I was preparing my Sather lectures, due to be delivered at Berkeley in the spring semester of 1986 on the theme of Christianity and the rhetoric of empire.[29] I wanted to argue that the huge mass of writing produced by Christians especially from the fourth century onwards played an important role in the process of the gradual Christianization of the Roman empire. It was often said that few contemporaries would have been aware of it, but I was struck by its sheer quantity,[30] as well as by the impact of regular preaching, and argued that it had effect because the writers attuned themselves to the rhetorical world of their time and were thus able to be persuasive. I also argued that the many apocryphal narratives and the mass of hagiographic writing and ascetic literature spoke to a thirst for stories and opened new imaginative possibilities in a society in the process of change. Imagination and fiction were as important as argument in the many-sided religious world of late antiquity and the Christian tendency towards stories, figurality (and indeed fiction) fitted well with my argument. I approached the subject chronologically and had to start by getting to grip with New Testament scholarship. I saw Christian writing as deeply connected with its social and political context, although my use of the term "totalizing discourse" in relation to the sixth century needed increasing modification as I began to concern myself with the seventh century and later. This fascination with Christian literature has continued to occupy me throughout my career.[31]

Arriving in Berkeley in a mild January from a cold grey England was a revelation, as were its coffee and sandwich culture, the urbanism of San Francisco, and the beauty and grandeur of the Pacific coastline. My graduate seminar on Eusebius's *Life of Constantine* included several members who went on to become well known academics themselves, but I missed overlapping with Peter Brown, who was then in Princeton. Nevertheless my book on Procopius had been published in the previous year in his then

---

29. *Christianity and the Rhetoric of Empire. The Development of Christian Discourse* (Berkeley and Los Angeles, 1991).

30. See also "Education and Literary Culture," in: *Cambridge Ancient History,* XIII , ed. Averil Cameron and Peter Garnsey (Cambridge, 1997), 665–707.

31. "New Themes and Styles in Byzantine Literature, 7th-8th Centuries," in: Averil Cameron and Lawrence I. Conrad, eds., *The Byzantine and Early Islamic Near East I: Problems in the Literary Sources* (Princeton, 1992), 81–105; "New Themes and Styles in Later Greek Literature—a Title Revisited," in: *Greek Literature in Late Antiquity. Dynamism, Didacticism, Classicism,* ed. Scott Fitzgerald Johnson (Aldershot, 2006), 11–28; "New Themes and Styles Revisited Again: Literature, Theology and Social and Political Change," in: *New Themes, New Styles in the Eastern Mediterranean, Christian, Jewish and Islamic Encounters, 5th–8th Centuries,* ed. Hagit Amirav and Francesco Celia [Late Antique History and Religion, 16] (Leuven, 2017), 1–18.

new series with the University of California Press, The Transformation of the Classical Heritage.[32] Our lives have gone in parallel or overlapped at different times, always in ways that were important for me.

In 1981 I had been a Summer Fellow at Dumbarton Oaks in steamy Washington and met Elizabeth Clark in one of the places on Wisconsin Avenue. This proved the beginning of another lifetime friendship. In the next few years she published her early books on *Jerome, Chrysostom and Friends* (1982), *Women in the Early Church* (1983), and the *Life of Melania* (1984). I had first become attuned to the theme of ancient women in 1967 during our year at Columbia, and in 1989 Amélie Kuhrt and I edited a volume arising from the ancient history seminar at the Institute of Classical Studies and containing chapters on women in a number of different ancient societies.[33] Elizabeth Clark's work reinforced my view of the centrality of discourse in forming attitudes and linked early Christian writings about the Virgin Mary with general attitudes to women in early Christianity. To this were added the tales about female saints like Thecla in the second- and third-century apocrypha and the often exotic lives of late antique female ascetic heroines like Pelagia or Mary of Egypt.[34] I was less interested in finding out about the actual lives of Christian women than in the sometimes extreme language used about them, which was itself connected with the broader issue of Christian asceticism. The same period saw the publication in English of the first three volumes of Foucault's *History of Sexuality*,[35] and Peter Brown was at work on *The Body and Society: Men, Women and Sexual Renunciation in Early Christianity*, published in 1988. All this formed the background to my Sather lectures in 1986. I was drawn towards critics who were exploring asceticism in terms of the discourses of

---

32. *Procopius and the Sixth Century* (London and Berkeley and Los Angeles, 1985); see also "History as Text: Coping with Procopius," in: *The Inheritance of Historiography, 350–900*, ed. Christopher Holdsworth and T. Peter Wiseman (Exeter, 1986), 53–67.

33. *Images of Women in Antiquity* (London, 1989). Another seminar at King's College was on the *Life* of the patriarch Eutychius by Eustratius, an important source for the sixth century: "Eustratius's Life of the Patriarch Eutychius and the Fifth Ecumenical Council," in: *Kathegetria: Essays Presented to Joan Hussey on her 80th Birthday*, ed. Julian Chrysostomides (Camberley, 1988), 225–47; "Models of the Past in the Late Sixth century: The *Life* of the Patriarch Eutychius," in: *Reading the Past in Late Antiquity*, ed. Graham Clarke (Canberra, 1990), 205–23.

34. Pierre Petitmengin, *Pelagie la pénitente: metamorphoses d'une légende*, 2 vols. (Paris, 1981–84); Benedicta Ward, *Harlots of the Desert* (London, 1987); and Sebastian P. Brock and Susan Ashbrook Harvey, *Holy Women of the Christian Orient* (Berkeley and Los Angeles, 1987)—all belonged to the 1980s.

35. See "Redrawing the Map: Christian Territory after Foucault," *Journal of Roman Studies*, 76 (1986), 266–71.

deconstruction and postmodernism,[36] and published an article on the textual representation of early Christian women in a collection I edited with the title *History as Text*.[37]

By now I was becoming interested in the emergence of Islam[38] and wanted to look more closely at the transition from the sixth century to the seventh and eighth; I was able to do so during a Wolfson Research Readership from the British Academy in the early 1990s during which I was able to visit many of the late antique sites in Israel and travel to Cyprus (Jordan was to come later). I was also reading the textual evidence on icons, much of it difficult to disentangle. Given my preoccupation with the power of discourse I was struck by the violence of the language used against rival Christian groups and Jews, not only in theological texts but also in chronicles and other writing; it raised broader questions of intolerance,[39] which have since been much taken up by others, and was a thread that ran through much of my work thereafter; extending to the nature of heresiological works as well as to an ongoing interest in how the Byzantines tried to establish and enforce orthodoxy.[40] This reading of Greek Christian texts also lay behind

---

36. "Ascetic Closure and the End of Antiquity," in: *Asceticism*, ed. Vincent L. Wimbush and Richard Valantasis (New York, 1995), 147–61.

37. "Virginity as Metaphor: Women and the Rhetoric of Early Christianity," in: *History as Text*, ed. Averil Cameron (London, 1989), 184–205; and see "Early Christianity and the Discourse of Female Desire," in: *Women in Ancient Societies. An Illusion of the Night*, ed. Susan Fischler, Leonie Archer, and Maria Wyke (Basingstoke, 1994), 152–68 (repr. with an "Afterword" in: *The Religious History of the Roman Empire. Pagans, Jews and Christians*, ed. John A. North and Simon R.F. Price [Oxford Readings in Classical Studies] (Oxford, 2011), 505–30).

38. Especially after the conference held in Madison, Wisconsin in 1984, published as *Tradition and Innovation in Late Antiquity* (n. 11). I went on to start the series Studies in Late Antiquity and Early Islam together with Lawrence I. Conrad and Geoffrey King, published by the Darwin Press, Princeton, and co-edited or edited three volumes of workshop papers: *The Byzantine and Early Islamic Near East I: Problems in the Literary Sources* (Princeton, 1992) (with Lawrence I. Conrad); *The Byzantine and Early Islamic Near East II: Land Use and Settlement Patterns* (Princeton, 1994) (with Geoffrey R. D. King); *The Byzantine and Early Islamic Near East III: States, Resources and Armies* (Princeton: 1995). The sceptical *Hagarism* by Patricia Crone and Michael Cook had been published in 1977, and we were much engaged with the source problems for early Islam; a key later publication in the series was Robert Hoyland, *Seeing Islam as Others Saw It: A Survey and Analysis of the Christian, Jewish and Zoroastrian Writings on Islam* (Princeton, 1997).

39. "Apologetics in the Roman Empire—a Genre of Intolerance?" in: *'Humana sapit'. Études d'Antiquité tardive offertes à Lellia Cracco Ruggini*, ed. Jean-Michel Carrié and Rita Lizzi Testa [Bibliothèque de l'Antiquité Tardive, 3] (Paris-Turnhout, 2002), 219–27.

40. "The Jews in Seventh-century Palestine," *Scripta Classica Israelica*, 13 (1994), 75–93; "Texts as Weapons: Polemic in the Byzantine Dark Ages," in: *Literacy and Power in the Ancient World*, ed. Alan Bowman and Greg Woolf (Cambridge, 1994), 198–215; "Byzantines and Jews: Some Recent Work on Early Byzantium," *Byzantine and Modern Greek Studies*, 20

a contribution on dialogues and disputations in 1991. I was becoming more aware of the mass of late antique material in Syriac and already argued that the *Adversus Iudaeos* "debates" should be read in the context of a wider study of dialogues in Greek, to which I turned in earnest much later.[41]

I had often attended the annual Byzantine symposia founded by Anthony Bryer at Birmingham in 1967, and by 1983 I was chair of the British National Byzantine Committee. Bryer and I founded the Society for the Promotion of Byzantine Studies in 1983 on the model of the Hellenic and Roman Societies, with Bryer as secretary, myself as chair, and Steven Runciman as President. I was happy enough to use the term Byzantine in my publications, and I wrote on the tenth-century *Book of Ceremonies* in 1987,[42] but I was not seen as a Byzantinist, for example by Donald Nicol, the Koraes Professor of Byzantine History, Language and Literature and head of the tiny department of Byzantine and Modern Greek at King's College. At the same time I had been impressed by the structuralist approach to late antiquity in Evelyne Patlagean's *Pauvreté économique et pauvreté sociale à Byzance, 4e–7e siècle* (Paris, 1977), which I had reviewed in *Past and Present*,[43] and was identifying myself more and more with the field of late antiquity as it developed after Peter Brown's *World of Late Antiquity*.

Both these concerns—late antiquity and Byzantium—carried forward into the 1990s, but the focus of my teaching changed for two reasons: first, the move away from the restrictive University of London syllabus taught until then in all its large constituent colleges, King's College included, and second, a decision at King's to develop the teaching of Byzantium. I became the founding director of the new Centre for Hellenic Studies and

---

(1996), 249–74; "Blaming the Jews: the Seventh-century Invasions of Palestine in Context," *Travaux et Mémoires*, 14 (*Mélanges Gilbert Dagron*) (2002), 57–78; "Jews and Heretics—a Category Error?," in: *The Ways that Never Parted: Jews and Christians in Late Antiquity and the Early Middle Ages*, ed. Adam H. Becker and Annette Yoshiko Reed (Tübingen, 2003), 345–60; "How to Read Heresiology," *Journal of Medieval and Early Modern Studies*, 33.3 (Fall 2003), 471–92; also in *The Cultural Turn in Late Ancient Studies. Gender, Asceticism and Historiography*, ed. Dale Martin and Patricia Cox Miller (Durham, NC, 2005), 193–212.

41. "Disputations, Polemical Literature and the Formation of Opinion in the Early Byzantine Period," in: *Dispute Poems and Dialogues in the Ancient and Mediaeval Near East*, ed. Gerrit J. Reinink and Herman L. J. Vanstiphout [Orientalia Lovaniensia Analecta, 42] (Leuven, 1991), 91–108.

42. "The Construction of Court Ritual: The Byzantine *Book of Ceremonies,*" in: *Rituals of Royalty. Power and Ceremonial in Traditional Societies*, ed. David Cannadine and Simon R. F. Price [Past and Present Publications] (Cambridge, 1987), 106–36

43. "Late Antiquity: the Total View," *Past and Present*, 88 (1980), 129–35.

oversaw the establishment of the digital *Prosopography of the Byzantine Empire* at King's College. For the first time I began to teach courses on later periods and gave a second inaugural lecture on popular and academic attitudes to Byzantium.[44] As with late antiquity, I was interested in the ways in which Byzantium has been seen, and viewed it through the lens of Edward Said's conception of Orientalism. The question of how to approach Byzantium has been a continuing preoccupation ever since, and in 2008, after a lecture I had given at Princeton, I set out my feeling that when not exoticized, Byzantium tends to be absent or at least side-lined.[45] This provoked lively responses, and later I went on to set out some of the difficulties in approaching Byzantium and Byzantine culture in *Byzantine Matters*.[46] Moving into Byzantium proper from late antiquity took me into a very different academic milieu, and, although there are now many more Byzantinists, one which remains underdeveloped and prone to inherited and nationalist biases; I argued at the end of *Dialoguing in Late Antiquity* that Byzantinists would do well to pay more attention to late antiquity, and indeed the relation of late antiquity to that of Byzantine studies has become a key issue.[47] I have been more relaxed about periodization and nomenclature than some others because Byzantium was necessarily a hybrid. It grew out of the Roman empire, but with its very long history it was also medieval and had an inherited Greek culture and language. No state can stay the same for hundreds of years—Rome itself did not and neither did Byzantium nor the world around it.

Moving back to Oxford in 1994 to be the head of a college was a change of a different order altogether. From then until 2010 I was the Warden of Keble College, one of the largest colleges in the University of Oxford, and a college with an interesting history. I was its first woman head and one of the first three women elected in the same year to head former men's Oxford colleges. In my first year there was only one woman

---

44. *The Use and Abuse of Byzantium*, Inaugural Lecture, King's College London (1992); see "Byzance dans le débat sur l'Orientalisme," in: *Byzance et l'Europe, XVIe–XX siècle*, ed. Marie-France Auzépy (Paris, 2003), 227–42; and "Byzantium between East and West," in: *Présence de Byzance*, ed. Jean-Michel Spieser (Lausanne, 2007), 112–33.
45. "The Absence of Byzantium," *Nea Hestia*, January 2008, 4–59 (in English and Greek).
46. *Byzantine Matters* (Princeton, 2014); "Thinking with Byzantium," *Transactions of the Royal Historical Society*, 21 (2011), 39–57; "Seeing Byzantium: A Personal Response," in: *Wonderful Things: Byzantium through its Art. Papers from the Forty-first Spring Symposium of Byzantine Studies, Courtauld Institute of Art and King's College, London, March 2009*, ed. Liz James and Antony Eastmond (Farnham, 2013), 311–18.
47. See "Late Antiquity and Byzantium—an Identity Problem," *Byzantine and Modern Greek Studies*, 40.1 (2016), 27–37.

fellow, and I did my best in the next few years to bring in more. Being Warden was an absorbing and rewarding role that brought me close to the actual working of the University (which now has twenty-four thousand students, half of them graduates) in ways of which I had been entirely unaware as an undergraduate. It also gave me access to the extraordinary riches of the Bodleian Library and daily contact with academics and students in an equally extraordinary range of disciplines. The same curiosity that drove me to continue thinking and writing also now led me to seek to understand and where possible to influence the practices of an extremely complex institution. I was closely involved in the running of the University overall and in the relations between the central University and its then thirty-eight colleges. Being one of the three or four judges for the Wolfson History Prize, given for a significant but also accessible contribution to history, for which we had to assess up to two hundred books every year in all types and periods of history, was also an enjoyable and also educative experience. In addition, I chaired the national committee dealing with changes to the fabric of English cathedrals and led a controversial review of the "Royal Peculiars" (Westminster Abbey, St George's Chapel, Windsor, the Chapel Royal, and the Chapels in the Tower of London and Hampton Court Palace).

Some Oxford roles I was assigned related to the way in which the history of the University was intertwined with that of the Church of England, for instance chairing the committees appointing "Select Preachers" to deliver the University Sermons,[48] or deciding who should be invited to give the regular Bampton lectures, founded in 1780 "to confirm and establish the Christian Faith, and to confute all heretics and schismatics." Keble College itself was founded in 1870 to promote the aims of the Oxford Movement, which began from the Assize Sermon preached by John Keble in 1833 in the University Church of St. Mary the Virgin, and portraits of John Keble and his friend John Henry Newman hang in its senior common room.[49] The Chapel at Keble is a masterpiece of Victorian Gothic architecture and decoration, and its greatest treasure is the original of *The Light of the World*, painted by the young Holman Hunt in 1853 and given to the

---

48. I gave the Sermon on the Grace of Humility, endowed in 1684 together with one on the Sin of Pride, and discussed the phenomenon of false humility: Averil Cameron, "On the Grace of Humility," *Theology*, March/April (1999), 97–104.

49. Newman "went over" to the Roman Catholic Church in 1845 and was the most prominent of several highly placed Tractarians to convert; this was a bitter blow to John Keble, and afterwards the only occasion on which he and Newman met was in 1866, when Keble was dying.

College in 1873 by one of its many Tractarian benefactors. Keble's formal religious affiliation ended when it adopted new Statutes in 1969, but Oxford's remaining religious links are complex, and Keble College's role in the history of the Church of England is an important one. The College is still the patron of some sixty-five livings in the Church of England, and my duties sometimes included participating in the appointments of incumbents. I was surprised that no history of the College had been written, and with Ian Archer I later set about editing an illustrated volume, *Keble Past and Present*, which came out in 2008. It was indeed a loss that after the move I did little course teaching, and it was often frustrating when committees and other duties kept me from seminars I really wanted to attend, but the outstanding doctoral students I was able to supervise were an ongoing joy.

The power of language to change history continued to intrigue me after I moved to Oxford. I was still struck by the vast amount written by Christians in the name of trying to establish correct belief and now also by the problem of reconciling written authorities and visual depictions (in art-historical terms the problem of text and image), the ways in which Byzantine religious art itself acted as an authoritative language, and the manner in which these habits of thought and language carried over into late antique and Byzantine thinking and writing about Judaism and Islam. Recent years have seen one of the great achievements of the last decades, the publication of new critical editions, translations, and commentaries on the acts of the major ecumenical councils, and this also raises the question of the relation of historical scholarship on late antiquity and Byzantium to traditional patristics. That was the theme of the lecture I gave at Duke University in 2002 in connection with the journal *Church History*, and of my address to the North American Patristic Society in Chicago in 2009, and I made it the subject of my Ptarmigan Lecture to the Faculty of Theology and Religion (formerly simply Theology) at Oxford in 2018.[50] I continued to insist on the need for historians to address the role played by Christian literature, to interpret this broadly, and to develop a better methodology for integrating it into historical writing on late antiquity and (especially)

---

50. "Christian Literature and Church History," Duke University, 2002; "Not the End of the Affair: Discourse and Resistance in Late Antiquity," North American Patristic Society, Chicago, 2009; it was also the theme of my lecture on "Late Antiquity and Literature: What's the Problem?" at Elizabeth Clark's retirement conference at Duke in 2014; these remain unpublished, but see "Christian Literature and Christian History," in: *Enrico Norelli, Markion und der biblische Kanon, Averil Cameron, Christian Literature and Christian History, Hans-Lietzmann-Vorlesungen* 11/15 (Berlin, 2016), 29–53; and "Late Antiquity and Patristics: Partners or Rivals?," *Journal of Early Christian Studies*, 28.2 (2020), 283–302.

Byzantium. I see the often difficult reception of Byzantium within this frame: Byzantium is an idea, even a mirage, the term I used many years ago (above, n. 26), as we see in the many narratives constructed round it.[51] They rely heavily on assumptions based on its visual art and the persistent appropriation of Byzantium in poetry and literature, including works by Yeats, French dramatists, and the prose of Edward Gibbon.

Can religion in late antiquity be reduced to "culture"?[52] That is a worry I have had about the way that the field of late antiquity has developed, especially in the United States. It was a breakthrough when in the 1960s Peter Brown chose to write a psychological and contextual study of St Augustine, and when a few years later Timothy Barnes wrote his (very different) Oxford doctoral thesis in ancient history on Tertullian, but without ever being a theologian myself I am convinced that historians cannot ignore theology; indeed Christian "theology" was itself the result of a historical process in which writing and interpretation were critical. I see the formulation of what was considered to be orthodox as part of this process, and the identification of heresy as a gradual exclusion of unacceptable or losing views. I do not take Christian dogma or patristic statements as given, and I believe that historians dealing with religious texts and religious developments in late antiquity must recognize that theology and theological scholarship cannot be regarded as wholly separate from what they are doing themselves. In 2015 Elizabeth Clark published a thoughtful paper in this journal with the title "From Patristics to History in the *Catholic Historical Review,*" in which she surveyed the coverage of book reviews in the journal over its century of history and documented the changes in the study of early Christian history that they represent. She distanced herself from theology, on the grounds that her article was focusing on history,[53] and she reviewed the shifts in approaches to the period of early Christianity and late antiquity, as well as the changes within the Roman Catholic church, especially in recent decades. Rhetoric makes only a brief appearance, but in an earlier contribution she pointed to a move in late antique or "late

---

51. "Byzantinists and Others," in: *Byzantium in Dialogue with the Mediterranean*, ed. Daniëlle Slootjes and Mariette Verhoeven (Leiden, 2019), 6–23; "Byzantium Now—Contested Territory or Excluded Middle?" *Scandinavian Journal of Byzantine and Modern Greek Studies,* 6 (2020), 91–111.

52. "Culture Wars: Late Antiquity and Literature," in: Libera Curiositas. *Mélanges d'histoire romaine et d'Antiquité tardive offerts à Jean-Michel Carrié,* ed. Christel Freu, Sylvain Janniard, and Arthur Ripoli [Bibliothèque de l'Antiquité Tardive, 31] (Turnhout, 2016), 307–16.

53. Elizabeth A. Clark, "From Patristics to History in the *Catholic Historical Review,*" *The Catholic Historical Review,* 101.2 (2015), 27–71, on 32.

ancient" studies from the 1980s onwards from an approach based on social theory to one focusing on discourse and attention to literary theory,[54] an approach that has been termed "the new intellectual history."[55] Yet when a historian moves from the analysis of a particular text or text to broader issues of historical change and the formation of a mainly Christian society, theology has to be part of the story. This is why for instance the phenomenon of iconoclasm in eighth- and ninth-century Byzantium (and its reappearance in the twelfth century) cannot be reduced simply to social factors or for that matter seen as only a matter of discourse.[56]

When I retired from Keble College in 2010 I accepted the invitation to become the chair of a new research centre, the Oxford Centre for Byzantine Research, with the aim of raising funds to extend and consolidate the coverage of Byzantine studies in the University. At its inauguration I spoke on the theme "Was Byzantium an Orthodox Society?" questioning the assumptions that are routinely made and calling for a more critical approach. It was a theme that had already occupied me.[57] Rather than being a given, Byzantine Orthodoxy was painfully constructed over a long chronological period from early Christianity to late Byzantium, with many setbacks and false starts, and through highly contested processes. This was what I wanted to convey when in 2015 I accepted the challenge of writing a very short history of Byzantine Christianity (published in 2017 by SPCK). It was aimed at non-specialists, some of whom are attracted to Orthodoxy for romantic and often mistaken reasons, and while topics such as lay piety and daily life are indeed crucial, I wanted to explain the tortu-

---

54. "From Patristics to History," 65–66; cf. Elizabeth A. Clark, "From Patristics to Early Christian Studies," in: *Oxford Handbook of Early Christian Studies*, ed. Susan Ashbrook Harvey and David G. Hunter (Oxford, 2008), 1–39; Clark herself made such a move with her books *Reading Renunciation* (Princeton, 1999) and *History, Theory, Text* (Cambridge, MA, 2004).

55. Review forum on Clark, *History, Theory, Text: historians and the linguistic turn*, in: *Church History*, 74 (2005), 812–36, especially the comments by Mark Vessey.

56. Contrast Brubaker and Haldon, *Byzantium in the Iconoclast Era* (Cambridge, 2015) with Jaś Elsner, "Iconoclasm as Discourse: from Antiquity to Byzantium," *The Art Bulletin*, 94.3 (2012), 368–94.

57. "Enforcing Orthodoxy in Byzantium," in: *Discipline and Diversity*, ed. Kate Cooper and Jeremy Gregory [Studies in Church History, 43] (Woodbridge, 2007), 1–24; "Byzantium and the Limits of Orthodoxy," Raleigh Lecture in History, *Proceedings of the British Academy*, 154 (2008), 139–52; "The Violence of Orthodoxy," in: *Heresy and Identity in Late Antiquity*, ed. Eduard Iricinschi and Holger Zellentin [Texte und Studien zum antike Judentum, 119] (Tübingen, 2008), 102–14; "The Cost of Orthodoxy," Second Dutch Annual Lecture in Patristics, 2011, *Church History and Religious Culture*, 93 (2013), 339–61; *Byzantine Matters*, 87-111.

ous steps by which contemporaries formulated Orthodox doctrine as well as the highly political issues that remain today. Doctrine and verbal definitions were important in Byzantine Christianity, and the ecumenical councils were at their heart. Everyone was affected directly or indirectly by the outcomes and by the way they carried through into law, administration, and daily life.

I had been intrigued since the early 1990s by the choice of the dialogue form for polemical and catechetical works including the Christian "dialogues" with Jews known as the *Adversus Iudaeos* literature, and the related collections of questions and answers.[58] Such dialogues cover a vast range of literature in Greek (as well as Syriac and Latin) that continued until after the fall of Constantinople in 1453, and which had never been studied together. I reacted against the idea expressed in Simon Goldhill's book *The End of Dialogue in Antiquity* (2009) and elsewhere that Christianity somehow shut down real dialogue and decided to approach these issues more directly, first by collecting the relevant material—not so simple a task as it may seem, since many of the Byzantine examples still require basic study, or even critical editions, and others are known only indirectly through other mentions, refutations, or translations into other languages. This led to lectures in Budapest, Princeton, Dumbarton Oaks, and Oxford. *Dialoguing in Late Antiquity* (Washington DC, 2014) resulted from the Haecker Lecture, a series of four given in Heidelberg in 2011.[59] *Arguing it Out* (Budapest, 2016), which drew on the part of this work that related to the twelfth century, in which I considered the debates between Latins and Orthodox, as well as Byzantine discussions with Jews and Muslims, resulted from my Natalie Zemon Davis lectures at the Central University, Budapest in 2014, given in the presence of Natalie herself, whom I had met and admired years before in Princeton.[60] There is still much to do, but meanwhile the *Adversus Iudaeos* texts and the questions and answers have received attention from other scholars, while a conference held at Keble College in 2014 that ranged over the whole period from late antiquity to the end of Byzantium and beyond resulted in a comprehensive volume co-

---

58. Above, n. 41; and see "Dialogues: A World of Imagination," in: *Dialogues and Disputes in Biblical Disguise*, ed. Peter Tóth (in press).
59. Published in German as *Dialog und Streitgespräch in der Spätantike*, The Haecker Lecture, Ruprecht-Karls-Universität Heidelberg 2011 [SpielRäume der Antike, 3] (Stuttgart, 2014).
60. I had visited the Central European University several times, and become friends with many people there; my former student Volker Menze is Associate Professor in the Department of Medieval Studies.

edited with Niels Gaul.⁶¹ We opened up a vast field of mostly neglected writing in Greek and Syriac, and our conference and the collected volume attracted welcome attention to the subject and produced some original and important contributions.⁶² These ostensibly sober records of actual conversations in fact took many different forms, from the highly literary or philosophical to the mundane, and are yet another example of the power of language to shape history.

Conclusion

As I look back, I see the importance of my early background at Oxford and in Classics. I had no clear pathways when I started out, and I realise that I have been lucky to have been able to follow where my curiosity led. It drew me towards late antiquity and then to Byzantium, and from classicising Greek texts to the Roman empire, literary theory, archaeology, art history and reception, and more.⁶³ Perhaps in retrospect I have gone in too many directions, but common threads are to be found not in data gathering but in the critical analysis of texts, a continuing interest in religion as a historical force, and the theory and practice of history.

While I have certainly written a good deal about Christianity in those periods and I have been President of the Ecclesiastical History Society and chair of the Directors of the Oxford Patristic Conference, I see myself as a historian of late antiquity and Byzantium in a wider sense. The historical role and development of religion, especially Christianity, have indeed occupied me since very early in my career, and as I moved forward chronologically into Byzantium I was confronted with more such issues. Nevertheless, I have seen them in a wider historical context rather than as discrete subjects in themselves;⁶⁴ it worries me that so many of the huge

---

61. *Dialogues and Debate from Late Antiquity to Late Byzantium*, ed. with Niels Gaul (Milton Park, 2017).

62. Alberto Rigolio and Foteini Spingou, who worked with me on the project, have both published excellent studies: Foteini Spingou, "A Platonizing Dialogue from the Twelfth Century. The *Logos* of Soterichos Panteugenos," in: *Dialogues and Debate*, 123–36; Alberto Rigolio, *Christians in Conversation: A Guide to Late Antique Dialogues in Greek and Syriac* (Oxford, 2019).

63. The *Festschrift* that I received in 2006 has the happy title *From Rome to Constantinople* (ed. Hagit Amirav and Bas ter Haar Romeny (Leuven, 2006).

64. Broader reflections on historical method: "History and the Individuality of the Historian: the Interpretation of Late Antiquity," in *The Past before Us: The Challenges of Historiographies of Late Antiquity*, ed. Carole Straw and Richard Lim [Bibliothèque de l'Antiquité tardive, 54] (Paris, 2004), 23–31; "Nazaten van Byzantium," *Nexus*, 69 (2015), 126–40 (in Dutch) and "The Present in the Past and the Past in the Present," in: *The Past as Present: Essays*

number of current publications on late antiquity focus almost exclusively on Christian texts.

I belong to the academic system of the UK rather than that of North America, but my exposure to the latter has been an important influence. I did not have the experience of North American graduate school described by other contributors to this series, but of the places that have influenced me most I would place Columbia, Berkeley, Dumbarton Oaks and Princeton[65] alongside London and Oxford, and among my key personal connections Peter Brown (who also had an Oxford background, though very different from mine, and who shares in my debt to Arnaldo Momigliano) and Elizabeth Clark. Almost equally important have been the places and people I have got to know in lecture and conference visits over the years. An invisible hand has clearly also been at work at various points in my career. It has been a rich experience as step by step I pursued my curiosity where it led, and it is a main part of who I am.

---

in Honour of Guido Clemente, ed. Giovanni Cecconi, Rita Lizzi Testa, and Arnaldo Marcone [Studi e Testi tardoantichi, 17] (Turnhout, 2019), 133–50; and see also "Christian Conversion in Late Antiquity—Some Issues," in: *Conversion in Late Antiquity: Christianity, Islam and Beyond*, ed. Arietta Papaconstantinou and Neil McLynn, with Daniel Schwartz (Oxford, 2015), 3–21.

65. Including further stays in Princeton, in 2005 as a Visiting Fellow in the Program in Hellenic Studies, in 2014 for the Faber lecture, and in 2018 to give the keynote lecture at the retirement conference for John Haldon.

Recovering the Multiple Worlds of the Medieval Church: Thoughtful Lives, Inspired Critics, and Changing Narratives

JOHN VAN ENGEN*

The author describes his formative influences, his mentors, and his scholarship in Medieval history at the University of Notre Dame.

Keywords: Gerhart Ladner, Rupert of Deutz, Cenobitism, Christianization, Hildegard of Bingen, Bernard of Clairvaux, Marguerite Porete, Devotio Moderna, Dutch Reformed Communities.

IN THE FAR CORNER OF RURAL NORTHWEST IOWA where I grew up in the 1950s, churches loomed large. Yet they were in retrospect comparatively new. A map of Iowa dated to 1855 indicated as yet not a single town in my region and supplied two names for the rivers, one native, the other likely an attempt at translation. Native Americans (Lakota/Dakota) traversed these lands for centuries, and their presence lingers still in placenames, especially "Sioux," given to my home county, also to the two largest cities in the region, and more. It was a land of tall grass prairie, slightly rolling, its soils rich, making it attractive as well to European-American immigrants. The first to settle my hometown, some twenty years after that map, established a Methodist and a Catholic Church, these however both closed before my memories began. As a boy that shuttered Catholic church intrigued me, its shattered glass windows, sealed off interior, and adjoining churchyard. The ordinary in churches for me was something else. Between the later 1880s and early 1920s, Dutch immigrants poured into this region by the hundreds. Mostly Reformed (Calvinist) in religion, mostly from the rural north and east of the Netherlands, and mostly poor, they sought land and a chance at setting up households of their own. As one grandfather put it: he was not going to spend his life as a "*knecht*" (hired-hand) milking the cows and shoveling out the barns of "*mijnheer*" ("Mister": the owner). I grew up in a small town, but my uncles and aunts and cousins virtually all worked small family farms.

---

*Professor Van Engen is the Andrew V. Tackes Professor Emeritus of Medieval History at the University of Notre Dame.

Today, in the world of agribusiness, the last cousin has just moved off my grandfather's farm into retirement.

These immigrants came from a part of the Netherlands often called its "Bible-belt" and began at once to organize congregations and build churches. Most brought with them firm convictions, many too varied contestations over belief and practice, differences carried over in part from disputes that had roiled churches across the Netherlands in the wake of the French (and Dutch) Revolutions. The Netherlandish Reformed Church (Hervormde Kerk), with its quasi-established status largely dissolved, had set to work reconstituting itself amidst, on one side, new intellectual initiatives challenging inherited teachings and, on the other, revivalist communities (*Reveil*) keen to restore older traditions. Some groups leaned pietist, others more strictly Calvinist, some more latitudinarian and toward "modern" society, others more inward and focused for instance on schools for their children of a distinctively Christian character (like the Catholic parochial schools emerging in that era too). Once in America, some leaned to assimilation and the English language, some clinging for a generation or two still to Dutch and singing mainly the Psalter in church.

In my town of something over a thousand people, Hull, nearly all farmers or shopkeepers, there existed, as I grew up, five churches, all of them Dutch Reformed in character, each of a slightly different leaning or origin and spread among three denominations. Differences between them could be serious and divisive, or minimal and hardly noticed, if still nonetheless present—or so it seemed to me. My father and mother came from slightly differing strands, and my cousins therefore too. Colloquial talk among uncles and aunts about those attending another church could be gut-splittingly funny at times, or not so funny. For me it all tended to sharpen a kind of alertness toward these matters of belief and practice. By contrast Catholics, Lutherans less so, existed only somewhere beyond the pale (hence my curiosity about that abandoned church), an unknown beyond shibboleths inherited from Reformation diatribes. I recall little sense of history in all this, yet somehow connection to something larger and sprung from elsewhere.

Church came as a given, simply part of life. A relative who grew up with my father and became a novelist (under the pen-name Frederick Manfred) set some of his books in this world of immigrant farm families. He drew at times—too often in the view of some relatives—upon characters or vignettes taken from the Van Engen family (his mother's), including a person drawn on my Grandfather Van Engen, who had died before

John Van Engen
Andrew V. Tackes Professor of Medieval History, Emeritus
Department of History, University of Notre Dame

I was born. In one scene he (as neighbor, cousin, and church elder) attends a dying woman in her farmhouse, the novelist's mother in actual fact, and oversees calling the children into her bedroom to say their goodbyes. In yet another he is feared by the minister for questions he might ask about the sermon after church. Whatever the haze here of memory and story, this world of church and farm life persisted, amidst change, into the years after the Second World War, as did those differing church loyalties. My mother, a farm-girl, pragmatic, and shrewd, mostly kept my sisters and me from being drawn in too deeply. I have never forgotten her rendition of a saying from the Sermon on the Mount (Matt. 5:45) muttered to me on one occasion: "What's the matter with these people? Do they have shit in their eyes? Can't they see God's rain falls on all alike?" Rain, remember, loomed large for farmers, especially amidst the droughts of the late 1950's, as did manure before the industrial production of fertilizers.

Social history would reach a high-water mark during my graduate student years, and for medieval historians this meant attention directed toward peasants too, that great majority of the medieval population whose labor fed most others including clergy and lords. While my own predilections would incline to cultural and religious history, I read in it too and appreciated those who saw here enterprising figures as well as many scrabbling for basic existence. My own medieval ancestors were likely often landless (as my grandfather and great-grandfather were), and non-literate. It bemused me, I confess, to read fellow scholars who wrote well enough about all this, yet with little apparent instinct for life as labor day-in day-out on land and with animals, the hardships as well as returns. Others, I realize, could well smile at my plunging into the study of monks and nuns and forms of religious life remote from my own experience. That aside, it also seemed instinctively evident that such peasants in countless rural parishes would participate in their own mix of beliefs, doubts, practices, and squabbles, again some zealously or even enterprisingly, some just getting by.

What becomes embedded in a person amidst one or another kind of upbringing deserves attention too if we are to understand or critique our own work with any integrity. John Calvin's 'republican', or more bottom-up, ecclesiology, by sixteenth-century standards at least, conferred responsibility for the church and its leadership on communities (or at least a portion of their leaders). This 'republicanism', as I experienced it four centuries on, was no democracy of free churches with one-person leaders, a form held in contempt as well as suspicion. But neither were there any bishops in my world. Church was constituted by elected elders and assemblies, fostering a sense—for good and ill—that this all rested importantly on them, males in the first instance of course then, though not exclusively. But central too was the deference shown a minister, also his books and training, with preaching reserved exclusively to him. In my community this figure, "reverend" in English, was commonly addressed as *'domine'*. In fact, it turns out, the Dutch Reformed had preserved the medieval form of addressing priests ('lord' or 'sir'), without our having any notion of the word's origin or meaning. I heard my mother use it as a sign of reverence as well as affection for someone who could gravely admonish but also look out for you in times of trouble. Some too proved tyrants, lords indeed, seriously testing 'republican' oversight. Nor was this 'republican' order any bulwark against splintering and worse, at times fostering it. Still, it presumed discussion and deliberation as part of a person's religion, and at its best embedded a sense of shared responsibility. To transfer some form of this onto an earlier age (including early modern Protestantism) marked by authoritarian leaders, sacred or secular, would be false. Yet what we can learn about the workings of medieval parishes, especially in the later middle ages—priests in charge of the chancel, laypeople of the nave, wardens of assigned accounts and tasks, patrons or guilds or confraternities contributing altars and stained glass-windows, people finding places of belonging at the baptismal font, church porch, churchyard, and so on—all suggests more interactive forms of ownership and responsibility, at least for some classes of people, than we sometimes credit, or than generally held indeed in Catholic churches for a century following the Ultramontane Restoration prior to Vatican Council II.

This Dutch Reformed tradition also, again going back to Calvin's Geneva, valued education, and these immigrants had founded two colleges already in my home region when I left to attend another, Calvin College in Grand Rapids, Michigan. Still, these farm families also kept children home to work after the eighth grade, this true for my mother and father both, not of their choosing. So this was a new world for me. At Calvin I found superb teachers, also some first-rate research professors. I was introduced to the ontological argument as a first-year student by Alvin Plantinga (a recent recipient of the Templeton Prize), or rather to that argument as one may diagram it in symbolic logic on a chalkboard, not as a Latin prose-poem read meditatively—though both arguably can work. In my senior year the professor with whom I was studying Greek and Latin, Robert Otten, offered an intensive one-month course in Medieval Latin with passages from Einhard's *Life of Charlemagne* and Benedict's *Rule* (works then wholly new to me). I have still the bound copy of the *Rule* he ordered for us, marked for daily reading in chapter. I had no inkling then how central to my intellectual life (and pleasure) Medieval Latin would become.

At college I encountered a further aspect of this tradition: the worldview of Abraham Kuyper (1837–1920), a larger-than-life nineteenth-century figure whose vision for Reformed Christianity extended religion's reach into every facet of human life, learning, and activity, and in his case to founding a "free" Christian university in Amsterdam (1880) and becoming prime minister of the Netherlands (1901–05). His socio-religious vision was, put too simplistically, at once democratizing and totalizing. It reached down to include people from all social levels, then to be drawn together by a common theologically informed worldview, which was in turn poised for, indeed deployed in, dialectical exchange, if not combat, with other worldviews. It represented, as became clear to me later, a post-revolutionary Neo-Calvinist vision comparable to the Neo-Thomist one that came to prevail in Catholic circles at that same time. Kuyper's program generated an intense dedication to learning, thoughtful religion, and—fitfully—to progressive social engagement (labor unions, hospitals, and the like). At that point I found myself more inclined to keep religion at arm's length, wary too of any all-encompassing outlook in a world that appeared to me ever more multiple in the later 1960s. The serious and intellectually engaged education was what I found most compelling and in a real way inspired the path forward I would take.

A last word here about philosophical currents encountered in college. Indirectly I was introduced too to some aspects of continental ontology and epistemology as they figured in this Kuyperian tradition. His formal thought was more or less neo-Kantian in inspiration, presuming the subject's fundamental role in perceiving and giving shape to phenomena beyond the self—cast here as "pre-suppositionalism." The arrival of post-structural theory (for me after graduate school)—with its varied Heideggerian, Nietzschean and other philosophical roots, together with its critique of "positivism" and "objective" realities—hardly seemed news at the time, at least in some of its core philosophical or cognitive moves. It also hardly seemed the whole story. Subjectivity was conceivably a truth about human knowing, if it were paradoxically in itself a truth. Yet this hardly obviated, or reduced to eternal swirl, the hard work of grappling still with learning and self-understanding and religion and responsible action in society. It only made clearer to me the role of a reflective interpreter and narrator.

In my junior year—at the time I was an English major—friends told me about a history course in Ren-Ref to be taught wholly from primary sources. The class and its texts gripped me, also the intellectual buzz that came in trying to unpack them. That summer this teacher, Edwin Van Kley, took me for coffee and suggested I could go on reading such texts for ever and ever as a history major, and of all sorts, from literature to politics to religion. I was convinced at once, wrote a senior thesis on Erasmus's sardonic jab at warrior popes, his *Querela pacis* ("complaint of peace"), and applied to graduate school to study Renaissance humanism. My teachers pressed me to go to UCLA with its medieval and renaissance center. I set out to study Renaissance history and later also taught it. But its intense focus at the time there on social class and political conflict did not fully capture my interests, or perhaps suit my aptitudes, though it sensitized me to materials and questions in ways lastingly profitable.

Early on I took a course in Medieval Church History with Gerhart Ladner and encountered in him a figure that resonated: a student of *Geistesgeschichte* as practiced earlier in central Europe, with degrees in both art history and diplomatics, at ease too in theology. In the early 1930s, he had entered the Catholic Church but his upbringing was that of a bourgeois assimilated Jew in imperial Vienna, with rabbis in previous generations and his parents socializing now in the circle of Freud. Graduate seminars, held at his house in the hills above UCLA, differed only slightly, it seemed to me in retrospect, from what he had likely experienced as a student in Vienna during the later 1920s, with philology as the leaven to learning in the humanities—a subject on which my colleague Jim Turner has now written compellingly.[1] Texts in Latin distributed the week before were read and interpreted in class: philology yielding ideas, and ideas grasped as moving history, in this case particularly medieval ideas of "reform." His books and articles—always deeply, even forbiddingly (as it seemed to some of my fellow graduate students) anchored in primary sources—nonetheless implicitly addressed issues alive in the current era. By insisting on the historic role of "reform" in European history and the church, he was joining debate with those who proposed "revolution" or "restoration" as the way forward, even as his book on *The Idea of Reform* (1959) contributed to the momentum issuing in Vatican Council II. So too his focus on the "portrait" in medieval art, if quietly challenging Renaissance claims in writing art history, grew out of his own deeply incarnational view of the human. Studying medieval religion and culture was for him an energizing scholarly enterprise, but no less importantly an existential undertaking.[2] His course on medieval church history first gave that subject shape for me, also revealed its astonishingly broad scope with endlessly varied possibilities. For his seminar, staying then initially in the fifteenth century, I wrote a massive paper on Antonino of Florence (d. 1459) and the place of reform in his so-called *Summa Moralis*. Here was an author located in Medici Florence, a work written by an Observant Dominican friar who was also a bishop, a canon lawyer, a student of usury and economy, a chronicler, and an author of vernacular tracts on confession, and for whom there was then no place in standard narratives, and in some ways still is not.

I chanced upon a possible dissertation topic, something quite different, while reading Jean Leclercq's *The Love of Learning and Desire for God*, a work that indirectly spawned many dissertations in that era. Initially it was not monks so much that attracted me as this whole new landscape of writing and culture, one as capacious in its materials, also as influential over time, it seemed to me, as the world Charles Homer Haskins had set out in his twelfth-century classical renaissance, other scholars in that rise of university learning yielding scholastic philosophy and theology, and still

---

1. James Turner, *Philology: the Forgotten Origins of the Modern Humanities* (Princeton, 2014).
2. Gerhart Ladner's personal outlook comes through in his two presidential addresses and an honorary lecture at UCLA: "Greatness in Mediaeval History," *The Catholic Historical Review* 50 (1964), 1–26; "*Homo Viator*: Mediaeval Ideas on Alienation and Order," *Speculum* 42 (1967), 233–259; and "The Middle Ages in Austrian Tradition: Problems of an Imperial and Paternalistic Ideology," *Viator* 3 (1972), 433–462. For an overview of his work, see Van Engen, "Images and Ideas: The Achievements of Gerhart B. Ladner," *Viator* 20 (1989), 85–115.

others in emerging "national" vernacular literatures. Leclercq, charged by his order with a new edition of Bernard of Clairvaux, had reviewed thousands of manuscripts, drawn attention to overlooked or neglected writers and texts in hundreds of articles, and in 1956 presented this whole literary and cultural world to fellow monks (and implicitly a wider public) as a "monastic theology" implicitly alternative to the scholastic one then reigning in Catholic circles and as well in many textbook accounts of medieval intellectual life. There he noted Rupert of Deutz (c.1075–1129) in passing as a thinker and writer of interest. The few other references I could find cast him as old-school, even a comic or pathetic figure (influentially, by M.D. Chenu). Noteworthy however I thought was his reading of Scripture as the works of the three persons of the Trinity unfolding in history, this nearly three generations prior to Joachim of Fiore—and Ladner agreed.

When I then turned to Rupert's voluminous writings in earnest (four volumes of J.P. Migne) during two years spent mostly in Heidelberg's Historisches Seminar, I found column after column of biblical commentary, possibly the most prolific writer of his time, often creative, sometimes almost poetic, at times echoing but rarely citing predecessors (unlike most commentary since the Carolingian era). But how was one to write a history dissertation out of hundreds of pages of biblical commentary? Beryl Smalley had shown one way, but Rupert's writings were of another sort. Evident in him, I saw, was a very self-conscious author, his commentaries in many cases presented as thematically titled books. I immersed myself in the texts, learned his voice in its moves and moods, and began to recognize key themes. Further, through prefaces and some occasional works, his bold engagement in contemporary controversy emerged, religious, political or intellectual, and that led me to reading other authors. He now came to life for me as an engaged public actor as well as a cloistered interpreter, and that in fraught times which the writings presumed rather than set out. I became thus increasingly taken with rendering him an intelligible figure at work in multiple landscapes, a self-conscious *persona* who penned an autobiographical *Apologetica sua* a few years after Guibert of Nogent's *Solo Songs* and before Peter Abelard's *Letter on his Calamities*, and a polemicist, thus requiring that I delve too into local history in Liège and Cologne.[3] It was only in a later article, "Wrestling with the Word," that I focused more narrowly on his persistent claim to a special spiritual *"intellectus"* (understanding) as an expounder of Scripture, whence he then queried an ordering of the church that charged Judah and

---

3. Van Engen, *Rupert of Deutz* (Berkeley, 1983).

St. Peter with its leading as prelates rather than Joseph or Daniel or St. John as visionary biblical interpreters.[4]

The dissertation was long and not a book. I was fortunate to gain a position in the History Department at the University of Notre Dame (hard times then too) where for forty years I would benefit from the marvelous resources of its Medieval Institute. As I then set about rewriting the dissertation into a book I worked to free Rupert's life and writings from various predisposing categories: "Benedictine" (over against Cistercian), monastic theology, German (he was likely a romance speaker from around Liège), German symbolist, conservative, and so on. Such categories had effectively foreclosed any effort to imagine him self-consciously engaging his intellectual and religious world in his own way. While revising, I conceived a plan as well to open up that larger scene by way of distinct essays, roughly one per chapter. As things turned out I wrote only one, on the so-called "Crisis of Cenobitism,"[5] challenging a then reigning narrative which had new monks triumphantly displace the decadent old. Though such typologies were wielded in some contemporary polemic, they did not correspond to what I found in trying to contextualize Rupert: Black Monks widely flourishing, often in or near towns, and in roles partly foreshadowing those mendicants would take up a century later. Decadence was not so much the issue, at least no more than the usual run of human affairs. At issue historically was a radical rethinking of monastic life amidst apparent success, men and women of means, often of education too, fleeing towns, submitting to vile manual labor, and affixing their lives to the fine points of an ancient rule. And it succeeded, wildly, also spawned a whole new kind of spiritual writing—what Leclercq was actually responding to and pointing towards. All of this cannot be reduced to old or new monks, scholastic or monastic theology. Their lives, writings, and aspirations were far more curiously entangled in fact, Giles Constable's *Reformation of the Twelfth Century* later treating them all together. But for all this we have, still, no satisfactory or compelling narrative fully capturing these forces that would spawn such success and yield too both new structures and new writ-

---

4. Van Engen, "Wrestling with the Word: Rupert's Quest for Exegetical Understanding," in *Rupert von Deutz—Ein Denker zwischen den Zeiten*, ed. Heinz Finger, Harold Horst, and Rainer Klotz (Cologne, 2009), 185–99.

5. Van Engen, "The 'Crisis of Cenobitism' Reconsidered: Benedictine Monasticism in the Years 1050–1150," *Speculum* 61 (1986), 269–304.

6. I commented later on this indirectly in two pieces: Van Engen, "The Twelfth Century: Reading, Reason, and Revolt in a World of Custom," in *European Transformations: The Long Twelfth Century*, ed. Thomas F.X. Noble and John Van Engen (Notre Dame, 2012),

ings of even greater influence.[6] This then started me gnawing at issues of narrative, how or whether they can be capacious enough to keep in motion all the historical and religious energies at play in a given moment. As for my own first project, I began, I came to see in retrospect, by pursuing a theme (Rupert's theology of history), then expanded into reconstructing a multifaceted life and body of writings, and then pushed toward somehow reconfiguring our received narratives to make room for and represent a more complexly dynamic cultural and religious scene.

Soon after tenure I took up another issue of narrative and historiography, a subject born more of teaching and broader in scope. My subsequent essay on the "Christian Middle Ages" would garner more attention than any other work I have done.[7] At issue was how we think or talk about medieval Europe as a society and culture accounted as "Christianized," a matter controverted too for the early modern period.[8] French revolutionaries had grandly repudiated two evils they saw as having bedeviled Europe's old order, "Feudalism" and "Christianism." Nearly ever since medieval historians have been left to sort out what these were, or if they were. To raise doubts about the extent of medieval Europe's "Christianization" was hardly new—Protestants had done it for centuries, then enlightened philosophers, and medieval reformers in fact regularly long before either of them. In the wake however of a broader secularizing from the 1960's, the horrors of the Holocaust, Vatican Council II, and a dissolving Restorationist vision of the medieval church so influential for so long (1830s–1950s), historians now began to look back on Europe's religious past more critically and posit a religion of the people sharply distinguished from that of Latinate clerics, also to critique notions of the Middle Ages that appeared too "churchy" or romantic or to move too quickly past its darker sides.

My intent in this was first of all to render intelligible, also to myself, a historiography full of paradoxes, mirroring European history itself over the past two or three centuries in its varied takes on medieval religion. But I also meant to push back against what seemed to me a simplistic reductionism in the treatment of some religious phenomena and a too easy dismissal of any

---

17–44; and "Medieval Monks on Labor and Leisure," in *Faithful Narratives: Historians, Religion, and the Challenge of Objectivity in History*, ed. Andrea Sterk and Nina Caputo (Ithaca, 2014), 47–62.

7. "The Christian Middle Ages as an Historiographical Problem," *American Historical Review* 91 (1986), 519–52; and "The Future of Medieval Church History," *Church History* 71 (2002), 492–523.

8. Central to the early modern discussion was Pierre Delumeau, who contributed his own "Journey of a Historian" to this series. *Catholic Historical Review* 96 (2010), 435–48.

religion accounted as not coming from the "people," it conceived as far more folkloric in character with things "Christian" relegated to a self-interested clerical caste. The following year R.I. Moore would publish his influential *Formation of a Persecuting Society*—it in some ways, among much else, interestingly channeling the spirit and complaints of medieval anticlericalism. All this came paired with a turn to anthropological models drawn from non-European and non-literate societies (these since come under critique) as potentially better guides to the character of religion among Europe's non-literate people. For me, of Protestant heritage (though often then read as Catholic), to construe the religion of dissenters or of certain cults as of the "people" and consequently more authentic seemed romantic but also old news in so far as it amusingly echoed traditional Protestant polemic.

Still, to be clear as the article may not fully have been, in so far as these initiatives brought balance to a study of medieval religion that had often been all too singularly focused on the learned or the professed religious (from whom of course we have by far the most sources), or drawn without nuance from normative Christian writings, or concerned too exclusively with Europe's Christian majority, this new wave of scholarship brought needed and productive corrections. Over the past thirty years medieval religious history has actually flourished as nearly never before. The conversation too has moved on: more varied approaches to religion itself, more nuanced explorations of how literate and oral cultures merge and diverge in religions born of a sacred text, fresh attention to crossovers between materiality and spirituality, and now also to global comparisons. For myself I find the term "Christianization" a static abstraction which nonetheless implies or even requires a larger narrative arc even as it inherently presumes unspecified markers by which to judge its own actual presence or reality. It tends too to suggest continuities or uniformities I find at odds with a thousand years of religious movement and variation, often generated indeed by forces coming from within the Christian religion itself. So I avoid the term. But the term "christening" I find useful, even important. It points toward a sense of collective identity and personal belonging among medieval Europe's majority baptized peoples, if in practice and perception yet still highly varied. It signals too expectations and obligations that came with a rite performed on infants, a citizenship both cherished and at times chafed at. At the same time this christening effectively set apart or "othered" those outside the privileged majority, thus medieval Europe's Jews, Muslims, and non-baptized. Medieval writers would use the term *Christianitas* for christening on occasion but more often for what followed from it religiously, socially, and politically, while humanists (nearly all of them christened) proffered the classicizing term

Europa, if then sometimes glossed to explain it as referring to the land of the "*Christiani*." In an article honoring my friend and colleague Thomas Noble, and also in the conclusion to a volume on "medieval Christianities," I pointed toward some aspects of this complex enmeshing as evidenced already in the Carolingian era.[9]

On my first extended leave after tenure, I proposed to ask how things looked if we bracketed out the educated and the professed religious as well as those called dissenters or heretics, the two groups then receiving the most attention. What could we know about the religion of all the others, the great majority in mostly rural parishes? I spent that leave in the Low Countries, residing with my family in the beguine court at Louvain. This project took me now beyond cloisters or schools and into manuscripts and archives. I knew the work on "*pastoralia*" of Leonard Boyle and his heirs and had myself browsed in the pastoral manuals that began to multiply from the thirteenth century onwards. But I wanted to get closer to the ground if possible, especially in the thirteenth century when parishes first emerge more largely into view in the north, if not yet so manifest and flourishing as they would be in the fourteenth and fifteenth centuries. After months of probing archives, also examining manuscript materials at the Royal Library in Brussels (and elsewhere), I came to a provisional realization—notwithstanding religious notes or economic lists priests and canons might scratch into their codices—that at this date and in that region the parish remained, apart from occasional economic records and surviving liturgical books, a world mostly of customary and oral practices. One could read the emerging prescriptive manuals, also against the grain, and make surmises, also draw inferences from *exempla* (preachers' stories) and literary tales. But what could one truly infer about actual patterns of practice or belief? What was the felt impact for them of shared rites and of a calendar at once religious and agricultural? What meanings did they draw from biblical stories, images, and processions? A parish meant unavoidable obligations (tithes and more), but also a place of local belonging, its font for christening, its porch for weddings, its churchyard for burials, its side-chapels for praying. It was a religious world of doing and of learning by

---

9. Van Engen, "Conclusion: Christendom c. 1100: On the Cusp of the Twelfth Century: Latin Christendom and the Kingdoms of the Christened," in *Early Medieval Christianities*, ed. Thomas Noble and Julia Smith (Cambridge, 2008), 625–43; and "Christening, the Kingdom of the Carolingians, and European Humanity," in *Rome and Religion in the Medieval World: Studies in Honor of Thomas F.X. Noble*, ed. Valerie L. Garver and Owen M. Phelan (Burlington, VT, 2014), 101–28.

doing, this true in the main as well for many or most local clerics and priests—seminaries, remember, would come along after Reformation and Trent. A good generation ago Brian Stock argued that non-literate dissenters or heretics might become "textualized" into certain beliefs or practices by way of someone presenting or expounding a book's teachings—which doubtless happened. But the homespun model for this, it strikes me, beyond a classroom, was any parish church, presuming a priest there with a decent hold on his books (some complaints about this) and doing his job (some complaints about that too)—the complaints themselves revealing local parishioners who cared.

A year's work produced many notes, raised some possibilities, but generated no book. In a later essay I noted that visiting shrines, venerating chosen saints, making local pilgrimage, hearing a friar preach, and much else of this sort might evidence more individual choices, if we presume the parish as a place marked notably by obligations under a priest/ *dominus*.[10] Yet choices were made at rural home parishes too: how often to attend services and which, whether to join this or that procession, and on through a long list. What seems mistaken, or at least overblown, is from evidence of extraordinary cults or purposeful dissenters (specially recorded as causing trouble or appearing extraordinary) to infer a broader or more authentic people's religion. Those unusual or dissenting figures, we must be clear too, often saw themselves precisely as the truly Christian (some Cathars possibly aside), the ones going beyond or outside the ordinary and the customary on offer in their local parish. Commentators, to be sure, could be scathing on the ignorance or greed of local curates. Yet it is also worth recalling that the lay and worldly-wise Geoffrey Chaucer chose to depict an ordinary parish priest as nearly the only type among his church figures not treated satirically or ironically, possibly in part owing to his humbler lower social estate but expressly for his earnestness and care. But that again was at the turn of the fifteenth century, not the thirteenth, and in England, not the Low Countries. Times change; regions matter.

Debates over how to understand and represent medieval religious life arose too because historians had turned more vigorously and creatively to hagiography, miracle collections, shrines, and much more as revealing of what was first called "popular" and then "lived" religion. This looked to recover potentially vast stretches of medieval religion passed over or dis-

---

10. Van Engen, "Practice Beyond the Confines of the Medieval Parish," *Educating People of Faith: Exploring the History of Jewish and Christian Communities*, ed., Van Engen (Grand Rapids, 2004), 150–77.

missed by early "scientific" historians (except for the "historical" bits), this conceived and presented now as cultural history as much as religious. My own penchant or aptitude had from the beginning run more to other sources historians might equally find puzzling or even impenetrable, such as biblical commentary, canon law, and theology. These too moved history and were moved by history. Lived religion was present and disputed in medieval law and theology, even as shrines and reliquaries harbored theologies together with legal claims and rights. At a time when social historians were much occupied with notions of lordship, I noted the sacred sanctions lords might presume along with their raw exercise of human power or those sacred sanctions alternatively invoked against lords as "tyrants." Moreover, the social experience of lordship itself inflected conceptions or perceptions of divine lordship, evident in scholastic thinkers like Bonaventure and Thomas Aquinas if one reads or listens carefully from within this social context.[11]

On returning from leave, I became director of Notre Dame's Medieval Institute, and for fully a dozen years my scholarly work proceeded primarily at article rather than book length. It also crisscrossed varied topics. Robert Benson first introduced me to the study of medieval canon law during my last year in graduate school. It became one of the ways I thought about medieval history and the medieval church, if here too leaning more to its religious and conceptual dimensions than its institutional or political. Canon lawyers made the medieval church run, certainly from the twelfth century, even as most popes after 1150, bishops too if they had a university education, came from the ranks of lawyers. Neither the Restoration idealists of the nineteenth century nor today's sharpest critics of medieval clerics, have, it seems to me, quite taken this onboard. Moreover, once Christianity became medieval Europe's established religion, canon law emerged as its one "common" law, taught from the later twelfth century alongside Roman law (in recent times called *ius commune*). Canonists however came as varied in thought and practice as Europe's Christian peoples, not teaching or acting alike on necessarily any key matter, and schooled moreover to think *sic et non, pro et contra* even if they had finally to arrive at a certain position or defend one for an employer. In graduate seminars at Notre Dame, I regularly offered courses in history centered on canon law, each

---

11. Van Engen, "Sacred Sanctions for Lordship," in *Cultures of Power: Lordship, Status, and Process in Twelfth-Century Europe*, ed. Thomas N. Bisson (Philadelphia, 1995), 203–30. Similarly, "'God is no Respecter of Persons': Sacred Texts and Social Realities," in *Intellectual Life in the Middle Ages: Studies for Margaret Gibson*, ed. Leslie Smith and Benedicta Ward (London, 1992), 243–64.

with a different thematic focus, thus the status and rights of non-Christian peoples, the claims of custom, the world of sex and marriage, issues of heresy and inquisition, and so on. Students entered wary; many or most left converted. In the medieval church law became so pervasive a presence that from the later twelfth century confession too came to be thought of or treated as in part an "internal" court.

Ernst Kantorowicz drew attention to a move across the later twelfth century "from liturgy to law," and in an essay honoring Robert Benson (one of his students), I considered the emergence of law rather than liturgy as determinative of who counted as a monk, nun, or friar.[12] A decretal (papal letter become precedent law) accounted definitive in the matter (*Porrectum*) was issued by Pope Innocent III in 1199, defining the constitutive act as voluntarily swearing obedience to a rule and submission to a religious superior. Put contextually and from the other side, a person could not be deposited in a religious house indefinitely as a child without a choice at puberty, nor be accounted "religious" for having worn the habit a year and a day (an inherited ritual notion and practice), nor made a "religious" simply by virtue of the liturgical rite itself (regarded earlier as quasi-sacramental). Lawyers affirmed this on the pattern they had just worked out for marriage, that mutual voluntary "I do" which they and theologians had together, if in tension, agreed as constituting marriage, lawyers originally preferring consummation, it now accounted as the act "verifying" the willed "I do." Medieval society's two paradigmatic estates, marriage and professed religion, were thus "made" and entered into only by way of a personal act of will—over against a social world that still presumed familial oversight. Further, this principle came eventually to be understood at all social levels and so thrived that it ballooned into a problem in the form of clandestine, if nonetheless valid, marriages. At the core here was full recognition accorded the power of human intent as determinative of entry into these two key socio-religious estates. Now, this ruling (*Porrectum*) came moreover, I further worked out, in a letter addressed to none other than Joachim of Fiore, the great apocalyptic thinker. He, in his capacity as abbot of his new Florensian order, had appealed to the pope in frustration after someone left and disputed any further claims on his person. In our usual telling of medieval history, its greatest apocalyptic thinker and rulings in canon law appear, and indeed operate, in distinct narrative spheres. In practice they did not.

Schooled theologians were far fewer in number and far less present in administrative posts. But they were hardly ignorant of the sociology of the

---

12. Van Engen, "Religious Profession: From Liturgy to Law," *Viator* 29 (1998), 323–43.

church. No medieval historian these days would deny the social and intellectual distance between a doctor of divinity and a non-literate peasant—if nonetheless both christened, expected too to give account of their lives at the end to the same Judge, and both sharing more than a few common ritual practices. With burgeoning schools, the gap may well have widened, at least faith conceived as knowledge. Regarding this great majority of the christened population, theologians came to speak of an "implicit faith" held by those "intending to believe what the church believed."[13] Here again intent becomes the baseline, not faith as explicitly articulated knowledge, though, even as marriage was to be consummated, so all mature christened were in principle to prove they could recite the Creed, the Our Father, and from the thirteenth century the Ave Maria. Scholars who see in non-literate peasants more a quasi-independent "popular" religion have dismissed this notion as patronizing, even delusory—and with some right. Yet in it we should hear too university theologians trying hereby to account for, even make room for, what they could see plainly enough sociologically and religiously, while at the same time still holding that people christened at birth, belonging to a parish, and sharing in its rituals were to be presumed as fully among the faithful whatever their level of articulation. "Faith" gets construed here in practice more like "allegiance" than articulated belief, fairly or no, while presuming as basic, and present, again truly or no, a willed intent. It is worth noting that in inquisitional settings what brought punishment down upon someone was, after being "corrected," a personal or willed refusal nonetheless to recant and simply say or believe as the church said or believed. Protestants, with their theological emphasis upon faith as such in Christian life, would subsequently dismiss this whole notion with disdain. All the same, Protestants and Catholics alike in the sixteenth century demanded the death penalty of any who rejected the christening of infants and held out for baptisms undergone instead by willing adolescents or adults, a practice held to subvert rather than form a common religious or believing community—so tightly had over a thousand years christening and community become foundationally bound together.

Lynn White, Jr., the visionary founder of UCLA's Medieval and Renaissance Center, also one of my teachers, insisted upon an inclusive program that extended to religious culture as well, thus Judaism and Islam along with Byzantine Orthodoxy and Latin Christianity. At Notre Dame, my departed friend and colleague Michael Signer and I organized a con-

---

13. Van Engen, "Faith as a Concept of Order in Medieval Christendom," in *Belief in History*, ed. Thomas Kselman (Notre Dame, 1991), 19–67.

ference that approached medieval Jews and Christians as living alongside each other in towns and streets, in converse as well as in tension and amidst occasional bouts of violence—in my opening sentence a world of "intimacy and distance at the same time."[14] Our point was not to look past the violence or its awful beginnings in 1096 but to consider an ambience harder to capture or narrate, an everyday mutual awareness marked by interaction as well as wariness. As I knew from my earlier work, Rupert had spoken with, though not converted, a Jew in Deutz/Cologne who later became a Premonstratensian canon (Herman quondam Judaeus). On request he also wrote a work, part dialogue, part polemic, and for noteworthy reasons. A fellow abbot and friend reported that some younger monks in Cologne were rattled by Jewish arguments and critiques, and in need of intellectual and scriptural fortification. (Remember too that the Hebrew Bible makes up more than three-fourths of the Christian Scriptures.) This same dynamic was at work, I found, in Ralph of Flaix's Leviticus commentary, the largest and most influential on the Christian side in the twelfth century. He knew about the pogroms and their aftermath, knew personally a former Jew, now a monk, born of that calamity, and was alert to the centrality of Leviticus for Jewish formation. Ralph worked to generate a persuasive Christian reading while seemingly almost haunted by these varied other presences. Such dynamics went both ways. None of this denies the anti-Judaism built into parts of the medieval Christian liturgy or the coercive powers resident in a christened majority and sometimes brutally and capriciously exercised. But at issue more broadly is how to make Jews and Christians together part of medieval Europe's story (Muslims too, but I have no credentials there), also how to emancipate each in some cases from their own narrative ghettoes.

That leave in the Low Countries produced no book on parish religion, but out of it came nonetheless, and unexpectedly, a whole new line of research which over time yielded many articles, some editions and translations, and a book. During that year, memorable to me for months spent uninterrupted with manuscripts, also soccer games in the late afternoon with my boys on a lawn behind the beguine court, I spent evenings, more as an aside initially, translating texts from the Netherlandish movement called the Devotio Moderna.[15] I decided to call up manuscript copies of items I was working on—and was almost immediately hooked. It all marked for me too a move from the twelfth or thirteenth to the fifteenth century, and felt a very

---

14. Van Engen and Michael Signer, eds., *Jews and Christians in Twelfth-Century Europe* (Notre Dame, 2001), 1–2.

15. Van Engen, *Devotio Moderna: Basic Writings* (New York, 1988).

different world, exhilarating, with more source material than I could ever muster or master. Over time the projects that resulted came to require legal, institutional, and local history while still doing religion, and also brought closer access to people practicing religion. It came too, though this dawned only later, with its own battle royal over narrative. From the nineteenth century, Protestants had laid claim to this movement as proto-Protestant and proto-Humanist as well as tending lay (still echoed in nearly every popular account). From the 1950s Monsignor R.R. Post declared it thoroughly Catholic and mostly about cloistered monks and nuns in professed orders. In historical reality, as I and others would now put it, it began as a mix of clerics, lay women, lay men, and third-order Franciscans, and would persist as such in part, while also generating, initially in part as a legal front, a house of canons regular at Windesheim which then grew into the most successful new order of the fifteenth century—a blur of socio-religious groups then, each of differing status in the church and many, if not all, relating predominantly to urban settings.

I found myself skipping over old arguments about late medieval or Reformation, decline or renewal, also what was "new" in this so-called "present-day devotion," since they often acted, as I saw it, as religious magpies gathering any and all materials that suited while also writing new texts for themselves. That writing attracted me, in Dutch and Latin, then quite especially writing itself as integral to shaping a religious self, what Thom Mertens called "reading with the pen." Their organization intrigued me too: a mix of clerics and laypeople, women and men, the women far outnumbering the men, religious communes formed in towns by an ingenious blend of civil laws—two of their earliest figures having studied canon law, Geert Grote in Paris and Florens Radewijns in Prague. Others under pressure mustered texts from the church's own law to ward off inquisitorial intrusions, and stretched legal loopholes to justify ministries engaged in effect in preaching, spiritual guidance, and structured prayer. What I uncovered from this mix of sources was a world where inquisitorial threats could be blunted, religious communes established through civic laws, and a form of life not truly lay or truly clerical or professed sustained nonetheless as dedicated religion—until the Reformers, to whom it all looked too "monastic," shut it down. From these circles too came the most widely copied religious book of the fifteenth century, actually four pamphlets, Thomas of Kempen's so-called *Imitation of Christ*, later to touch figures as diverse as Ignatius Loyola and George Eliot.

These groups, like others before them, raised questions on the structural side as to whether such groups or individuals, presuming to act as spiritual aspirants, then fell under the church's protection or oversight or condemnation, likewise where and how they were to seek guidance and counsel, also in the confessional. Kaspar Elm had first drawn attention to all this. My reading of their situation in law and religion (even earlier of beguines and so many others) was as more ad hoc, tentative, and vulnerable than Elm's.[16] The book I then wrote was not a history of the movement or of a religious order.[17] It drew on a variety of sources published and unpublished, part of its attraction and satisfaction, to picture the workings and life of these groups in their creativity and messiness, their sternness and flexibility, a circle where the Eucharist was neither central nor under dispute, where personal spiritual journals were encouraged, departed members both women and men were written up in memoirs, and the making and reading of books was central. As for how to characterize them, as I read the sources they appeared suspect or rebellious to some, to others (probably more) holier-than-thou, to many others admired representatives of both piety and religious literacy. The book garnered prizes, but once again it was in article format that I tackled the larger narrative issues, what I called "Multiple Options."[18] I projected a complex and creative Later Middle Ages that, religiously at least, was not all Harvest or Decline (Huizinga, a century ago), with room for religious initiatives, quite varied and sometimes virtually contradictory, some surviving in part (including Lollards and Hussites) alongside others stopped or silenced, some arising with lay people, some within orders. Moreover, what we call the Renaissance in varied ways shared in it. Erasmus would come out of the Brothers, himself a professed Windesheimer for years, if complaining repeatedly about their austerity and inattention to high-end Latin learning. Luther praised the Brothers of the Common Life and saw monasteries as properly schools and to be preserved in that form (which the Brothers had in effect done with arrangements for young students). This world appeared to me more diverse, contentious, and creative than Duffy's fifteenth-century "traditional" church, at least on the continent. Parishioners too, if not to be confused with these more intense and dedicated types, were ever more drawn in, whose priests in these Netherlandish regions, despite raging diatribes

---

16. Van Engen, "Friar Johannes Nyder on Laypeople Living as Religious in the World," in *Vita Religiosa im Mittelalter: Festschrift für Kaspar Elm zum 70. Geburtstag* (Berlin, 1999), 583–615.

17. Van Engen, *Sisters and Brothers of the Common Life: The Modern Devotion and the World of the Later Middle Ages* (Philadelphia, 2008).

18. Van Engen, "Multiple Options: The World of the Fifteenth-Century Church," *Church History* 77 (2008), 257–84 (the presidential address for the American Society of Church History in 2007).

from Geert Grote, kept female hearth-mates at a level approaching sixty percent in some regions.

    Women made little appearance in my earlier research but in the Devout book had assumed significant roles. Medieval religious women and their writings have drawn ever more attention over the last generation and more, if often as their own focal point, this true often still in the study of medieval heresy as well. I was invited to write about Hildegard of Bingen (1098–1179) on her ninth centenary, and saw in her letters—some four hundred preserved, a number surpassed at this time only by Bernard of Clairvaux—an opportunity to situate her more integrally in a broader landscape. I approached her by way of the preserved incoming correspondence: Who did they think she was? What did they expect she could do for them? The answers were multiple, a panorama of religion (and politics) in her time: someone with a direct line to God and an answer hopefully to their pressing issue, a private counselor to prelates both women and men, to souls anguished by hidden sins, infertility, demons, a decision about crusading, and on and on—and some correspondents too cynically or ironically testing her, alongside others hoping to procure something from her in writing as virtually a contact relic. No other figure in Europe between 1150 and 1180 managed a comparable reach, all as an acclaimed seer, to be sure, a role she also cultivated however we understand her visionary graces and claims. On the other hand, Bernard, I also showed (contrary to the common story), treated her early approach to him disdainfully (his letter then subsequently doctored), and Pope Eugene III, though admiring of her, never "licensed" her (that also later doctored) and resisted her petitions and threats. Subsequently, type-casting as a "prophet" preserved her image and a package of such writings but also thereby contained or side-lined her as not in effect a player in any larger historical narrative—a mistake yet to be rectified. This mirrors a recurrent paradox: medieval women finding a voice in certain forms, admired for it (also by men and prelates) or doubted or ridiculed, but usually not integrated into the main (male) narrative. Bernard too however—son of a castellan north of Dijons, a zealous monk setting up a new house in a remote valley, in time the most powerful religious figure in his day—deployed his power by letters. Moreover, in early days he too was conscious of constructing a kind of authorization, if in a different way, rhetorical rather than visionary, evident still in famous letters into his later years.[19]

---

    19. Van Engen, "Authorship, Authority, and Authorization: The Cases of Abbot Bernard of Clairvaux and Abbess Hildegard of Bingen" in: *Shaping Authority: How Did a Person Become an Authority in Antiquity, the Middle Ages and the Renaissance?* ed. S. Boodts, J. Leemans, and B. Meijns (Turnhout, 2016), 325–62.

Marguerite Porete, a religious woman writing in French (more accurately, Picard), has been treated by historians almost entirely in terms of heresy and inquisition, with her *Mirror of Simple Souls Reduced to Nothing* linked to images of so-called "Free Spirits." For a volume of essays commemorating the seventh centenary of her inquisitorial murder at Paris in 1310, I approached her contextually as a religious seeker active in the Netherlandish region, as Valenciennes then was, if French-speaking. This also placed her in the orbit of other brilliant women writers, all of them, if hardly noted by historians, from the same medieval diocese (Cambrai: Beatrice, Hadewijch).[20] If we approach her and her book apart from pre-set narratives, we find in this woman a brilliant critic of the church as well as an expositor of religious life. We find too biting critiques of parish or dedicated religion as preoccupied with reckoning up practices and virtues, and a bracing invitation to spiritual alternatives in the form of radical interior abnegation, or emptying the soul into God, associated soon after with Master Eckhart (who likely knew her work, certainly her case). In this landscape, known too for its vernacular literary competitions, we find as well a highly independent thinker and writer, yet one also fully in touch with learned churchmen; a *persona* that is elite, even arrogant; likewise an impatient and disdainful and frustrated observer who names beguines first among her critics; a religious practitioner penetrating more deeply (and wittily), in my view, into the pitfalls and dilemmas of aspiring religious souls in her age than nearly anyone else. We should not read her story first of all by way of its terrible end but the other way round, even extending to her refusal to recant. We lose too much of her and of her insights into the religion of this age if we reduce her story to that of a persecuted medieval heretic. Nonetheless, she was the first medieval woman burnt for a book.

For the past decade I have worked at reconstructing and translating the works of another Netherlandish woman author, this one largely unknown and writing in Middle Dutch. Alijt Bake (1413–55), like Margery Kempe, would disappear for five hundred years. In fact she composed in six different genres including an "autobiography" and a formation manual for religious women, was a layperson into her twenties, a failed religious experimenter (likely as a recluse), and lastly, after a deep internal struggle, a canoness at a new Windesheim cloister in Ghent, then soon after elected its prioress (1445–55). There she understood herself called to act as a teacher and

---

20. Van Engen, "Marguerite of Hainaut and the Medieval Low Countries" in: *Marguerite Porete et le "Miroir des simples âmes": Perspectives historiques, philosophiques et littéraire*, ed. Sean Field, Robert Lerner, and Sylvain Piron (Paris, 2013), 25–68.

preacher, met with opposition and was deposed a decade on, dying soon after just before her forty-second birthday. Mother Alijt, as she was called, a woman of the gentry class with just enough Latin for the office, thought and composed entirely in Dutch and wrote out her own works. They have proved, for me, challenging to translate, her prose spilling out in alliterated and assonant doublets, in colloquial passages of her talking to and arguing with God and her Sisters, then passionate personal sentences that run on for a paragraph. We find next to nothing here of visions, a genre often associated with women authors, but we do find a direct repudiation of strict asceticism. She was deeply immersed in the sermons of Tauler and other Rhineland and Dutch mystic figures, seeking words herself to express the experience of wrenching spiritual poverty, an utter interior abnegation reducing all, God too, to Nothing (*niet*), this then paradoxically the way forward into a calling to teach and into what she was to teach. She alternates between saying she learned little from books, could not understand the ones she read (all men), and observing that Tauler came closest to capturing what she had experienced if he too fell short. The scholarly challenge has been to reconstruct her person and oeuvre from the ground up. Like Hildegard and Marguerite, she fits no generic narrative of women religious writers. Yet her works and actions offer glimpses into a religious leader and spiritual teacher amidst what was then the largest and most thriving city in the Low Countries, in a house not far from where Van Eyck painted his Adoration of the Lamb altarpiece a decade or so earlier.

It is nearly fifty years now since I started graduate school and first took Ladner's course on medieval church history. What I have recounted may seem less a "journey in church history" than a few disparate treks into a vast landscape. I set out with no conscious agenda, ideological or religious, other than to take seriously the people I studied and their religion. What I found is a medieval church that both is and is not a coherent historical subject. Textbooks exist, as do courses, and the term itself has long since become common in both historical and religious discourse. But if it is taken to signify a recognizable narrative arc or a singular set of institutional and religious features, that is misleading or simply wrong. Notions of a "medieval church" first took shape in post-Reformation polemic as each side quickly set in digging deeply (for which we remain grateful) to find and then wield any evidence supporting their view of what had transpired between the "early church" and the church of their day and allegiance. In truth both Protestants and post-Tridentine Catholics were heirs to what we now call the medieval church, each then taking for granted or claiming for themselves different bits of it, to all differing extents, both also repudiating bits, the part usually noted, Catholics in fact too, if far less than Protestants, while Anglicans would retain certain structural and cultural features more than the other two—the delight in part of Trollope's Barchester novels. In nearly every century since the sixteenth, moreover, groups have freshly re-envisioned these "middle ages" for their own purposes, with its religion often, if not always, a key aspect. In our day the critical rethinking of the last generation or two represents in part, consciously or no, the repudiation of an inherited Ultramontane and Restorationist vision: monarchical papacy, church and state, religious orders, scholastic philosophy and theology, people happily churched, and so on. A more fractured view of the medieval church, or churches, has now succeeded it, with more change over time, more critique of churchmen and praise of laypeople, more religious energy moving bottom up as well as top down, more mysticism and apocalypticism and less Thomism, more women and less attention to men, especially clerics. My own work mirrors some of this, though not consciously driven by it. In truth I thought of myself more as an explorer in a world I found fascinating, also for myself, and knew nearly nothing about.

The medieval church has been integral to at least three broad narrative streams in accounts over the last century or more. One is focused primarily on secular power and society with the church accounted a player or policymaker only as needed, another focused on the church itself together with its religion and thought but often with minimal contextualization, while a more recent third makes religion a central feature but approached mostly as culture. Each has its own legitimacy and purposes and audiences. Yet the three are not so easily separable. Those focused on the church together with its history and thought must acknowledge too its utter entanglement in medieval politics and society, with its own privilege and leadership and even saintly reputation resting as much on family genealogies and Latin literacy as on exemplary conduct or personal holiness. Those historians keyed mostly to social power and material wealth (land and peasant labor, eventually urban economies) must recognize too that religious outlooks and zeal could, and frequently did, wholly overturn people's lives and the society's institutions and laws and goods. Again, distinguishing aesthetic or affective or literary intentions and cultures from spiritual, and vice-versa, hardly proves easy. Medieval people grew up wholly enmeshed in such entanglements, also if they happened to be for instance set apart in a cloister, many of those reserved mostly or exclusively for nobility. Hildegard and Marguerite and Alijt were likely all of at least gentry class, while Rupert was an orphan with family status uncertain. On the other hand, not a few, clergy or laity, women or men, regularly and even passionately tried to separate the spiritual out from the material, the churchly from politics or land, often with explosive results for medieval European history.[21] Those same initiatives on the other hand might equally upend or transform the church and its institutions, even conceptions of the Christ and the Virgin, theologies, notions of religious life, expectations for parish life, and much more. Such initiatives, whether we treat them under the name of "reform" or some other rubric, always potentially threatened the status quo, even if paradoxically the church and its divine authority also worked as a conservatizing factor in both society and religion—the charge or expectation most familiar to us since the Revolution.

History is a rhetorical art, however much "science" we bring to bear by way of our sources and now a host of new techniques. Narrative is essential to its exposition, and interpretation, overtly or no, is embedded within it. Whether what we call the medieval church can be comprehended within a single narrative is an open question: to do justice all at once to people and institutions, religious aspirations and material power, community rituals and individual inspiration, university learning and oral custom, and so much more—and then amidst continuous change across ten centuries and multiple landscapes. I have started into more than one narrative myself, and left off in despair . . . and started again. Narratives however vitally shape what we communicate to students and audiences. I am partial too to irony and paradox as often capturing the conundrums of medieval religious life, this articulated more than once by Caroline Walker Bynum.[22] But they do not in themselves, as I see it, generate narrative, though they may well inform it. Narratives at their worst moreover reduce human players to stick figures, and stories to the white-hats and black-hats of old western movies. What were once Protestant or Catholic puppet figures in confessional polemic have now sometimes reappeared in type-cast figures of clerics and laypeople, churchmen and women, inquisitors and victims, and so on. Narratives likewise harbor, as we know, causes and agenda, and may also be simply wrong or misguided or dated. Past narratives of the medieval church were often driven by a predisposition toward evolving continuities, then more recently by disruptive and heroic outbursts of protest or dissent, and by notions too of ever renewing cycles of reform (for instance in monastic life). New narratives are needed to capture the fullness of this period, wherever one sets its beginning and end, not only for its inherent interest but to instill it anew with relevance and standing in the twenty-first century. The medieval church is an integral part of what I call at times

---

21. See "Twelfth Century" in n. 6

22. The subject of her contribution to this series: Caroline Bynum, "Why Paradox? The Contradictions of My Life as a Scholar," *Catholic Historical Review* 98 (2012), viii–455.

the "formative first thousand years of European history and culture." Our notions and portraits and narratives of that have in turn key roles to play in history considered now on a global and comparative scale. Without the narrative art we are at risk of losing in effect the history itself.

Despite these utterances on the larger issues of narrative with respect to the medieval church, my own work has tended to take up individual persons or writings or cases. To do justice to them in their contexts, to illumine the powers of religious experience within them, the searching or convictions or despair at work in their stories, actions, or writings—this has been central. Because literacy rates in the Middle Ages could be as low as ten percent or so, never topping forty percent except selectively, our access to such particular cases is also comparatively limited. Still, I hold out for our eliciting and acknowledging the presence of religious experience, of whatever kind it may be, and trying to understand it, however indirectly we may have to approach it. Thus my frustration with some recent interpretations of inquisitional records which treat inquisitors' charges mainly as foils deployed to enhance ecclesiastical power—though that may well have happened. One thereby however effectively obliterates any possible recognition, however indirect, of a person making their own religious choices or coming to certain convictions or practices or resistances—especially among those non-literate people who may indeed have chosen to go their own way or a new way. To do justice to people, to their religious experiences, their intellectual powers, their powers of critique, also their indifferent conformity—all this has intrigued and animated me from the beginning, and still does.

On the Road to Italian Church History

Paul F. Grendler*

I am an historian of the Italian Renaissance rather than a lifetime church historian. But because it is not possible to study Renaissance Italy without encountering church institutions in various circumstances, the majority of my books deal with the church in Italy in greater or lesser degree. That is the framework for this journey in church history.

The journey began on May 24, 1936, in Armstrong, Iowa, population 700, near the Minnesota border. My grandparents on my father's side came from Silesia, then part of Germany, now part of Poland, while my grandparents on my mother's side came from Luxembourg. All four emigrated to the United States between 1880 and 1900 and settled in small towns or farms in northern Iowa. A remarkable feature of my parents' lives was that both taught one-room rural schools, grades one through eight, in northern Iowa. My father taught from 1924 to 1942, and my mother from 1926 to 1935. Neither had the opportunity to obtain a university degree. But one could qualify as a teacher in a rural school with a few weeks of instruction. My father attended a teacher-training program one summer, probably in Spencer, Iowa. My mother learned how to teach at a summer program at Iowa State Teacher's College at Cedar Falls, much later renamed The University of Northern Iowa. That was it. They were obviously talented teachers. The story is that they met at a teachers' conference. They married in the summer of 1935 during the Great Depression and I grew up in modest circumstances.

My father stopped teaching in 1942 because it did not pay enough to support a growing family of two sons and a third on the way. He became a school custodian, which meant that he was in charge of heating and cleaning a school building. He served as the school custodian in several small towns. My mother helped my father by sweeping classrooms after school and I did the same in my first two years of high school. In those small towns one building, usually three stories and a large basement, housed all twelve grades with maybe a gymnasium attached. The heat came

---

*Paul F. Grendler is a professor emeritus of history of the University of Toronto. He now lives in Chapel Hill, NC, and can be reached at paulgrendler@gmail.com.

from a large coal-burning furnace for which the school custodian needed a license to operate. When I was ten our family lived in two large rooms in the Bradgate, Iowa, Consolidated School for the academic year 1946–1947, because of the shortage of housing right after World War II.

I was a voracious reader as a child. My father took me and my brothers fishing now and then and I brought along a book for when the fish were not biting. After a while I decided that the book was more interesting than the fish and stayed home. Every tiny town in which I lived had a public library which I haunted. Bradgate, population about 250, was such a town. Its public library consisted of some space in the fire house. One could sit on the running board of the fire engine and look at a book. It was open Wednesday and Saturday nights. The bookmobile brought a fresh load of books every three months from the Humboldt County Library located in Humboldt, Iowa. When I was almost out of books to read toward the end of periods between visits of the bookmobile, I was forced to look at the tiny permanent collection, which included a set of Shakespeare's complete works. I am sorry to say that I did not have enough curiosity to try Shakespeare.

My interest in history began as a child during World War II. My parents subscribed to a daily newspaper, *The Des Moines Register*, and my father listened to radio news commentators such as H. V. Kaltenborn (1878–1965). So I followed the progress of the war and first learned about far away countries. My parents kept track of domestic politics. For example, in the summer of 1948 when I was helping my father scrub floors and wash walls in the school building in Bradgate, he brought along a radio and we listened to the speeches and commentary at the national political conventions. Those were years in which the conventions were real and broadcast all day long. The interest in history continued when I was in high school in a larger town with a public library that was open several days a week and had enough resources to purchase books. It acquired the six volumes of Winston Churchill's *The Second World War* (1948–1953). I read them in study hall and everywhere else, every word, including the documentary appendices.

My parents were New Deal Democrats and I inherited their preferences. In 1952, when I was a junior in high school in Greene, Iowa, population 1,300 at that time, the high school sponsored a mock election. I delivered a passionate speech in favor of Adlai Stevenson to the assembled grades nine through twelve, some 160 students, while my chief academic rival, a girl, spoke for Eisenhower. My speech was so persuasive that Eisenhower won the student vote by a margin of two and one-half to one. I should not have been disappointed. The last time that Butler County, in

Paul F. Grendler

which Greene is located, voted Democratic in a presidential election was 1936, when it voted for Roosevelt over Landon by 2.4%. In 2020 Butler County voted for Trump 67% to 28%.

Although my parents never had the opportunity, they were determined that their children would be college graduates. As I approached graduation, the question was how would I get to college and where would I go? The answer to the first question was that while in high school I had many jobs, some interesting, others dreary, before and after school, and on Saturdays and in the summers, with the money going into a savings account. The where was solved in a different way. On a Saturday morning in the spring of 1953 I went to Waterloo, Iowa, about forty miles away, where I and forty to fifty other students wrote a three hour examination. So did other seniors in several other towns in an area of northeastern Iowa, southeastern Minnesota, southern Wisconsin, and western Illinois. The prize was free tuition at Loras College, a liberal arts college for men in Dubuque, Iowa, operated by the Archdiocese of Dubuque. I was one of the six winners. Although annual tuition was only $300, it meant a great deal to my parents and me.

What to study? I was always good in mathematics so my parents very sensibly thought that I should study to become a certified public accountant. But all I really wanted to do was play the piano and I also played the trombone. So I became a music major. Then my piano teacher thought that I needed to broaden my horizons and attend a conservatory of music. I prepared a tape playing a Beethoven piano sonata, not one of the more difficult ones, and sent it and my transcript and letters of recommendation to the Oberlin Conservatory of Music. To my pleasant surprise it accepted me. I began in the fall of 1956.

One of the glories of conservatories is that you are surrounded by music played by your fellow students, and you quickly realize how good you are not. And I lacked perfect pitch or excellent relative pitch. The highest to which I could aspire was a high school music teacher, a very honorable profession. But I did not think that I would be very good at leading teenagers in a band or chorus. So after one year in the Oberlin Conservatory, I transferred to Oberlin College. I have never regretted the years spent studying music. Over time and the failure to practice, my piano skills have diminished so much that I seldom play now. But when I retired from teaching and moved to Chapel Hill, North Carolina, I began to sing with choruses. Although my voice is mediocre, I sing the right notes. I have had the opportunity to sing such choral masterpieces as the Bach B minor Mass, and to perform with the North Carolina Symphony three times.

When I transferred to Oberlin College, again I had to decide what major to choose. My previous interest in history emerged and I chose European history. I was then fortunate to encounter an able and dedicated teacher. In my senior year at Oberlin I took three courses in nineteenth- and twentieth-century European history from George M. Kren (1926–2000), who was a one-year replacement for someone on leave.[1] As my interest in history blossomed, he recommended that I go to graduate school at the University of Wisconsin at Madison in order to study with his mentor there, George L. Mosse (1918–1999). I had no idea who Mosse was and I wasn't astute enough to look at his books. I took Kren's word for it and applied to Wisconsin plus several other places. My historical interests had shifted to the Reformation or the Renaissance and Reformation. At that time Oberlin had a small Protestant-oriented graduate school of theology. It was quiet, so I went there to study. The shelves of the main reading room held standard histories of the Reformation, which I began to read. The complex history of the sixteenth century attracted me.

---

1. For Kren's condensed biography, see: *The Second Generation: Émigrés from Nazi Germany as Historians: With a Biobibliographic Guide*, eds. Andreas W. Daum, Hartmut Lehmann, and James J. Sheehan (New York: Berghahn, 2016), 23, 34, 36, 397.

A final comment about Oberlin. Throughout my college career I always held jobs to pay expenses. In my last two years at Oberlin I was a waiter at the Oberlin Inn, which hired sixteen to twenty students, men and women, plus more students for special occasions, to be its waiting staff. In my last year my fellow student waiters elected me co-head waiter. Our duties were to serve as a buffer between management and the other student waiters and to train student waiters. In addition, I did the scheduling of all the student waiters, which was complex because of their academic schedules. Although I have been elected president of three scholarly organizations, this election by my peers still gives me equal or greater satisfaction.

To my pleasant surprise, Wisconsin accepted me. At that time Wisconsin was one of the three or four best history graduate schools in America. And Mosse accepted me as a graduate student. Again I was fortunate, because my undergraduate record was uneven, to put it mildly. What predictive value did grades in piano and music theory have for success in European history? I received no fellowship, which was understandable.

Mosse was a brilliant, original, and prolific historian, and a demanding teacher.[2] He wrote several books on sixteenth- and seventeenth-century Europe including a well-known textbook on Reformation Europe. He is best remembered today for his many books on nineteenth- and twentieth-century European cultural history including pioneering studies on the intellectual origins of the Nazi ideology.

In my first semester of graduate study at Wisconsin, Mosse lectured on the intellectual history of sixteenth-century Europe at 11 a.m. Monday, Wednesday, and Friday. His lectures were stimulating and provocative. After one of his first lectures I left saying, how can he interpret Luther in that way? So I skipped lunch and went straight to the library to look up the text (in translation) he had discussed. I found that yes, he had read the text, and yes, it could be understood his way. After that, I did not skip lunch. His seminars, held in his home, were even more stimulating. His students were writing master's theses and doctoral dissertations on sixteenth-, seventeenth-, nineteenth-, and twentieth-century European history. Hence, the papers and discussion flew from Calvinism to Marxism, to the Munich Revolution of 1919, back to the sixteenth century for a paper on the Heidelberg Catechism, for-

---

2. See George L. Mosse, *Confronting History: A Memoir* (Madison, WI: The University of Wisconsin Press, 2000); and *The Second Generation*, 414–16, and from the index.

ward to French Fascism, and elsewhere.[3] I was in awe of Mosse and the other students. And I was frantically trying to keep up him and them.

At that time graduate students at Wisconsin had to write a master's thesis. I settled on a topic in sixteenth-century French intellectual history. But instead of finishing my master's thesis in the summer of 1960, I played hooky and went to Europe. I found a very cheap student charter flight to Paris and I bought a youth hostel pass. I spent the summer hitch-hiking around Europe, from Paris to Ljubljana. I visited Berlin before the wall was erected and argued the merits of democracy and communism with East German students in bad German and fractured English. I discovered Italy. It was as if a light ignited in my head. I loved Italy, the sunny skies, the friendly people, and the history that was all around me as I walked the streets of Venice and Florence. I was so attracted to the country and its history that when I returned to Madison, I changed my focus from France to Italy. I wanted to study the Italian Renaissance. So I enrolled in a beginning Italian class. This was in addition to graduate history classes, holding a teaching assistantship, and finishing my master's thesis.

I wanted to study the Italian Renaissance but the department of history at Wisconsin had no historian in that field. Indeed, medieval history dominated and Renaissance studies were of little importance in American graduate education. A small example. At Wisconsin I did something permissible but uncommon. I did a minor outside of the department of history, in the history of philosophy. This meant taking four courses in philosophy and doing an oral examination. So I did a course on medieval philosophy, another on nineteenth-century European philosophers, and so on. There was no course in Renaissance philosophy or anything close to it. So I had the bright idea of doing a reading course in Renaissance philosophy. I prepared a list of texts—Marsilio Ficino, Giovanni Pico della Mirandola, Pietro Pomponazzi, Justus Lipsius, etc.—that I would read. But I needed the permission of the chair of the philosophy department to do a reading course. He practically threw me out of his office: there was no philosophy in the Renaissance! I did a course on Hegel instead. Years later *The Cambridge History of Renaissance Philosophy* (1989), a volume of nearly 1,000 pages edited by Charles B. Schmitt and others, appeared. I was happy to contribute an article.

---

3. Mosse was not the only excellent historian at Wisconsin. For more on the teachers, graduate students, and the academic environment at Wisconsin, see my oral history interview of January 22, 2022: Paul F. Grendler, "Oral History: Paul F. Grendler," interview by John Tortorice, University of Wisconsin-Madison, George L. Mosse Program in History, January 22, 2022, https://mosseprogram.wisc.edu/2022/03/07/grendler/

But the situation was changing. I was a member of a generation of graduate students and young scholars who benefitted directly from a major development in North American humanities scholarship including Renaissance studies. In my classes at Toronto I sometimes asked a trick question: which two political figures <u>indirectly</u> contributed the most to the growth of Renaissance studies in North America? The answers are Adolf Hitler and Benito Mussolini. They drove into exile a host of fine scholars, most of them young and Jewish. The majority went to the United States, a few went to Canada and England. They brought with them European scholarly traditions and much technical expertise. Most important, they understood European history in a way that only those who have lived it can.

The great European refugee scholars had a huge impact on practically all humanities fields in North America. Any scholar of my era who heard their lectures or read their books can testify to this. I was a direct beneficiary. George Kren, who taught me at Oberlin, was born in Austria. In 1938, at the age of twelve, he and his family fled Austria and came to the United States. George Mosse was the youngest son of a very wealthy Jewish publishing family in Berlin. The family left Germany in 1933 when George was fifteen. He came to the United States, earned a Ph. D. from Harvard, and taught at the University of Wisconsin. Some of the refugee scholars made major contributions to Italian Renaissance history. Thus, although the University of Wisconsin lacked an historian of the Italian Renaissance, I could read the books of Hans Baron (1900–1988), Felix Gilbert (1905–1991), and Paul Oskar Kristeller (1905–1999).

In the fall of 1961 I was again very fortunate. Mosse went on leave and the department hired Giorgio Spini (1916–2005) from the University of Florence to substitute for him for the fall semester.[4] This was probably on Mosse's recommendation, because they knew each other. The department of history made me Spini's assistant. That was because I was the only graduate student in the department interested in Italian history. Assistant sounds impressive. But I only checked references, graded some papers, mailed packages at the post office, and helped Spini to navigate the American university bureaucracy. I would meet him in the morning and his mail box would be full of pieces of paper. And he would ask me, "What do I do with all this?" And I would tell him which office of the university it came from, which communication he should

---

4. Spini, a Waldensian and a Socialist, was a brilliant and versatile historian who published books on sixteenth-, seventeenth-, and nineteenth-century Italy, plus a book on New England Puritanism.

answer, and which to throw away. Or I explained the campus group that was inviting him to speak. Spini was very helpful to me. Above all, he suggested a dissertation topic.

An important step on the road to doing Italian Renaissance history was the Fulbright-Hays Act of 1946, expanded in 1961. It made it possible for young American scholars to go to European libraries and archives to look at the sources at first hand. I applied for a Fulbright fellowship, Mosse and Spini wrote letters for me, and I received it. I also married in June 1962. The Fulbright stipend was enough for one person but provided no funds for spouses. So I borrowed a thousand dollars, and Marcella and I sailed for Italy on the SS Constitution in October 1962. After the year 1962–1963 in Italy, Mosse obtained for me a visiting position for the academic year 1963–1964 at the University of Pittsburgh where I did my first teaching and finished my dissertation.

I defended my dissertation in mid-July 1964. It was a sleepy affair because all the examiners and I had been awake until the small hours of the morning watching the Republican National Convention and Barry Goldwater's famous speech in which he said "Extremism in the defense of liberty is no vice." We were all a bit hungover. In the fall of 1964 I began to teach at the University of Toronto where I taught until I took early retirement in 1998.

I arrived at the University of Toronto at a time when the department of history was undergoing a vast expansion. It added several young and able European historians who became good friends. They included William Callahan in Spanish history, James Estes in German Reformation history, and David Higgs who taught French and Portuguese history. In the 1970s all sorts of things were going on in these countries, as Italy endured the Red Brigades, Spain almost reverted to Fascism in 1975, and Portugal emerged from dictatorship. We followed and discussed these events. There was also a vibrant community of Renaissance scholars outside the department of history including Konrad Eisenbichler, James Farge, James McConica, Erika Rummel, and others. The Collected Works of Erasmus project began in the 1970s, and I was a part of it from 1976 onward. It enabled me to keep in touch with scholars and the latest scholarship on the Renaissance and Reformation in northern Europe. I taught a variety of courses and directed dissertations in Italian Renaissance history. Antonio Santouosso, Thomas Deutscher †, Nicholas Terpstra, Paul Murphy, Mark Lewis S.J., and Mary S. K. Hewlett wrote their dissertations under my direction, and they are teaching in or have taught in Canadian and American universities and the Pontifical Gregorian University in Rome.

My first book was *Critics of the Italian World 1530–1560: Anton Francesco Doni, Nicolò Franco & Ortensio Lando*. Madison: The University of Wisconsin Press, 1969. Giorgio Spini had suggested Anton Francesco Doni (1513–1574) as a dissertation topic and I pursued it in Italy. The book was broader; it reconstructed and analyzed the works of three men who wrote voluminously for the vernacular presses of Venice and gave voice to dissatisfaction with contemporary Italy. One chapter is entitled "Religious Restlessness." The three writers energetically condemned clerical abuses and longed for a simple non-theological Christianity of Scripture and faith. They were attracted to Erasmus' "philosophy of Christ" and praised scriptural studies. Future scholarship confirmed that Lando (born between 1500 and 1512; d. 1555) did become a Protestant. This was my first small venture into religious history, an account of criticism of the Catholic Church in Italy and attraction to Erasmian and Protestant views as a better way. It led directly to my second book.

The Roman Inquisition and the Venetian Press, 1540–1605. Princeton, NJ: Princeton University Press, 1977, was a deep plunge into a controversial area of Italian church history, censorship by the Indexes of Prohibited Books and the Inquisition during the struggle against Protestantism in Italy. It is a study of joint ecclesiastical and state censorship of the press in Venice. For the first three-quarters of the sixteenth century, until the plague years of 1575 to 1578, Venice was the largest publishing center of Europe and the publisher of half or more of all the books printed in Italy. Moreover, the records of the Venetian Inquisition are found in the Archivio di Stato in Venice. The documents are almost complete and available to scholars. But they had received very little attention when I began to read them in the summer of 1967. I read every trial transcript looking for references to prohibited books, the printers and publishers of Venice, and anything else relevant.

If I may insert a non-scholarly note, I combined research and living in Italy in a most pleasant manner in the summer of 1967. I, my wife Marcella, and our eighteen-month-old son Peter, lived in a room in an inexpensive *pensione* on the Lido di Cavalino, a long sand bar near the beach on the Adriatic Sea located between the Lido di Venezia and the Lido di Jesolo. Unlike the other two *lidi*, the Lido di Cavallino was strictly zoned and not built up, but populated by orchards and this *pensione*. Six days a week I rose early, ate a cold breakfast on a tray just outside the door to our room, walked about a mile to catch a bus which took me to Punta Sabbione, where I caught a boat. I shared the boat with tourist industry employees who commuted to Venice daily. We arrived at Riva dei Schiavoni, where I caught a vaporetto to a stop near the Archivio di Stato. I read documents in the Archivio until it closed at 1:30, ate a quick lunch at a counter, then read manuscripts and books in the Biblioteca Marciana until 5 p.m. I then reversed the commute, arriving in time for a swim before dinner. In the meantime Marcella and Peter spent the day at the beach along with Italian families from the Veneto. We were the only English-speaking family at the *pensione* all summer. The research on the book continued during two years in Italy, 1970–1972, when I was a fellow at Villa I Tatti, the Harvard University Center for Italian Renaissance Studies.

My research revealed that the Index and Inquisition were effective only when the Venetian government decided to support the ecclesiastical authorities. That cooperation started slowly in the late 1540s; then the government strongly supported the Tridentine Index from the 1570s until the 1590s. However, a series of disputes between Venice and the papacy erupted in the 1590s. They reached a climax in the battle over the papal interdict that the papacy imposed, but Venice ignored, in 1606 and 1607. During the interdict the clandestine traffic in prohibited books became almost open, because the Venetian Inquisition did practically nothing. After the interdict the Venetian presses did not publish Protestant books, but they did publish other prohibited books. The book won the 1978 Marraro Prize of the American Catholic Historical Association and was translated into Italian.

The book uses the term Counter Reformation. It accepts that the papacy made a largely successful effort to prevent Italy from becoming Protestant, an effort that relied heavily, although not exclusively, on the Index of Prohibited Books and the Roman Inquisition. The book points out that the Venetian Inquisition tortured some suspects and released to the secular arm for execution a small number of recidivists. However, the church did not impose its will on a resisting civil society. The book does not see the Counter Reformation as an exclusively papal effort. And the efforts of the Index and Inquisition did not prevent Italians from obtaining some prohibited books from northern Europe. It is a nuanced study that presents a detailed examination of what happened, case by case and decade by decade, amid changing circumstances.

The accepted view of many historians, Italian and non-Italian, when the book was published was that the Counter Reformation shut Italy off from developments in the rest of Europe, thus preventing Italy from becoming modern, like other European, especially Protestant, states. This view goes back at least to Jacob Burckhardt, who wrote in 1860 that the Counter Reformation destroyed the Italian Renaissance. It became historical orthodoxy during the Risorgimento of the nineteenth century when the papacy opposed Italian unification. And it was widely held by Italian historians in the 1960s and 1970s, partly because much Italian historiography was *laico*, meaning anti-clerical, at that time. Although the Italian reviews of the book were polite, my book did not fit in. As interest in the Inquisition and Index grew in the 1980s and 1990s, there were conferences of Italian and English-speaking historians on the Inquisition and Index every second or third year. I was not invited to participate.

During the research for the book I made several trips to Rome to look for manuscripts concerning the Index, Holy Office, and anything else relevant in the Archivio Segreto Vaticano and the Biblioteca Apostolica Vaticana. Like other scholars, I knew that the archives of the Roman Congregations of the Holy Office and the Index were housed in the Palazzo del Santo Uffizio, the home of the Congregation for the Doctrine of the Faith, located at Piazza S. Offizio 11, just outside the walls of the Vatican. However, scholars were denied access. Even Ludwig von Pastor (1854–1928), who wrote the indispensable *The History of the Popes from the Close of the Middle Ages*, was denied access and criticized the policy.[5] There were a couple of exceptions. Luigi Firpo (1914–1989) gained access to look for documents concerning Giordano Bruno in the 1940s, and Paul Oskar Kristeller was able to obtain a microfilm of a document written by Francesco Patrizi da Cherso (1529–1597), a Platonic philosopher, in the 1960s. That was all.

However, being young and foolish, I gave it a try. In my visits to the Vatican archive and library from 1970 through 1972, I asked librarians, archivists, and anyone one else willing to listen about how I might be able to gain access to the Index and Holy Office documents. The advice received was to ask a curial cardinal to plead my case for access. Since I did not know any cardinals, I gave up the quest. Fortunately, a number of Italian scholars kept trying and their efforts were eventually crowned with success. A few scholars gained informal access in the late 1990s, and in 1998 the archives of the Congregations of the Holy Office and Index were opened to all scholars. This was absolutely the right policy and it has resulted in considerable good research. Scholars can decide for themselves if the opening of the Inquisition and Index archives has produced any documents that change the story presented in *The Roman Inquisition and the Venetian Press*.

---

5. Ludwig von Pastor, *The History of the Popes from the Close of the Middle Ages*, trans. Frederick I. Antrobus et al., 40 vols. (London: Herder, 1898–1953, here 1950), XII, 507–08.

Much more scholarship on the Index of Prohibited Books and the Inquisition followed my book. For the Index the most important was the Index des Livres Interdits project in eleven volumes of J. M. De Bujanda and his collaborators at the Université de Sherbrooke in Québec. I was pleased to participate by writing the historical introductions for two of the volumes.[6]

Over time I developed some research habits. It would be an exaggeration to call what I do a scholarly method, nor is it another theory about what history is. I start with a question: what happened and why did it happen? I try to ask a question that has not been asked before about a significant event. After formulating the question, I do not immediately review all the previous scholarship on the topic. I read just enough to become familiar with the scholarly terrain. Then, as soon as possible I start to read the primary sources, because I want to approach the topic with a fresh mind. After working in the sources for a period of time, I return to the rest of the bibliography, which I can then go through quickly, because I know what is useful and what is not.

I approach every Italian archive and library with trepidation, because each has different documents and a unique organization that reflects the state or institution it serves. The Archivio di Stato of Venice, a republic, houses Venetian state documents organized into governmental bureaus. Its documents and organization are different from what is found in the Archivio Gonzaga of the Archivio di Stato of Mantua, the archive of a princely house. Here much of the documentation consists of letters or reports to the prince. The Archivum Romanum Societatis Iesu is the archive of a religious order, again organized in a different way. Consequently, I sometimes bumble and fumble at the beginning of my research.

I search for any relevant scrap of information and constantly ask myself, where does this scrap fit? Often my initial question leads to better questions. After a while I form an hypothesis, a tentative reconstruction of events. But I also keep looking. If the hypothesis is a good one, additional pieces of information support and expand it. Or they force me to adjust it, or formulate a new hypothesis. When I am pretty certain that I understand

---

6. Paul F. Grendler, "Introduction historique," in: Jesus Martinez De Bujanda et al., eds., *Index de Venise 1549, Venise et Milan 1554*, [Index des livres interdits, 3] (Sherbrooke: Éditions de l'Université de Sherbrooke, 1987), 25–65; and, Paul F. Grendler, "Introduction historique," in: Jesus Martinez De Bujanda et al., eds., *Index de Rome 1590, 1593, 1596. Avec étude des index de Parme 1580 et Munich 1582*, [Index des livres interdits, 9] (Sherbrooke: Éditions de l'Université de Sherbrooke, 1994), 271–309.

what happened, I start to write an account that others can understand. History is still telling a story. Hence, I write a chronological and analytical narrative that tells the reader what happened and why.

The next research encounter with the church in Italy concerned catechism schools and religious orders teaching lay students. In 1989 I published *Schooling in Renaissance Italy. Literacy and Learning, 1300–1600.* Baltimore: The Johns Hopkins University Press, 1989. It is a broad study of the development of Latin humanistic schools and vernacular schools in the Italian Renaissance. It documented an educational revolution. The Italian pedagogical humanists of the fifteenth century discarded the late medieval Latin curriculum of verse grammars and glossaries, morality poems, a handful of ancient poetical texts, and *ars dictaminis*. In its place they substituted grammar, rhetoric, poetry, and history based on ancient Latin authors and texts just discovered or newly appreciated. They created the humanistic Latin curriculum that endured for centuries in Europe and North America. The book also describes the vernacular curriculum. That consisted of teaching various religious and secular vernacular texts plus mathematical, accounting, and writing skills needed for commercial careers. The book received the 1989 Marraro Prize of the American Historical Association and has been translated into Italian.

Schooling deals with the role of the church in education in two ways. First, it demolishes the old textbook myth that the church provided the bulk of education for lay students in the Middle Ages. Instead, most ecclesiastical schools in Italy disappeared by 1300. Communal schools and independent masters took their place. The former were schools operated by the *comune*, the town government. Each independent master taught in his home or in a rented room twenty-five to forty boys whose parents paid him for his services. Communal schools and independent masters dispensed almost all of the education that lay boys received through the Renaissance until the late sixteenth century.

Next, the book describes how church organizations unconnected to the papacy or bishops created new schools in the middle of the sixteenth century. Associations of secular priests and laymen and women created the Schools of Christian Doctrine beginning in Milan. These were catechetical schools that taught prayers, Christian doctrine, and limited reading and writing to boys and girls (in separate classes) for two hours or so on Sundays and religious holidays. Their primary purpose was to teach religion. But the organizers also taught reading and writing as a work of charity, and because elementary religious instruction and learning to read were practically synonymous. Children learned to read by memorizing, then learning, the syllables and words of printed prayers. One might call it catechetical literacy.

In addition, new religious orders of the Catholic Reformation dedicated to providing high-quality free education to lay boys rose in the second half of the sixteenth century. Unlike the Companies of Christian Doctrine, the religious orders established formal schools teaching about thirty hours a week in several classes of ascending difficulty. The Jesuits set the pace by founding their first school at Messina, Sicily, in 1548. The Piarists, the last of the four teaching orders, founded their first school in Rome in 1597. Some towns awarded operational control of communal schools to religious orders because the Jesuits, Barnabites, Somaschans, and Piarists provided a quality education to more students at a lower cost than the town could. Parents sent their sons to the religious order schools because the schools were free of charge and the teachers were good. The lower classes of the Jesuit, Barnabite, and Somaschan schools taught the same Latin humanistic curriculum, including the same texts beginning with Cicero's *Familiar Letters*, as the fifteenth-century humanists did, albeit with a more structured organization. The Piarists taught the vernacular literature and commercial arithmetic curriculum of the Italian Renaissance. The schools of the religious orders profoundly changed education in Italy, in Europe, and in other parts of the world that missionaries visited.

An historian who studies religious order schools examines how they served students, parents, and civil society. In addition, he or she becomes in part a church historian in order to examine the relationship of the religious orders to the rest of the church. Although the schools of the religious orders in *Schooling* occupied only thirty-eight pages in a book of 501 pages, they came to be a focus of my research.

My next major book was *The Universities of the Italian Renaissance*. Baltimore: The Johns Hopkins University Press, 2002. It is an account of the sixteen Italian universities that were teaching between 1400 and 1601. It was written at the prompting of Paul Oskar Kristeller. Possibly the greatest of the German Jewish refugee scholars who created the field of Renaissance studies in North America, Kristeller wrote some pioneering articles on Italian Renaissance universities in the 1940s and 1950s. He intended to write a book on them, because the only one in existence appeared in 1880.[7] But his many other projects prevented him from doing it. So he persuaded his

---

7. Ettore Coppi, *Le università italiane nel medio evo*, 2nd. ed. (Florence, 1880), and 3rd. ed. (Florence: Loescher & Seeker, 1886).

extremely able former student, Charles B. Schmitt (1933–1986), to write the book. Charles was then teaching at the Warburg Institute of the University of London. He was the perfect choice because he had already published articles on philosophy and science in Italian Renaissance universities. He was also one of my closest friends in the profession. My wife and I met Charles and his wife in Florence in the academic year 1962–1963 when we were both Fulbrighters. In early April 1986 Charles wrote to me—a real paper letter—that he was about to start the book. But first he had to go to the University of Padua to deliver some lectures. He went, gave the first lecture, then collapsed and died in Padua on April 15, 1986, at the age of fifty-three. It was a great loss to scholarship and to me.

Then one evening in July 1986 I received a telephone call from Professor Kristeller. He had never called me before. We were not close; I read his works and admired him from afar. Without preamble he strongly urged me to write the book that Charles could not write. I was very surprised, because this was three years before *Schooling* was published. But Kristeller seemed to know everything that was going on in the field. Taken aback, I only promised to consider his strong request. As I finished *Schooling*, the idea attracted me more and more. After I forwarded the *Schooling* manuscript to the press in 1987, I began research on *The Universities of the Italian Renaissance*.

As I was researching and writing the *Universities* book, I realized that it would correct two major misunderstandings in university scholarship. The first was that Italian universities were the same academic animals as universities in northern Europe and the Iberian Peninsula. Wrong. Italian universities were profoundly different. Italian universities concentrated on law and medicine; arts (meaning philosophy) was less important and theology hardly mattered until after the Council of Trent (1545–1563). Northern European and Iberian Peninsula universities concentrated on arts and theology, and taught little law and medicine. Italian university students were eighteen to twenty-five years of age. Students at northern and Iberian universities were twelve to twenty-one. Italian universities awarded only doctorates. Northern and Iberian universities awarded many bachelor and master's degrees, and only a handful of doctorates. Teachers in Italian universities filled academic chairs. Most teachers in northern and Iberian universities were regent masters, meaning students holding master's degrees teaching younger students. Italian universities had hardly any structure. Northern and Iberian Peninsula universities were organized academic communities with deans. The culture in Italian universities was lay because most of the professors and students were laymen. The culture in northern and Iberian universities was clerical, because most of the teachers and students were clergymen or youths preparing for ordination. Overall, Italian Renaissance universities somewhat resembled today's North American research universities, while northern and Iberian Peninsula universities were more like today's liberal arts undergraduate colleges.[8]

A major reason for the mistake was that medievalists studying northern European universities, most often Paris and Oxford in the Middle Ages, dominated university research. Insofar as medieval scholars paid attention to Italian universities, they saw them as like northern universities. And being medievalists they were not inclined to believe that an Italian Renaissance existed, which meant Italian universities of the fifteenth and sixteenth centuries did not matter. A fresh look would provide an accurate picture and encourage more research.

A second common mistake was the view that Italian universities were bastions of Scholasticism and, therefore, hostile to Renaissance humanism and to new research generally. The famous Italian historian Eugenio Garin (1909–2004) made this argument repeatedly and it lingers today.[9] The opposite was true. I discovered that Italian universities appointed major humanists to professorships in the middle of the fifteenth century and continued to do so through the sixteenth century. And humanism helped produce much new knowledge. Scholars influenced by humanism studying anatomy, medicine, and mathematics found inspiration and manuscripts from antiquity that spurred them to challenge received knowledge. Then they created new knowledge that left ancient learning behind.

Short sections of the *Universities of the Italian Renaissance* deal with the impact of the Counter Reformation. It notes that a handful of profes-

---

8. This is explained in more detail in several of my publications. See Grendler, "The Universities of the Renaissance and Reformation," *Renaissance Quarterly*, 57 (2004), 1–42 at 3–12. This is reprinted with the same pagination in Grendler, *Renaissance Education Between Religion and Politics* (Aldershot: Ashgate, 2006), Study I.

9. Eugenio Garin, *Scienza e vita civile nel Rinascimento* (Bari: Laterza, 1965), 119–20; English translation, *Science and Civic Life in the Italian Renaissance*, trans. Peter Munz (Garden City, NY: Doubleday, 1969), 90–91; Garin, *La cultura del Rinascimento* (Bari, 1961); second printing, (Bari: Laterza, 1971), 76–78, 85; Eugenio Garin, *Portraits from the Quattrocento*, trans. Victor A. and Elizabeth Velen (New York: Harper and Row, 1972), 128–29; the original passage in *Portraits* is found in Eugenio Garin, *La cultura filosofica del Rinascimento italiano* (Florence: G. G. Sansoni, 1961), 325.

sors were imprisoned briefly or left Italy because of their religious or philosophical views, or had to change passages in their books. And philosophers had to deal with the issue of how to approach the immortality of the soul. In 1513, before the Protestant Reformation began, the Fifth Lateran Council condemned the view that the human soul was mortal, the Averroist position of the unity of the intellect, and the position attributed to Aristotle that the world was eternal (and not God's creation). However, it did not prohibit professors from discussing these propositions. It only directed them to demonstrate philosophically that the soul was immortal, in so far as this was possible. The last phrase was an escape clause that allowed philosophers to argue that the immortality of the soul could not be proven philosophically but was known through faith. *The Universities of the Italian Renaissance* briefly describes how Italian university philosophers adopted a variety of positions on the immortality of the soul and the other condemned positions. What is impossible to determine was the degree of self-censorship that may have resulted.[10]

Universities also points out that Protestant students, especially from Germany and England, continued to attend Italian universities throughout the sixteenth century. Civil governments welcomed them, but expected that they would not practice Protestantism openly or show their contempt for Catholicism publicly. Naturally, some students did the latter. Nevertheless, civil governments in university towns did not allow local inquisitions to prosecute them. The book demonstrates that Italian professors lacked complete freedom of inquiry in the sixteenth century. On the other hand, professors in Protestant universities did not have complete freedom of religion and philosophical discourse either. It is likely that professors and students in Italian universities had as much, and possibly a little more, freedom of inquiry and religion, than their counterparts in the rest of Europe. *The Universities of the Italian Renaissance* received the 2002 Marraro Prize of the American Historical Association and a CHOICE Outstanding Academic Book citation.

In 1996 I was asked to be the editor-in-chief of a proposed encyclopedia of the Renaissance to be published by Charles Scribner's Sons in association with The Renaissance Society of America. My first task was to decide, in consultation with the very able managing editor, Dr. Stephen Wagley of Scribner's, what subject areas would be covered, and to choose

---

10. For this and the following paragraph see Grendler, *Universities of the Italian Renaissance*, 186–95, 281–97; and Paul F. Grendler, *Humanism, Universities, and Jesuit Education in Late Renaissance Italy* (Leiden: Brill, 2022), 310–40.

distinguished scholars to serve as subject associate editors. I decided that it would cover all aspects of the Renaissance, which meant that I needed to find twelve associate editors, some with expertise in areas not always given detailed attention in encyclopedias, such as Jewish studies and the history of women. An area meriting an associate editor was church history, and we were fortunate that Nelson H. Minnich agreed to serve as associate editor for church history.

The conception behind the encyclopedia is that the Renaissance was both a cultural movement and a period of history. The encyclopedia begins in Italy about 1350. It then broadens geographically to embrace the rest of Europe in the middle to late fifteenth century. The coverage ends chronologically in the early seventeenth century with a number of key transitional political events. And the artistic, intellectual, and literary Renaissance had mostly run its course by the early seventeenth century as well, with a few exceptions such as John Milton (1608–1674), whose works are studied in English Renaissance literature courses. The encyclopedia is intended for scholars looking for accurate information and basic bibliography on topics outside their specialities, plus university and upper-level high school students, and inquiring general readers. Preparation was exciting and stimulating, because it meant working with many distinguished scholars, an outstanding group of associate editors, and a dedicated and very competent group of people at Scribner's. Despite a few anxious moments when contributors did not produce articles and substitutes had to be found at the last moment, it was a satisfying experience.

It appeared on Christmas Eve of 1999 as *Encyclopedia of the Renaissance*. Edited by Paul F. Grendler et al. 6 vols. New York: Charles Scribner's Sons, 1999. It consists of 3,000 pages with 1,188 articles written by 642 authors, many of them not based in North America, and 800 illustrations. It was both a scholarly and commercial success. It was awarded the 2000 Dartmouth Medal of the Reference Division of the American Library Association as the Best Reference Book of 1999, and the 2000 Roland H. Bainton Reference Book Prize by the Sixteenth Century Studies Conference. Other awards included CHOICE Outstanding Academic Book for 2000, American Library Association Outstanding Reference Title 2000, *Library Journal* Best Reference Source 1999, *Reference Books Bulletin/Booklist* Editor's Choice Best Reference Title 1999, and RUSA Outstanding Reference Source 2000. It was reprinted in 2000. As of 2022, it has sold over 7,000 complete sets and an unknown number of individual volumes. Major purchasers have been university, college, high school, and public libraries. For the first year or so after publication, I received lists of the purchasers. I was pleased to learn that the Humboldt County, Iowa, public library, from which I benefitted as a child, purchased a set.

A few years later I worked with the staff of Scribner's to create a much shorter version intended for grade nine readers: *Renaissance. An Encyclopedia for Students*. Editor Paul F. Grendler. Four volumes. New York: Charles Scribner's Sons, 2004, pp. 1,038, which contains 461 articles plus 243 illustrations, charts, and maps.

The next book, *The University of Mantua, the Gonzaga & the Jesuits, 1584–1630*. Baltimore: The Johns Hopkins University Press, 2009, is a study of the creation, short life, and violent death of a university. I saw tantalizing references to a civic-Jesuit university in Mantua in documents in the Archivum Romanum Societatis Iesu in 1999. But I could find only a nineteenth-century article and a short article of 1972 based on a laureate thesis about such a university. So I spent a week at the Archivio di Stato of Mantua on my way to a conference in Parma in December 2001. I found a treasure trove of documents about a real and lively university and returned for more research in 2003.

The Peaceful University of Mantua (*Pacifico Gymnasio Mantuano*), its official title, began to teach in early November 1624 and died in 1629–1630, the victim of the War of the Mantuan Succession, the plague of 1630, and the terrible sack of Mantua on July 18–20, 1630. But it was worth a book-length investigation for several reasons. It was an original topic. It offered an opportunity to study in detail the creation of a university, as a Gonzaga duke organized the university, raised money, and recruited professors of law and medicine, including raiding other universities for star professors. Because the University of Mantua had some innovative professors, it offered a window into some new developments in medicine and other research areas in seventeenth-century Italy, a period less studied.

The University of Mantua book also revealed information about how a religious order fit into an Italian civic university. Lay professors taught about sixty percent of the lectures at Mantua. They taught several branches of civil law, canon law, medical theory, medical practice, anatomy, surgery, medical botany, chemistry, and a course on Tacitus. The Jesuits taught about forty percent of the lectures. They taught Scholastic theology, cases of conscience, Scripture, metaphysics, natural philosophy, moral philosophy, logic, Latin humanities, and Greek. The Jesuit professors were part of the larger university, but also retained their own academic culture.

I became aware that Jesuits taught in different kinds of universities in Catholic Europe between 1553 and 1773. And I sought to explain this in my next two books. For the understanding of readers, the different forms of Jesuit universities are summarized here in the order of the extent of Jesuit control and involvement in the operations of a university.

1. The first was the Jesuit university. That is, a university that the Society completely ruled and taught in without exception. In a Jesuit university the Jesuits did all the teaching. But because the Jesuits did not teach medicine and at most taught only a course in canon law but not civil law, Jesuit universities were not complete universities as Europeans understood them at the time. There were only a small number of Jesuit universities in Europe before 1773.
2. The second was the civic-Jesuit collegiate university of northern Europe and the Iberian Peninsula. The Jesuits and the civil government shared governance of the university and teaching responsibilities. Jesuits dominated the humanities and philosophy instruction and ruled this part of the university. They taught some theology but did not dominate the faculty of theology. The civil authority ruled law and medicine and appointed the professors in these disciplines. But because northern and Iberian Peninsula collegiate universities taught a limited amount of law and medicine, the Jesuits had a strong and often dominant institutional role in the university. The majority of European Jesuit universities were civic-Jesuit collegiate universities.
3. The third was the civic-Jesuit Italian law and medicine university. The Jesuits taught the humanities, philosophy, and theology, and governed this part of the university more de facto than de jure. The civil authority appointed all the law and medicine professors and governed the overall structure of the university. Because the greatest number of professors taught law and medicine, and the vast majority of students came to study and obtain degrees in law and medicine, the institutional and instructional position of the Society in the university was smaller and weaker than in a civic-Jesuit northern European and Iberian Peninsula civic-Jesuit collegiate university. The culture of the university was more civic than Jesuit.
4. The fourth form of a university with Jesuit involvement was the civic university completely ruled by the civil government, either city or prince. However, the civil authority invited one, two, or three Jesuits to teach in it. But the Society had no institutional role in the university. It did not govern any part of the university. There were few such universities.

My next book studied every Italian university in which the Jesuits participated, or tried to participate, between 1548 and 1773. As I sought a publisher for this book, I discovered that English-language university presses now wanted to publish only short books of a maximum of 250 to 300 pages, and they refused to do footnotes. Of course, university presses are suffering from diminishing sales and other problems. But such blanket prohibitions make no sense.

A happy exception was The Catholic University of America Press led by Trevor Lipscombe which published *The Jesuits and Italian Universities 1548–1773*. Washington, D.C: The Catholic University of America Press, 2017, a 525-page book with footnotes, and sold it at at the very low price of $35 in paperback. The book is a comprehensive history of relations between the Jesuits and Italian universities. It studies four successful civic-Jesuit Italian law and medicine universities (Mantua, Parma, Fermo, and Macerata) and three civic universities in which one or two Jesuits taught but the Society had no institutional position (Ferrara, Pavia, and Siena). It describes one bold but failed Jesuit attempt to obtain professorships in an established university (Turin) and two tentative attempts that also failed (Catania and Perugia). It chronicles failed attempts to create civic-Jesuit universities (Messina, Palermo, and Chambéry). And it describes the strong, sometimes extraordinary, hostility of the universities of Bologna, Padua, and Rome against the Jesuits even though the Jesuits never tried to become professors in them.

For the study of church history, the hostility of the universities of Padua and Bologna toward the Jesuits was instructive. In 1591 professors and some students from the University of Padua went to the Venetian Senate, and loudly claimed that the Jesuits in Padua had created a counter university in competition with the University of Padua and against the laws of the Republic of Venice. The Senate ruled that the Padua Jesuits could teach only fellow Jesuits. In similar fashion the University of Bologna in 1641 barred the Jesuit school in Bologna from teaching university-level courses (chiefly philosophy and theology) to non-Jesuits. This restriction was later partially eased.

Because Italian universities were full of law professors and the Jesuits responded, the university-Jesuit conflicts generated many documents arguing church-state jurisdictional issues. There were also felicitous cooperative arrangements that enabled Jesuits and lay professors to work together. The book explores the philosophical and pedagogical similarities and differences between Jesuit professors and non-Jesuit professors. The book received the 2018 Marraro Prize of the American Catholic Historical Association.

Jesuit Schools and Universities in Europe 1548–1773. Leiden: Brill, 2019, is a short book of 122 pages. It was written by invitation of my friend Robert A. Maryks for the series Brill Research Perspectives in Jesuit Studies that he edits. It presents an overview of Jesuit schools and universities across Europe with some detailed information about Jesuit colleges and schools in France. It continues to explore the different forms of Jesuit universities and schools across Europe.

Humanism, Universities, and Jesuit Education in Late Renaissance Italy. Leiden: Brill, (May) 2022, reprints with light modifications nineteen articles previously published between 2006 and 2019 and one new article. Another friend, Cristiano Casalini of Boston College, who edits the Brill series History of Early Modern Educational Thought, invited me to prepare the volume. It begins with a programmatic definition of Renaissance humanism followed by nineteen chapters concerning themes, historical figures such as Erasmus of Rotterdam, modern historians, and events, connected with humanism, universities, and Jesuit education in equal measure. Some chapters deal with church history. Chapter twelve studies Giacomo Antonio Marta (1557 or 1558–1618), a professor of law who wrote extensively about church-state jurisdictional matters. His upbringing and friendship with Jesuits should have made him a papal defender. But Marta strongly opposed papal jurisdictional claims and defended the state. Finally, I am preparing a comprehensive examination of Jesuit pre-university schools in Italy tentatively entitled "Jesuit Schools in Italy 1548–1773." It is intended to be a companion to *The Jesuits and Italian Universities 1548–1773* of 2017.

I began to study Jesuit educational history because I realized that Jesuit lower school classes continued the humanistic curriculum that the Italian Renaissance pedagogical humanists pioneered. I continue to study Jesuit schools and universities because Jesuit schools were an early form of free public education that is so important to the modern world today and that I strongly support. And there is the thrill of uncovering new material. There is so much documentation for religious-order education, and the history of European education generally, that has never been examined. The excitement of searching for and finding new material, understanding it, and then writing a history that explains the story to others does not grow old.

These are the steps of a church history journey. They describe how I became an historian of the Italian Renaissance and then a church historian.

Reminiscences and Reflections

ROBERT BIRELEY, S.J.*

The author describes his formative influences, his mentors, and his work in early modern Catholicism, and he lays out his argument for the importance of undergraduate history.

Keywords: Anti-Machiavellianism; early modern Catholicism; Emperor Ferdinand II; Jesuit court confessors; Maximilian of Bavaria; undergraduate history

I was born in Evanston, Illinois, the first suburb north of Chicago, on July 26, 1933, just as Hitler was coming to power in Germany and a few months after Franklin Delano Roosevelt became president in the depths of the Great Depression. Evanston was a great place to grow up; it was anything but a Catholic ghetto, and it was characterized by considerable socioeconomic diversity. Protestant churches dominated but there were four vibrant Catholic parishes, one of them Polish-speaking, and our family of five participated actively in St. Mary's parish where I attended the parish school. We did not socialize much with Protestants—indeed, Catholic students were prohibited from patronizing the YMCA just down the street from the parish school. But we did get to know some of them well. A Protestant family with six children, the Schulzes, lived next door to us, and both my sister and I spent considerable time in their house. The oldest daughter was one of my sister's closest friends, and they remained such until my sister died twelve years ago. Many years later I prayed at the deathbed of both Mr. and Mrs. Schulz. There was Mr. Kasten, who had been dismissed as principal of the local Lutheran school and then served as a handyman in the neighborhood. I used to help him shovel snow during the winter, and once he invited me into his home and showed me his volumes of the collected works of Martin Luther.

During the 1940s my father used to make a couple of business trips to New York every year. He would always return with a copy of the *New York Times*, which was then the newspaper of record. I would read

---

*Father Bireley is professor emeritus in the Department of History at Loyola University Chicago, email: rbirele@luc.edu.

through it carefully, and it helped to introduce me to the world of politics and history.

In September 1947 I made my first acquaintance with the Jesuits when I began high school at Loyola Academy on the campus of Loyola University on the north side of Chicago (it moved later to suburban Wilmette). In freshman year I took a course in Western civilization taught by the football coach and in sophomore year a course in American history. The latter course was taught by the excellent Walter Bamberger, for whom I wrote my first "research paper" on the financing of the New York Central Railroad, a topic that fascinated me. Juniors and seniors were divided into the classical course featuring further study of Latin and Greek, the scientific course that featured chemistry and physics, and a third course that featured modern European history and Spanish. History did not rank high. I entered the classical course. At Loyola I also developed an interest in social issues, especially race, partly as a result of religion courses from a highly idiosyncratic but effective teacher and visits to the slums on the south side of Chicago. I also read on my own a book on the French worker priests and a biography of Walter Reuther, the leader of the United Automobile Workers.[1]

During my years at Loyola Academy I experienced a growing attraction to the Society of Jesus, and at a retreat in the middle of my junior year I decided to apply for admission to the Society. I have never looked back. I entered the Society of Jesus on August 8, 1951, at the novitiate in Milford, Ohio, outside Cincinnati. The first two years there as a novice introduced me to the way of life in the Society, and the second two years were devoted mostly to literary studies in the "juniorate." I received an excellent literary education at Milford and subsequently in philosophy and theology. A failure in the system was the relative neglect of science.

A major decision was made about the future of my study toward the end of my fourth year at Milford. In the late 1940s Jesuit Superior General Jean-Baptiste Janssens had issued circular letters "On the Social Apostolate" and "On the Intellectual Apostolate," urging Jesuits to devote more attention to these ministries. Interest in the social apostolate was high among us Scholastics (Jesuits preparing for the priesthood), an interest that I shared partly because of my experience in high school. The province prefect of studies came to Milford to discuss the studies that students wished to

---

1. I cannot now identify the book on the worker priests; the biography of Reuther was probably Irving Howe, *The UAW and Walter Reuther* (New York, 1949).

Robert Bireley, S.J.
Professor Emeritus
Department of History, Loyola University Chicago
Photograph by Mark Beane

pursue beyond the required philosophy and theology. Students were expected to start working toward a master's degree as they studied philosophy, to prepare for later teaching in one of the province's high schools. I expressed my desire to pursue a master's in sociology in line with my interest in the social apostolate. But the prefect told me that the province had enough Scholastics studying sociology and that it needed more history teachers for the high schools. History would thus become the subject in which I would pursue a master's degree. I have never regretted this decision.

For fall semester 1955 I moved to West Baden College, a Jesuit seminary in southern Indiana (the Celtics star Larry Bird came from nearby French Lick), for three years of philosophy studies where I completed the necessary undergraduate courses in history and then began my study for a master's degree in history. The one history professor was Charles Metzger, one of the first American Jesuits to pursue an advanced degree at a secular university, having garnered an MA at Oxford and a PhD at the University of Michigan with a specialization in American colonial history. I attended his survey courses of American and English history as one of a small group of students. Father Metzger would come to class with a few notes on the back of an envelope, then deliver a perfectly coherent, 90-minute lecture that was stimulating and at times eloquent.

Two events pushed me toward an interest in contemporary Germany during my years in philosophy. During the summer we Scholastics traveled up to Chicago for courses at Loyola University with which West Baden College was affiliated. There I took a course on modern Germany by Raymond Schmandt, another outstanding lecturer, and then the graduate seminar "On Modern Totalitarianism" taught by the charismatic if disorganized Edward Gargan who later taught at Wesleyan and the University of Wisconsin–Madison and served as a president of the American Catholic Historical Association. For him, I wrote a paper on "H. L. Mencken, Nietzsche, and the Nazis," in which I examined Mencken's early sympathy for the Nazis. Back at West Baden in fall 1957 for a course on modern political parties, I prepared a seminar paper on "Adenauer and the Christian Democrats in Germany." My interest was now turning to the relationship between religion and politics, especially in the Christian Democratic parties that sprouted up in Europe in the wake of World War II. The professor encouraged me to publish the paper; it appeared eventually in *Thought: A Journal of Catholic Thought*, a now defunct periodical published by Fordham University Press. It was my first publication.

In August 1958 I began three years teaching European civilization to freshmen and American history to sophomores at St. Ignatius High School in Cleveland, the next phase in my formation as a Jesuit called "regency." In my third year I introduced an Advanced Placement course in European history for juniors and seniors at St. Ignatius, the second AP course there following chemistry. The text used was the *History of the Modern World* by Robert R. Palmer and Joel Colton (New York, 1950). Many years later I got to know Professor Palmer at Princeton. In my final year I also taught American history to sophomore honors students. In the second semester each student was required to select a twentieth-century American, write a twelve-page book review of two biographies of the individual, and produce a twenty-page term paper on some aspect of this person's life. College students today would rebel at these requirements. The teaching in high school certainly prepared me for teaching in college. Meanwhile, I completed my master's degree in history at Loyola with a thesis on "The Reaction of Five American Catholic Periodicals to the Rise of Nazism, 1928–1936."

Now it was time to begin a four-year study of theology; ordination to the priesthood took place at the end of the third year. At that time Germany and France dominated in the study of theology, and Jesuit superiors were glad to accommodate nearly anyone who desired to travel to Europe for theology studies. I had two reasons for studying theology in Germany. The first was to secure an excellent theological education. The second was to master German so that I could undertake doctoral studies in modern German history after the completion of my theological studies. So I began four years of theological study at the Jesuit Hochschule Sankt Georgen in Frankfurt am Main. The international experience was invaluable. Gordon Zahn's controversial book *German Catholics and Hitler's Wars* (New York, 1962) appeared shortly after I left for Germany.

Toward the end of my studies there I began to think about a future doctoral program. A few older German Jesuits alerted me to the extensive diary of Father Friedrich Muckerman, which was housed in the Jesuit Archives in Cologne. Muckerman had been a significant journalist and literary figure in Germany in the 1920s and early 1930s who firmly opposed Hitler. After Hitler came to power in 1933 he slipped out the back door of the residence in Cologne when the Gestapo knocked on the front door. He fled to Holland where he began to edit an anti-Nazi periodical, *Der deutsche Weg*, and smuggled it into Germany. Under tremendous pressure from the German government he was forced to leave Holland and headed to Vienna, Rome, and Paris; he was one of the last persons to speak on Paris radio before the Germans occupied the city. He then fled to Vichy France and, when the Germans occupied it, left for Switzerland, where he died in 1945. His diary promised to be excellent source material for a dissertation. But when a leading German Jesuit inquired in Rome whether I might have access to it, he was told that the time was not yet opportune.[2] This experience made me begin to wonder about access to documents if the Church in the Nazi period became the subject of my research. I also heard that some German academics were withholding certain documents until their own students could exploit them.

After my ordination to the priesthood on August 28, 1964, I attended a conference of the Katholische Akademie in Bayern that dealt with the Church in the Nazi period. There I met Professor Konrad Repgen, then at Saarbrücken but planning a move to Bonn, and I asked him about future study with him. He referred me to his friend, Professor Dieter Albrecht, then at the University of Mainz but shortly would depart for Regensburg. Both of them had written on the Nazi period; only later when I arrived at

---

2. This diary was later published as Friedrich Muckermann, *Im Kampf zwischen zwei Epochen. Erinnerungen,* ed. Nikolaus Junk (Mainz, 1973). In Germany it became a mini-bestseller.

Harvard did I realize that early modern Europe was the principal field of both of them. Before I returned to the United States, I had a long lunch with Albrecht at his home in Mainz. He was to become a patron and friend.

My first year back in the United States was spent in tertianship, the final stage of my Jesuit formation. By now, superiors had authorized me to proceed with doctoral studies in history. I applied to Harvard and Yale, thinking that if both rejected me, I would return to Europe. Yale turned me down, but Harvard accepted me, and so I began my doctoral studies there in fall 1966. I was thrilled to be able to study at Harvard, and I was not to be disappointed.

As I started at Harvard, I was still undecided whether to make modern Germany or early modern Germany my principal field of interest. In my first year I took lecture courses on early modern France and modern Germany with Franklin Ford, then dean of the faculty of arts and sciences and the second person in the university hierarchy. Gradually my interest was shifting to early modern Germany and early Jesuit history. Up to this point much had been published on the early years of the Jesuits and on their many missions throughout the world. But the history of the Jesuits in Europe from the last third of the sixteenth century to the suppression of the Society in 1773 had attracted relatively little attention from the academic community in the English-speaking world. My interest in the relationship between religion and politics also played a role here. I had often read about the influence of Jesuit court confessors on politics in the early modern period, but as far as I could tell, there was no systematic treatment of the topic. But where to start?

During a survey course of Professor Theodore Rabb on early modern Europe I reread C. V. Wedgwood's *Thirty Years War* and came to realize that Maximilian, Duke and later Elector of Bavaria, had been a major figure on the Catholic side throughout the whole Thirty Years' War. What about his confessor? While browsing through the card catalog at Harvard, I found that my friend Albrecht had written extensively about Maximilian[3] and that the Jesuit Adam Contzen had served as the duke's confessor during the crucial years of the war from 1624 to 1635.

Contzen also, I quickly learned, had a substantial list of publications that featured religion and politics. I wrote Albrecht, asking whether he

---

3. Albrecht had also provided an introduction to the German translation of Wedgwood's *The Thirty Years War* (London, 1938).

considered Contzen a suitable subject for a dissertation, and he encouraged me to move ahead. Ford then agreed to serve as my director, and he was to give me valuable assistance.

At Harvard, we were required to take comprehensive oral exams in four fields. In May 1968 I passed exams in medieval history, early modern German history, early modern intellectual history, and modern German history. I am grateful that Harvard insisted on the examinations in four fields; this required the achievement of a certain breadth of historical knowledge. A few years later I heard Konrad Repgen deliver a lecture in Rome in which he stated that dissertations had grown in quality in recent years but lamented the lack of general knowledge on the part of many historians. I am afraid that the latter situation has worsened.

I then spent the summer and fall plowing through the more than 800 pages of Contzen's *Ten Books on Politics* (1620; 2nd ed. 1629).[4] In February 1969 I flew to Europe to begin research on my dissertation in Munich, Rome, and Vienna. On my first day in the Geheimes Staatsarchiv in Munich, the friendly attendant showed me a book that had just appeared by Ernst Albert Seils, *Die Staatslehre des Adam Contzen SJ* (Lübeck, 1969). My first thought was: there goes my dissertation! But the book—an excellent study of Contzen's political thought—included nothing about his activity as confessor to Maximilian. I spent six weeks working in the Jesuit Central Archives in Rome where I found 109 letters from Jesuit Superior General Muzio Vitelleschi to Contzen during the latter's years as confessor to Maximilian, many of them with significant political content. I was really on to something.

I then returned to work in the Geheimes Staatsarchiv and Allgemeines Staatsarchiv in Munich. There I found drafts of correspondence with the phrase "To be revised in accord with Fr. Contzen's remarks" in Maximilian's own hand. I also made use of a set of documents that the Germans had been unable to decipher. These were the pocket-size notebooks of Bartholomaeus Richel, who was Maximilian's longtime vice-chancellor and the mediator between the prince and his privy council, as Maximilian did not normally attend the council meetings. The notebooks were written in a mishmash of German, Latin, and Italian, and they pointed clearly to the influence of Contzen. My research showed that after Catholic forces gained the clear upper hand in the war that had broken out in the Empire, Contzen and his counterpart in Mainz had advocated for Emperor Ferdinand's disastrous Edict of Restitution of 1629 that reclaimed the lands that the

---

4. *Libri Decem de Politicis.*

Protestants had confiscated from Catholics since the Peace of Augsburg of 1555. The initiative for the Edict came from Munich and Mainz. The principal argument of Contzen was that God was summoning Maximilian to this drastic measure and that to refuse to do so was to sin and to stain the reputation of the Bavarian Wittelsbachs. This was clearly a religious argument that characterized the militant party at the court of Munich. Aligned against it were the moderates who rejected the theological argument of the militants. Policy could not be based on an alleged divine revelation, they contended. They called for a favorable peace that would consolidate the gains achieved by the Catholics and warned against overplaying the Catholic hand, as doing so would bring previously neutral Protestant states and foreign states into the war. This is exactly what happened with the invasion of Gustavus Adolphus of Sweden and the defection to him of Saxony and Brandenburg. At the Peace of Prague of 1635 the moderate party finally won out. Moreover, I also argued that Maximilian acted against his own immediate political interest while giving priority to the interest of the Church and the Empire. My thesis also showed the importance of individual decisions in history at a time when many historians downplayed this in favor of a Marxian emphasis on social forces.

I returned to Harvard in early summer 1970 after the upheaval at the university of the 1969–70 academic year, and I prepared a complete draft of the dissertation during the summer and fall before turning to teaching at Loyola University Chicago in January 1971. When offered a teaching fellowship at the university I declined, figuring that I had acquired enough teaching experience at St. Ignatius. I was eager to escape the category of graduate student. In summer 1971 I rewrote the whole manuscript and submitted it to Ford and to second reader William Bouwsma on July 31, the feast of St. Ignatius. They returned it to me two weeks later with their approval, and I received my PhD the following June.

Albrecht, who had provided me with valuable assistance during the writing of the dissertation although he did not completely agree with its findings, offered to have the dissertation published in the Schriftenreihe der Historischen Kommission der bayerischen Akademie der Wissenschaften, and he oversaw its translation into German by his mother-in-law and one of his graduate students. So it appeared in 1975 as *Maximilian von Bayern, Adam Contzen, S.J., und die Gegenreformation in Deutschland 1624–1635* (Göttingen, 1975).

My findings did not go uncontested, as they ran counter to the general interpretation of Maximilian as a religious prince whose priority was always the advancement of his own and Bavaria's interests. In his masterful biography of Maximilian, *Maximilian I. von Bayern* (Munich, 1998), Albrecht discussed our relative positions and moved closer to mine without completely accepting it.[5]

The main theme of my scholarship now became the relationship among politics, religion, and morality, in practice and in theory. While conducting my research on my dissertation I had noticed in various archives as well as in the literature many traces of the Jesuit William Lamormaini who served as confessor to Emperor Ferdinand II for almost exactly the same period as Contzen had served Maximilian. Why not move over to Vienna to investigate Lamormaini's part on the much more expansive imperial stage in Vienna? So this became my new project. I was fortunate to receive an NEH Fellowship for Younger Humanists (I was thirty-nine, just one year under the cut-off point of forty). The grant enabled me to spend the academic year 1972–73 working in European archives, especially those in Rome and Vienna. I spent the fall in Rome. There in the Roman Archives of the Society of Jesus I found more than 1000 letters from Vitelleschi to Lamormaini for the period 1624 to 1635, many of them with substantial political content, as well as other correspondence with the imperial court. These documents proved invaluable in assessing the relationship between Lamormaini and Ferdinand and offering many insights into the workings of the imperial court. Lamormaini was much closer to Ferdinand than Contzen was to Maximilian. The Vatican Library and Archives then contained the regular weekly reports from the nuncio in Vienna plus other correspondence. A delight in working at the Vatican was the regular mid-morning visit to the coffee bar between the library and the archives where other scholars circulated congenially.

The second half of that year found me in Vienna researching in the venerable Haus-, Hof- und Staatarchiv, with forays to the Benedictine Monastery outside Györ in Hungary that proved fruitless and to the Czechoslovak State Archives in Brno that turned out to be highly rewarding. During the negotiations over the Peace of Prague of 1635, Emperor Ferdinand had convoked a conference of twenty-four theologians to determine whether he could, in conscience, agree to the terms that had been proposed. Cardinal Franz von Dietrichstein, bishop of Olomouc, had chaired the conference, and his papers, I knew, were in the archives in

---

5. A master's student at the University of Munich, writing before the publication of Albrecht's biography, compared the positions of Albrecht and myself on Maximilian and decided in favor of my position.

Brno. There just might be something in Brno from the conference. It was difficult obtaining a visa for Brno when the shadow of the suppression of the Prague Spring still hung over Czechoslovakia, but finally it came through. None of the students working in the archive would so much as look at this American, but the archivist herself was friendly and helpful. When she brought out the first box of the Dietrichstein papers, I was thrilled to find a twenty-six-page protocol of the conference written in the clear hand of the Capuchin Basilio d'Aire, one of the participants. It was, along with the Richel notebooks in Munich, one of my most satisfying archival discoveries. Lamormaini spoke more than any other participant, but he did not submit a position paper. The protocol confirmed my theory about the religious nature of the war.

Once again in Vienna, as in Munich and other Catholic courts, the struggle between the militants led by Lamormaini and the moderates was evident. I had come now to distinguish between a religious and a holy war. A religious war was fought to advance or to defend religious interests. A holy war, which had a long tradition going back to the Hebrew wars in the Old Testament, was a war fought at the summons of God and with the promise of divine assistance. Both Maximilian and Ferdinand shared the latter view of the Thirty Years' War from roughly 1627 to 1635, and it found its expression chiefly in the Edict of Restitution. Both rulers surrendered this position at the Peace of Prague of 1635, which prepared the way for the Peace of Westphalia. Religion continued to be a feature of the Thirty Years' War, but its importance declined.

After my return to Chicago for the 1973–74 academic year, I continued working on the book manuscript. In April 1976 my colleague and good friend Hanns Gross and I organized the annual Newberry Library Renaissance Conference on the topic "Renaissance and Counter-Reformation in the Empire." We assembled an all-star cast that featured Robert J. W. Evans who had recently published *Rudolf II and His World: A Study in Intellectual History 1576–1612* (Oxford, 1973); it was his first trip to the United States, and he delivered the keynote address. Later that spring I returned to Europe to fill in some gaps in my research. An illness then provided me with the time to finish the book. In fall 1979 a colleague suffered a heart attack in the second week of classes, and I volunteered to assume his course on Western civilization up to 1650 in addition to my regular load. It was my first experience lecturing to nearly 200 students. By the end of the semester I was exhausted and had to spend a week in the hospital. My doctor advised me to cancel my commitment to serve as a guest professor at The Catholic University of America that spring. So I had time to finish *Religion and Politics in the Age of the Counterreformation: Emperor Ferdinand II, William Lamormaini, S.J., and the Formation of Imperial Policy* and sent it to Lewis Bateman, who guided the volume through the production process at University of North Carolina Press until its publication in 1981. (He later assisted in the publication of three more of my books, two at North Carolina and two at Cambridge University Press.) I then had the opportunity to defend my position at the international conference "Krieg und Politik 1618–1648," which took place at the Historisches Kolleg in Munich in 1984. My contribution, "The Thirty Years' War as Germany's Religious War," appeared in 1988 in the volume that resulted from the conference.[6] I dedicated this essay to Ford on his sixty-fifth birthday.

It was now time to turn to another topic, one that would not require a large amount of time in European archives now that extended residence in Europe was becoming increasingly expensive. I had frequently taught Machiavelli, and despite the attractive style and valuable thoughts on government found in *The Prince* and the *Discourses*, I have harbored a profound distaste for his basic thought. I find it strange that so many scholars can view his thought so positively. How can anyone take seriously the recommendation of the infamous Cesare Borgia or Romulus, the assassin of Remus, his mythological brother and cofounder of Rome, as models for political conduct? In the central passage of *The Prince* he wrote: "any man who under all conditions insists on making it his business to be good will surely be destroyed among so many who are not good. Hence a prince, in order to hold his position, must acquire the power to be not good, and understand when to use it and when not to use it, in accord with necessity."[7] A ruler could not be successful, where success was measured by the foundation and maintenance of a powerful state, without violating natural and Christian law at times. According to Friedrich Meinecke, a historian of Machiavellianism, "not only had genuine moral feeling been seriously wounded, but death had also been threatened to the Christian views of all churches and sects."[8] Machiavelli departed sharply from the tradition of

---

6. *Krieg und Politik 1618–1648. Europäische Probleme und Perspective*, ed. Konrad Repgen unter Mitarbeit with Elisabeth Müller-Luckner [Schriften des Historischen Kollegs 8], (Munich, 1988), pp. 85–106.

7. *Machiavelli: The Chief Works and Others*, trans. Allan Gilbert (Durham, NC, 1965), 1:57–58.

8. Friedrich Meinecke, *Machiavellism: The Doctrine of* Raison d'État *and Its Place in Modern History,* trans. Douglas Scott (New York, 1965; orig. publ. as *Die Idee der Staatsräson in der neueren Geschichte*, 1924), p. 49.

Aristotle and Cicero against whom he was consciously writing. More than any other individual, he bears the responsibility for the negative view of politics and politicians that we often encounter in our culture today. He has exercised a baleful influence on Western culture.

Machiavelli had raised starkly the issue of the relation of politics to morality and religion and in doing so provoked discussion that gathered force in the later sixteenth century and continues to the present day. We are told that there was a notable increase in the number of books on politics published in Italy and that groups assembled to discuss "cose di stato" in Rome and Genoa.[9] Many writers took up their pens to argue against Machiavelli. Most of them condemned Machiavelli from a traditional philosophical or theological position that was not difficult to do. But there was one group of writers who, taking for granted the philosophical and theological objections to Machiavelli, attempted to refute him on his own turf—that is, on the means to establish and maintain a powerful state. They aimed to show that his program simply would not work, and they then proposed a program that would work. Of this group whom I identified as properly the "Anti-Machiavellians," I chose the six most prominent Catholic writers: Giovanni Botero, *On Reason of State* (1589)[10]; Justus Lipsius, *Six Books on Politics* (1589); Pedro de Ribadeneira, *The Christian Prince* (1595); Adam Contzen, *Ten Books on Politics* (1620); Carlo Scribani, *The Christian Politician* (1624); and Diego Saavedra Fajardo, *Idea of a Christian Prince* (1643). They were the subject of my next book, *The Counter-Reformation Prince: Anti-Machiavellianism or Catholic Statecraft in Early Modern Europe* (Chapel Hill, NC, 1990). I prepared the first draft of this book during my fellowship at the Institute for Advanced Study in Princeton in 1986–87. It was a wonderful year filled with intellectual exchange, and I made several close friends, including Arnold Angenendt from Münster and Robert Markus from Nottingham. I also had the opportunity to chat with Robert R. Palmer, whose textbook I had used many years before.

The Anti-Machiavellians stood for a significant element of Counter-Reformation spirituality: the full Christian life could be lived in the secular

---

9. Rodolfo Savelli, "Tra Machiavelli e S. Giorgio. Cultura giuspolitica e dibattito istituzionale a Genova nel Cinquecento," *Finanze e ragion di stato in Italia e in Germania nella prima età moderna*, ed. Aldo Maddelena and Herman Kellenbenz, [Annali dell'Istituto storico italo-germanico, no. 14], (Bologna, 1984), pp. 261–64.

10. I am now preparing a translation of and an introduction to Botero's *Della Ragion di Stato* for the series Cambridge Texts in the History of Political Thought.

world. This conviction distinguished the spirituality of St. Ignatius Loyola's *Spiritual Exercises* as well as St. Francis de Sales's *Introduction to a Devout Life*, perhaps the two most influential devotional works of the Counter-Reformation. They also reaffirmed a major strain of the Renaissance: that the active life and especially participation in politics represented a noble Christian calling. Moral action, the Anti-Machiavellians argued, was by its very nature useful; immoral action was counter-productive. A standard example was the lie. It was always unprofitable because, in the long run, it undermined trust and confidence in its perpetrator. Moral action was reasonable, whereas immoral action was unreasonable. Machiavelli was unreasonable as well as irreligious and immoral. The Anti-Machiavellian concern with practice fostered the moral analysis of individual actions and the careful application of general principles to a specific situation, or casuistry, which was a growing feature—often a controversial one—of the Counter-Reformation. What in a particular instance constituted a lie? A great deal of ink was spilled over this issue. The Anti-Machiavellians did share positions with Machiavelli on many questions. They agreed with him that the support of subjects was absolutely essential for any ruler or regime, and all but one of them accepted his pessimistic view of human nature and thought that fear was more important than love as a constituent of this support. This contrasted with a fundamentally optimistic vision of the Christian's relationship to the world that characterized the Counter-Reformation. Most of them emphasized the importance for a powerful state of economic development: the promotion of agriculture, commerce, and industry. Botero was an early mercantilist. This was a moral means to a powerful state that benefitted both ruler and subjects. Machiavelli had ignored it.

At this point I wavered about my next project. A new obligation came my way when I was named superior of a small Jesuit community at Loyola University, a position I held from 1992 to 1998. Then out of the blue an invitation arrived from Jeremy Black to prepare a book on the Catholic Reformation for the Macmillan series European History in Perspective. This resulted in *The Refashioning of Catholicism, 1450–1700: A Reassessment of the Counter Reformation* (Basingstoke, UK/Washington, DC, 1999), which I shall discuss later. I then decided to return to the topic of the court confessors but would expand my reach to the whole Thirty Years' War (from 1618 to 1648) and to four courts (Munich, Vienna, Paris, and Madrid). A leave of absence from my duties as superior gave me the opportunity to spend four months of further archival work in Rome in 1995, and I was able to spend a delightful year at the National Humanities Center in North Carolina in the academic year 1998–99. Eventually there appeared *The Jesuits and the Thirty Years War: Kings, Courts, and Confessors* (New York, 2003).

Jesuit Superior General Vitelleschi, who served from 1615 to 1645, emerged as the principal figure in the book. He displayed considerable skill as he dealt with the four courts and the Jesuits at the courts who were often at serious odds with one another. The Jesuits certainly could not be counted as a monolithic organization; there was no general "Jesuit" policy during the war. Nor was there any consensus within the order about what the relationship ought to be between religion and politics. Letters to Rome from Jesuits in Munich and Vienna complained about the activity of Contzen and Lamormaini. Vitelleschi aimed, above all, to maintain harmony within the Society and to secure support at the various courts for the initiatives of the papacy for peace. Jesuit influence was most pronounced at the two German courts of Munich and Vienna. Other religious orders had been weakened considerably by the Reformation, and the Jesuits had become for the time the dominant order. But the successors of Contzen and Lamormaini, Johannes Vervaux in Munich and Johannes Gans in Vienna, were moderates who served as confessor to Maximilian and Emperor Ferdinand III until the end of the war. Vervaux, a native of Lorraine, seems to have enjoyed a closer personal relationship with Maximilian than the irascible Contzen. He undertook a few diplomatic missions for Maximilian, although this was prohibited by Jesuit regulations, and traveled to Paris for the duke in 1645. In Vienna Ferdinand III, who succeeded his father in 1637 and was no less religious than his father, still took the step of greatly reducing the influence of ecclesiastics, including Jesuits at court. Thus Gans remained a relatively marginal figure.

The Jesuits faced a challenging situation in France. From their earliest days they had encountered opposition from Gallican elements at the Sorbonne and the Parlement of Paris. From 1594 (after an assassination attempt on Henry IV) until 1603, they were exiled from most of the kingdom. They had a huge investment in France: fifty-eight colleges in 1623 and 13,000 students in 1627. They depended heavily upon the king for support against their enemies, a situation that continued nearly up to the French Revolution. This explains the extremely deferential attitude always maintained by Vitelleschi toward Louis XIII and especially toward Richelieu once he became chief minister in 1624. Up to that point several confessors played a role at court, but the cardinal now effectively controlled them. In 1637 Nicholas Caussin, confessor of Louis XIII, along with a young nun who had been a favorite of Louis XIII before her entrance into the convent, attempted to unseat Richelieu in the interest of peace in Europe and relief for the French peasantry burdened with heavy taxes for the war. Richelieu outfoxed them, and Vitelleschi exiled Caussin to the

Jesuit college at Quimper on the western coast of Brittany—nearly as far as one could get from Paris and remain in France.

Of the courts that I examined the Jesuits exerted the least influence in Madrid. Tradition required that the king choose a Dominican for his confessor and the queen a Franciscan. But the Jesuits did provide the confessor for the count-duke of Olivares, who was the leading minister in Spain from 1621 to 1643. Hernando de Salazar held this position for a time as well as other governmental posts. Because his activities violated the policy of the Society, which prohibited the conduct of such offices by Jesuits, Vitelleschi tried to remove him and eventually succeeded. The militant spirit of the Counter-Reformation did not breathe as powerfully in Madrid as it did in Munich and Vienna. For political reasons, the Spaniards favored some concessions to the Protestants in the empire in order to encourage a peace there that would free the emperor to assist them in their conflict in the Netherlands. Olivares urged Vitelleschi to remove Lamormaini, the advocate of a militant policy, from his post as confessor to Ferdinand II, and he even threatened to exile the Jesuits from Spain if Vitelleschi failed to act. But Vitelleschi called his bluff and refused to budge on the matter. Vitelleschi complained that the Spaniards considered him French and the French considered him Spanish.

My interest in Ferdinand II remained after the publication of *Ferdinand II, William Lamormaini, S.J., and the Formation of Imperial Policy*, and I published two articles on him in the early 1990s.[11] In the past forty years magisterial biographies had appeared of major figures of the Thirty Years' War such as John Elliott's *The Count-Duke of Olivares: The Statesman in an Age of Decline* (New Haven, 1986), and Dieter Albrecht's *Maximilian I*, and there were many fine biographies of Louis XIII, Cardinal Richelieu, the Duke of Lerma, Philip III and Philip IV, Gustav Adolf, and others. Indeed, two biographies of Ferdinand III were then in the works and have since been published.[12] But there has been very little on

---

11. Robert Bireley, "Ferdinand II: Founder of the Habsburg Monarchy," in *Crown, Church and Estates: Central European Politics in the Sixteenth and Seventeenth Centuries*, ed. R. J. W. Evans and Trevor Thomas (London, 1991) pp. 226–44, and Robert Bireley, "Confessional Absolutism in the Habsburg Lands in the Seventeenth Century," in *State and Society in Early Modern Austria*, ed. Charles W. Ingrao (West Lafayette, IN, 1994), pp. 36–53.

12. Lothar Höbelt, *Ferdinand III (1608–1657). Friedenskaiser wider Willen* (Graz, 2008), and Mark Hengerer, *Kaiser Ferdinand III. Eine Biographie* (Vienna, 2012). Purdue University Press is now translating the latter.

13. Johann Franzl, *Ferdinand II: Kaiser im Zwiespalt der Zeit* (Graz, 1978), was out of date and based on limited sources.

Ferdinand II.[13] So I decided to try my hand at it. Once again, a medical problem came to the rescue. In spring semester 2007 I had to undergo a knee replacement, and this freed me for the semester so that I might get a running start (so to speak) on the book. After the completion of the first draft I sent it to a colleague for evaluation. Her valuable criticisms were so extensive that I almost gave up on the project. But the chair of Loyola's History Department, Timothy Gilfoyle, encouraged me to continue, and so I did. Finally the work appeared as *Ferdinand II: Counter-Reformation Emperor, 1578–1637* (New York, 2014). In it, I argue that, more than any other individual, Ferdinand II contributed to the formation of the Habsburg Monarchy in Central Europe on the pillars of the dynasty, the Catholic Church, and the aristocracy. At the end of the Thirty Years' War the monarchy emerged under Ferdinand III as one of the European powers, and it avoided the upheavals that convulsed France, England, and the Spanish Empire in the 1640s. His moderate form of absolutism incorporated the estates into his government. He firmly established the Habsburg succession in the Empire after two weak emperors. The Counter-Reformation and Catholic Reform in Central Europe owed more to him than to any other secular ruler, I contended. But he erred seriously with the Edict of Restitution of 1629 and especially with the refusal for a long time to modify it, and so he bears responsibility for the prolongation of the war. I now await the verdict of colleagues.

Over the years I have periodically taught a course on the Catholic Reform, now better known as early modern Catholicism, at the undergraduate and graduate levels. When I began teaching at Loyola University in 1971 the Protestant Reformation, especially in Germany and England, dominated the study of the religious changes of the sixteenth century in the Anglophone world. This approach could be seen in textbooks, conferences, and college courses. Theological issues were often the center of attention, and confessional positions frequently colored the work of historians. The late-medieval Church was portrayed as corrupt and decadent, badly in need of thorough-going reform. Reformation courses often ended with the Peace of Augsburg of 1555 that legalized the Confession of Augsburg in the Holy Roman Empire. There was increasing treatment of the social sources of the Reformation—in particular, the Peasants Revolt—that was fostered by historians from the Eastern bloc. Little space or attention was given to the Catholic Reform or other developments in the Catholic Church in the early modern period, and the treatment that was given it often focused on the Inquisition, the papacy, and the Jesuits. All this has changed now. My guess is that there are many more publications on the Catholic Church in the early modern period than there are on the Protestant Reformation.

What are the reasons for this profound development? One is the ecumenical movement that emerged with a new vigor after World War II in light of the challenges of communism, Nazism, and a generally more secular world. Christians had to come together to meet these challenges. Historians played a major role in resolving or modifying many of the conflicts between Catholics and Protestants by taking a more balanced look at the issues that divided them. The hard lines that had divided Protestants and Catholics were softening. Catholics were coming to a much more sympathetic assessment of Luther. Second, there was the entrance into the field of early modern Europe of many students with no strong confessional commitment and with an attachment to professional objectivity as well as of many more Catholics. A particular feature of this interest in early modern Catholicism was the attention given to the history of the Jesuits. Studies on the Jesuits have become à la mode. There are several reasons for this, in addition to the fact that they were a leading force in early modern Catholicism. First, they compose a truly international organization that has existed for nearly five centuries; there is no other comparable institution in the world apart from the Catholic Church itself. Second, they have a rich central archive in Rome that is well organized and easily consulted. Third, they were in the forefront of the effort to accommodate Catholicism to the peoples of Asia and the Americas and to a lesser extent of Africa, so they offer rich material on the meeting of cultures.

Comparative studies of the Protestant Reformation and early modern Catholicism began to appear in the late 1950s with Ernst Walter Zeeden's work on Konfessionsbildung (formation of the confessions) that showed the parallels in the development of the Reformation churches and early modern Catholicism.[14] Both the Protestant churches and the early modern Catholic Church were recognized as having similar roots in the late Middle Ages, and recent scholarship has upgraded the condition of the Catholic Church on the eve of the Reformation. Even the Inquisition has received a more sympathetic and certainly a more nuanced treatment. Historians now trace the continuing impact of the Protestant Reformation and the Catholic Reform well into the eighteenth century. Further comparative studies came with the work of John Bossy, who found in both Protestantism and in early modern Catholicism a decline from the religion of

---

14. Ernst Walter Zeeden, "Grundlagen und Wege zur Konfessionsbildung in Deutschland im Zeitalter der Glaubenskämpfe," *Historische Zeitschrift,* 185 (1958), 249–99, rpt. except for pp. 276–86 in *Gegenreformation,* ed. E. W. Zeeden (Darmstadt, 1973), pp. 85–134; E. W. Zeeden, *Die Entstehung der Konfessionen. Grundlage und Formen der Konfessionsbildung im Zeitalter der Glaubensspaltung* (Munich, 1965).

medieval Europe, and Jean Delumeau, who contended that large areas of rural Europe had not been effectively Christianized during the Middle Ages and that fear characterized both Catholic and Protestant religion in the early modern period.[15] Principally German scholars developed Zeeden's Konfessionsbildung into the theory of confessionalization (Konfessionalisierung) that continued to point up the parallels between the confessions while emphasizing the role of the state and social discipline in their evolution. Now the adequacy of confessionalization as an explanatory theory to describe the religious changes of the sixteenth century has been called into question as too schematic and rigid to do justice to the complexities of the growth of the Protestant churches and the Catholic Church and for failure to recognize the properly religious features of the Protestant Reformation and the Catholic Reform.

My own contribution to this discussion appeared in my *The Refashioning of Catholicism 1450–1700*. Here I proposed that the Protestant Reformation and the Catholic Reform can best be understood as competing responses to the changing world of the sixteenth century and that they fit into the general pattern of church history that recognizes the need of the Church to accommodate to changing culture and society if it wishes to reach the people. This accommodation is both passive and active: Culture and society affect the Church, which in turn influences them. Conflict frequently occurs over the accommodation, some decrying any change as a sellout and others pointing out the need for the Church to keep up with the times. My concern was with Catholic accommodation, but I tried not to lose sight of the Protestant side.

This struggle over accommodation appeared already in the Acts of the Apostles where the issue was whether all Christians should be required to observe many facets of the Jewish law. As Gentiles began to stream into the Church, this became a vital issue and it caused considerable conflict in the Church before it was resolved. The issue of accommodation arose once again during the Patristic Age, which was encapsulated in the words "What has Jerusalem to do with Athens?" To what extent ought the Church take on features of Greek and Roman culture? Later in the early Middle Ages the issue arose once again with the invasion of many Germanic tribes into Europe with their warrior culture. One result of this was the Christian knight who took the cross of the Crusade. In our own day we experience

---

15. Jean Delumeau, *Catholicism between Luther and Voltaire: A New View of the Counter Reformation*, trans. Jeremy Moiser (London, 1977; orig. publ. as *Le catholicisme entre Luther et Voltaire*, Paris, 1971); John Bossy, *Christianity in the West, 1400–1700* (New York, 1985).

this crisis over accommodation with greater acuteness than in any previous stage of church history given the rapid change that characterizes society and culture today. It is into this broad pattern that the Catholic Reform and the Protestant Reformation fit in the early modern period.

What were these fundamental changes of the sixteenth century to which the Church was called to respond? The first was a widespread desire for church reform, for a spirituality of life in the world that would speak to a growing number of educated laity, and for the need to address the challenge of the Reformation itself. The second was the rise of the state, a process that dated from the high Middle Ages but reached a new stage in its development with the three monarchies of Spain, France, and England as well as other states. The cultural changes of the Renaissance constituted the third change: the return to ancient sources including the Bible, humanism and education, individualism, and the invention of the printing press. Then the fourth change included demographic and economic expansion and accompanying urbanization. Finally, there was the expansion of Europe across the globe but especially into Asia and the Americas.

Not surprisingly there were many parallels between the Catholic and Protestant reactions to the new world of the sixteenth century. It is worthwhile noting some of these similarities without losing sight of the fundamental doctrinal differences. Two general features characterized the Catholic as well as the Protestant response to the changes. The first was the further development of a spirituality for the layperson in the world where the *Spiritual Exercises* of Loyola and the *Introduction to the Devout Life* of de Sales stand out on the Catholic side. Luther and John Calvin also both aimed at the Christianization of life in the world. Second, there was the pursuit of order after a period of widespread theological and ecclesiastical upheaval. This can be seen in the Catholic Church in the Council of Trent and in a consolidation of authority in the papacy, and in the Protestant churches in their numerous confessions and church orders. In addition, both Catholics and Protestants turned to education as a means of evangelization; this was the age of both the catechism and the school. The Catholic Church saw the foundation of new religious orders of both men and women who took education as a principal area of their ministry. Casuistry along with moral theology developed in the Catholic Church, somewhat less among the Protestants, to help resolve the moral issues that arose with the changes such as the legitimacy of usury which at the time meant the taking of any interest. In the Catholic Church there took place perhaps the greatest expansion of missionary activity since the early Church, and this brought with it many issues of accommodation to an array of cultures and civilizations.

In addition to my publications projects, I had the honor to serve as president of the American Catholic Historical Association in 2008. Father Joseph Chinnici, O.F.M., then president of the Franciscan School of Theology in Berkeley, California, and my predecessor as president of the Association, was a great help to me in this office, and I continued the changes that he had inaugurated in the Association and that came to fruition in subsequent years. In my presidential address "Early Modern Catholicism as a Response to the Changing World of the Long Sixteenth Century,"[16] I developed the ideas of my *Refashioning of Catholicism 1450–1700*.

My focus over the years has been on research and undergraduate teaching. Graduate teaching has generally not attracted me, and I have had only two students who have completed doctorates under my direction. Indeed, I have occasionally thought of myself as at heart a high school teacher who likes to do research. The start of a new semester, especially of the fall semester with the arrival of new students and new faces before me, has often given me a sense of exhilaration. During my more than forty years at Loyola University Chicago I first taught two sections and later one of the survey course History of Western Civilization to 1650 in the first semester and History of Western Civilization Since 1650 in the second semester. In my later years I taught only the first half of the survey because we did not have enough faculty members ready to teach the first half. One of my primary goals was always to teach the students how to analyze a book and write a seven- to eight-page book review; I have written more than 100 book reviews myself, many for *The Catholic Historical Review*. I have especially enjoyed team-teaching undergraduate honors courses at Loyola with colleagues from English, modern languages, philosophy, theology, and fine arts. Indeed, I have learned much from them. For a few years I served as director of the History Honors Program.

Teaching these introductory courses became for me a form of mission to convince students of the importance of the study of history for their own human development. It is a major building block in a liberal education, I told them. This is why the university requires history as an essential part of the curriculum. I laid out for them in an early lecture the reasons why they should study history. The case for history made by leading historians in professional publications and in the op-ed pages of newspapers I have found to be usually weak and unconvincing; in some cases it seems to be reduced to instruction in critical thinking that, of course, history does pro-

---

16. Robert Bireley, "Early Modern Catholicism as a Response to the Changing World of the Long Sixteenth Century," *The Catholic Historical Review*, 95 (2009), 219–39.

vide. But there is much more. Indeed, history can lead to a certain wisdom. What I say here holds even more for the history of the Church. One of the problems faced by the Church today is widespread ignorance of its history. As both Christians and Americans, we obviously have to know the traditions from which we come; that is fundamental.

History, first, broadens my perspective by giving me a proper measure with which to evaluate my own time. We all should have an idea of what an ideal society would look like; it is perhaps more the function of philosophy or political science to help us to work out our vision of an ideal society. But if we measure our own society only against the ideal society, then we will always be depressed. Young people without any knowledge of history often fall into this trap. But history tells us that the ideal society has never existed and that some of the most heinous crimes have been committed in the effort to create the ideal society, as at the time of the French Revolution and especially of the various communist regimes. Racism, for example, still exists in our society. But if we review the history of the postwar era in American history, we have to recognize that we have made enormous progress since that time. This does not mean that we give up efforts to improve the situation further, but it does give us a more balanced picture of it. We bemoan the corruption at various levels of our government, but is it really worse than it was in the Roman Republic, or in the French Revolution, or in the Tammany Hall of Boss Tweed? And what about foreign countries today? Often in those countries, what we consider corruption they consider to be only the normal cost of doing business. This is not to say that we ought to cease efforts to lessen corruption but to admit that given the human condition, we can never hope to eliminate it completely without taking draconian measures that would make the situation even worse.

Second, history teaches us tolerance and understanding of others, vital qualities in our pluralistic society. On the personal level most of us want to be sympathetic and compassionate individuals. We come to know another person largely as we come to know his or her personal history. History helps us to translate this attitude to the social and political level. The educated person is characterized by the ability to understand the viewpoints of others, where they are coming from, and this normally requires a knowledge of their history. This does not mean that I agree with everyone; this is obviously impossible. But I must make the effort to understand why they think the way that they do. A case in point is the long-standing conflict between the Israelis and the Palestinians. There is much to be said on the side of each party. Why is it that many Jews often feel hostile toward Christians? Here, study of the Holocaust is in order. Views of many

African Americans can only be understood against the historical background of slavery. Many people have strong feelings on both sides of the immigration issue in the United States. Why do so many Russians apparently support the aggressive policies of Vladimir Putin? To understand this a knowledge of the recent history of Russia and the Soviet Union is necessary. No matter what position I take, I must be willing to understand the other side; here, history is critical.

Third, history teaches us about the complexity of human affairs; it helps us to avoid the oversimplified, sound-bite statements that are often the instruments of demagogues. Monocausal explanations of events like the Civil War, World War I, or the contemporary rise of terrorism are always misleading. Very rarely in history is it simply "the good guys versus the bad guys." Normally there is something to be said for both sides in a conflict or interpretation. This does not mean that more cannot be said for one side than the other and that I cannot advocate for a particular side. Here we can think of the various judgments of the role in history of the Crusades or of Christopher Columbus. From history, we learn that simplistic positions do not do justice to reality.

Fourth, history expands and complements our own experience. We do not have to learn everything by personal experience—for example, that fire inflicts a burn when I put my hand into it. From history I come to realize the depths to which human beings can sink, for example, in the perpetrators of the Holocaust or the genocide in Rwanda, as well as the heights to which they can rise, as we see in the heroes of the Resistance in Germany or in Mother Teresa. Good historical fiction can be placed here. There is perhaps no better description of what it was like to be a German infantryman in the trenches in World War I than Erich Maria Remarque's classic *All Quiet on the Western Front.* I still cannot read the concluding passages of this novel without tears coming to my eyes.

Fifth, history along with other subjects helps the student to formulate a philosophy of life. Students come to college often with a vision of life that is implicit. One goal of a college education is the formulation of a more or less explicit philosophy of life that in a Catholic university, one hopes, is a Christian one. History acquaints them with what great thinkers and artists of the past have identified as basic human problems and the answers that they have proposed. During their undergraduate years they should have the time and opportunity to work on this project that they may well not have later as their life progresses. They will undoubtedly modify it as they acquire more experience. But in college, they have the opportunity to get a running start.

I realize that what I have written here is itself highly idealistic. How many college students today are capable of embracing these liberal values? But we have to make the effort, and, more generally, in making the argument in the public sphere for the study of history we have to emphasize these liberal values. History does, as we all know, help prepare students for many types of work in their future, but there is much more to it than that. We want to provide them with the opportunity to become active citizens and Christians.

I have been very happy with my life as a Catholic historian at a Jesuit, Catholic university. The Catholic university has a major role to play in the American Catholic Church, and I am glad to have had a part in it as the Catholic university struggles to maintain its identity. I have spent many hours on university committees working to this effect. Occasionally, especially recently, I have doubted my effectiveness as an undergraduate teacher. In this regard two recent happenings brightened the picture for me. Just last year as I was having lunch in our Jesuit dining room, a young woman, the guest of another Jesuit, approached me. She told me how much she had enjoyed my survey course two years earlier; as a result, she had become a history major. Then I learned that a student from the late 1970s had endowed a scholarship in my name as an outstanding teacher. This greatly pleased me.

Historian with a Double Major: The Church and Feminism

Asunción Lavrin*

I became a historian of the Church by serendipity. But then, I have learned that many of my colleagues who also cultivate this field have confessed that they had a similar experience. It is a good club to belong to. As for the feminism side of my career, it was a well-thought choice, but it came much after I began navigating the waters of church history. The serendipity part came as a recently married twenty-three-year-old graduate student walked into the office of a historian at the University of California in Berkeley. He was Robert C. Padden, who had published a justifiably popular and well-researched book on the conquest of Mexico, the *Hummingbird and the Hawk*. He was not a historian of religion or the Church. Yet, he was sympathetic and friendly to this rather disoriented young woman who was seeking a good topic for research for her doctorate degree. He pointed to a title on women in convents in Mexico, the first in the field, by historian Josefina Muriel, and suggested that there was more to do on both women and convents, should that topic be of my interest. For some reason still unclear to me, I was. And that is how it all began.

A bit of background history is necessary at this point. I arrived in the U.S. from my native Cuba with a solid college education that covered three years of Latin and three years of Greek—most of which are now gone—history of art, history of world literatures, philosophy and, yes, western history. I loved them all, but inside me I knew I preferred history. Exactly what period or what area? I was unsure, but there was plenty of time ahead. I won a scholarship to study at a place named Radcliffe College, about which I knew nothing, but was glad to travel to, and begin my next adventure in life. I arrived with hardly any experience of spoken English, although I could read it very well. After three weeks in a foreign students' summer initiation camp—what a joy to meet other young people from so many different countries—I had all the preparation I was going to get to tackle that place, Radcliffe, and its relative, Harvard University.

---

*Asunción Lavrin is a professor of History, Emerita, at Arizona State University. Her email is lavrin64@gmail.com.

Needless to say, everything was foreign and marvelous, but it was hard work: writing in English, remembering a bibliography in that language, getting to know how professors taught and what they expected from students, navigating a new school environment with rules that pointed to getting a degree, exploring libraries, making friends. It was puzzling, but I was young and my professors were kind. Much later, I learned how "big" those professors were and appreciated the degree of their understanding of foreign students. Among such puzzling experiences, I met a young man from England who was attending business school at Harvard. Two years later he proposed and I accepted. It was that simple. By then he had transferred to the University of California at Berkeley, abandoned business school, and entered a program in Biochemistry and Immunology. He would get his doctorate in that field while I worked on my own.

And that is how I found myself in Berkeley, California, looking for a topic for a dissertation. Harvard was easier then than now: two years of graduate courses, an oral examination in three fields, and if one passed, one was a doctoral candidate. So, I became one. I had some excellent professors while at Harvard, but I cannot say that they were "mentors." They were kind, but our time together was short and passed fast, and none of them was available for a degree in Latin American history, one of the weak points in the program. My dissertation was read by a professor in the Spanish Department. I graduated in 1963, the first class of women historians in the history of Harvard University. Despite all obvious handicaps, I had become a full-fledged historian—or so I thought, at any rate. Life would teach me otherwise, but that was in the future then. I do consider myself a fast learner and also a self-made historian. I read the writings of the "great men" in History and at some point, I even taught courses in the development of History as a discipline, a great way to gain perspective and approach the discipline as a humble practitioner despite any university degree.

That background explains why my doctoral research topic was suggested by someone who was totally new to me. While I did not realize it then, I was launching into two "odd" fields of history: the Catholic Church, and the history of women, even though it was women religious. Women's history was not yet a recognized academic field, and they were nuns. Were they a different category? Time would tell. After accepting Professor Padden's advice, I wrote Harvard and filed for a dissertation with a nominal advisor there, but I was really on my own. The next challenge was to carry out research in Mexico. The Bancroft Library at Berkeley had a magnificent collection of documents, but a trip to the Mexican archives was absolutely essential, given the nature of my topic. The Bancroft Library

Asunción Lavrin
Photograph by Andrew Lavrin

continued to be my research anchor for several years, a place to read and explore. I remember fondly its head, Dr. George Hammond. After my first research trip to Mexico, I paid a visit to his office and pointed out to him that a complete section of the Mexican Archives of the Nation on "Temples and Convents" had been microfilmed. Would the Library be amenable to purchasing it? I was only a doctoral candidate and certainly not registered at the University of California as a student, but I had no hesitation in my naïveté. He was generous and had a big smile. He agreed immediately to buy the microfilm, and I was guaranteed some first-class materials close to my home base, although subsequent trips to my sources in Mexico remained essential.

At this point, the details on how I planned that first trip escape me, but I landed in Mexico City with the same kind of lack of experience and enthusiasm that seemed to be my trademark. The archives were housed in the same building that had sheltered the colonial viceroys and were then the presidential palace. The building also housed battalion No. 1 of the Mexican army. So, in my daily visits I saw government bureaucrats, archivists, researchers, and soldiers. When very dusty reams of colonial papers were tendered to me for the first time and in subsequent yearly visits, I knew I was "caught" forever. The sight and feeling of those old papers and the stories they revealed were addictive. I have followed the Mexican National Archives through two "moves" to other more appropriate buildings as the key anchor of all my research. At some point, I took a side research trip to the city of Guadalajara in pursuit of what were rumored to be "secret" convents' papers held by communities of cloistered nuns. I had to obtain permission from the archdiocese of Guadalajara to get the addresses of the convents because under the existing national laws enclosure was not "legal" and those communities were underground. So, I requested to be received by the archbishop in one of his open receptions for believers and other people seeking some favor or advice. I now know that José Garibi y Rivera, then archbishop, was elevated to cardinal in 1958, so I must have met a cardinal. Titles remain fuzzy in my memory but I do remember clearly that when my turn came to be introduced to him, I realized that I had never met a prince of the Church and I did not know what to do. He suavely assisted me by offering his ring for a reverential kiss. After that, I very humbly explained my mission. At some point, he asked me if Harvard University was a Catholic University. I had to confess it was not, but he seemed not to have been troubled by that fact or by my request, and I got the addresses. Unfortunately, the rumors about secret archives were not true. The nuns had little to offer on historical papers. However, I learned about the public library and the archives of the city, to which I later returned on another research trip.

Convents and Nuns: My First Love

While the Guadalajara nuns' lack of historical documents disappointed me, their ancestors in the seventeenth and eighteenth centuries were more generous, and their papers at the National Archive of the Nation and other venues in Mexico and in the U.S. have for decades supplied me with plenty of resources for my research.

Once I began my work, I realized that conventual accounts and administrative records were the most abundant, for obvious reasons: the affairs of this world were the anchor of the convents; without economic self-sufficiency they would not have been able to survive as religious institutions in search of the spiritual. Those records tied the convents to the economic layout of the land and its propertied class. While I had to construct a complete picture of nunneries as social, spiritual, and economic institutions, the weight of those financial records guided my first publications and attendance at historical conferences. In the late 1960s and throughout the early 1970s economic and quantitative history were at the cusp of their popularity and my data on the economic role of nunneries in the colonial economy was a revelation to fellow historians who had never thought that women in convents had anything to do with money or investments. In 1966 the *Hispanic American Historical Review* published my second article as a historian on the role of the nunneries in the economy of New Spain in the eighteenth century. It explained that nuns were real estate owners and investors, and were in the money lending business catering to rich merchants. Who would have thought! In 1967 the article won the annual prize for the best article published in 1966, the James Alexander Robertson Memorial Prize. I traveled for the first time to the American Historical Association annual meeting to receive it. The AHA was a man's bastion and I was surrounded by men. I was presented with a corsage to pin on my jacket for the annual luncheon. That has never happened again.

Catholic nunneries in Latin America were a totally unknown topic in those years, and I found historical journals were interested in my work. I continued to publish on convents in general and their administration in particular, and how they fit in the social and economic reality of a European colony in the Americas. The network of fifty-seven convents on Mexican soil sheltered the female social elite and was tied to Mexican society through a complex system of liens and loans and urban real estate. After an attempt at land-ownership in the seventeenth century, the prelates decided that the administration of rural properties should not be the main concern of women dedicated to God. Urban property ownership and loans or liens on real estate administered by men was more suitable to convents. My work added an unknown dimension to the predominant view that wealth was in the hands of miners, merchants, and hacienda owners. It was undeniably intriguing to think that those women, hidden from view behind thick walls, could and would be invested in real estate and were "bankers" to powerful men. Following this lead, I extended my enquiries into the nineteenth century to survey how nunneries as property owners and sources of cash dealt with the increasing hostile republican administrations of the new nation and published two more articles on the topic covering the nineteenth century up to 1860 when after years of struggle cloistered nunneries were banned in the country. Around that time *The Catholic Historical Review* published my only article with the journal in 1972, "Values and Meaning of Monastic Life for Nuns in Colonial Mexico," under the kind editorial policy of Father Robert Trisco.

By amplifying my interest on the economic role of nunneries to cover the economic role of other religious institutions such as confraternities, I sustained my research and publications on economic issues through the following decades. An intensive study of the relationship between the ecclesiastical capital and the social elites in Mexico (1985) appeared shortly after essays on the theme of sexuality in Mexican colonial history (1984), a review of studies on women's history in Latin America (1984), an inquiry into Sor Juana Ines de la Cruz's behavior as compared to that of "model" nuns in Mexico (1983, 1984), and a general historiography of the Church in colonial Latin America (1989). The Church and nuns did not lose their appeal to me; they were joined by a new "stream" of interest: women in the larger frame of history of the nineteenth and twentieth centuries.

My interest in secular women's history was a natural response to changes in the academic world in the late 1970s and onwards. By the mid 1970s women's history was knocking at the door of all fields. Some colleagues were still somewhat disoriented about its nature. For example, the inclusion of the example of a notorious transgender who dressed up as a man and behaved as man, even after being punished with seclusion in a nunnery, was regarded as a contribution to women's history. The inclusion of "notable women" or queens also pretended to fulfill the requirement of mentioning women in general surveys. "Gendering" was still a concept to be developed in full. I shared the "call" to women's history with other women in my field. Latin American history was then taught largely as political history populated by male archetypes: conquistadors, pre- and post-conquest kings and emperors, dictators, political redeemers, messianic male revolutionaries, and, when religion and church were involved, plenty of evangelizers, bishops and archbishops, male saints, or irascible inquisitors. Otherwise, we had mothers of the new republics, women revolutionaries, or audacious and exceptional women such as "the Evita" of Argentine Peronism. Building a stronger foundation for a better treatment of women in our history had to begin somewhere.

Since I was in the colonial period, I remained there. There were many basic questions still to be raised and answered, and those of us who began discussing women's history with our surprised—albeit sometimes delighted—male colleagues had to lay a general foundation of understanding of what women's history was. What were the social and cultural mechanisms shaping women's lives in general? Why was there a predictable dichotomy in women's lives that drove them into either marriage and family, or a cloister? Was the experience of "womanhood" the same for women in complex, multi-racial, and economically unbalanced societies? These were basic bread-and-butter issues that look very unsophisticated decades later, but were nonetheless our starting point. The known world of nuns guided me into the relatively unknown world of secular women, which I began tackling by using the same documents I had used when I was writing on nuns: dowries and wills, the legal pillars sustaining all women's lives and already in wide use by historians in European history. Dowries and wills furnished data of how men's and women's lives were defined and intertwined at two crucial moments in their lives: marriage and family formation, and death and the legacy of material wealth. They opened new vistas on the social and financial strategies of individuals as well as families.

Working with my friend and colleague, Edith Couturier, we developed a research project on the nature, scope, and consequences of those legal documents in two cities: Mexico City and Guadalajara, both sites of the only two judicial courts of the viceroyalty and with excellent notarial records. The result was another first—so much so that the two male readers for the same journal that eventually published it rejected it outright. Fortunately, the editor of the *Hispanic American Historical Review*, Michael Meyer, had two women historians as editorial advisors, Susan Deeds and Donna Guy, who had a more open view of the future trends of history and reversed the fate of the article. It was finally published in 1979, although it lost one of its sections on the meaning of both sources for the study of material culture, a topic I never returned to. When we presented a paper on this topic in an AHA panel dedicated to women, the room was filled to capacity. I suspect that many male colleagues had come as "observers" of a rare event. Since then, dowries and wills have been amply used by historians in my field as meaningful sources for the study of women's status, marriage, and social and economic connections among people—whether with small or large economic resources—as well as how their dowries provided the source of funds for pious and religious ends that benefited the Church.

Before the publication of that article, I had already decided to publish an edited book on women's history. I like team-working. Then, and now, collaboration continues to be essential to break into new fields of research and understand topics with the benefit of the broader and multi-layered angle of several contributors. I gathered the best work of a number of colleagues who had been investigating, in pioneering ways, on women and gender-relations issues in this vast new field. There was no one at the time ready to write a general or even a regional history of women in Latin America with the fragmentary information we had in hand. It was necessary to introduce the topic with well-researched essays that would interest others in following the example, carry out more research, and invigorate our field. First published in English in 1978, *Latin American Women: Historical Perspectives* was translated into Spanish in 1985 and amply read on the continent. For decades, younger historians in Latin America have approached me and have told me how they felt inspired by this volume and its essays, to begin to study the topic in their respective countries. That was precisely my idea on the usefulness of the project, and while all books lose their currency in time, I think that our pioneering effort fulfilled its purpose.

The next chapter in my development as a historian of women relied in no small degree on the variety of ecclesiastical resources housed in the Mexican National Archives. The Church is such a complex institution, and it was so naturally intertwined with the legal structure of the state in Spanish America, that it could furnish abundant materials for all social history topics. Along with women's history, the history of sexuality was fast becoming a field of its own. Data provided by colonial sources showed that a large number of children were born out of wedlock in Catholic New Spain. This issue demanded an answer. Studies of marriage patterns and choice of marriage partners as they were carried out then simply did not address the root problem of such a high incidence of births outside the perimeters of civil and religious laws. It was also a situation that affected women of the lower classes in a multiracial society: those single mothers and those often-mixed-race children had to be explained to understand the complexities of colonial society gender and racial relations. The Church had many venues to model and control sexual behavior. It seemed to me that in order to explain the reality of "deviant" out-of-wedlock births rather than "proper" legitimate births, we had first to learn more about the rules set out by the Church in its indoctrination and even delve into moral theology. They are the sources from which confessors distilled their advice and confessors impinged on everybody's lives. Spanish America was a Catholic society by law. Was it really a Catholic society in practice? As adults, men and women may obey or disobey the rules of ethical behavior they learned in catechism classes, and it was possible to ignore totally church teachings and instead follow one's own emotions. It was also possible to wed properly and follow the Church's moral guidance, but disobey it in many instances of weakness, later confessed, and possibly forgiven.

Those were the situations that interested me: not charting wedlock in numbers as in quantitative history, but connecting human behavior to Church indoctrination and understanding how people challenged such a strong institution of social control. The records on the Inquisition were a very good source for understanding the rules of vigilance set up by the Church supported by the State, and, at the same time, for finding examples of how they were challenged or broken by those caught in the conundrum of flesh vs. spirit. Cast against the principles of moral theology, the records of the

Inquisition are rich in testimonies that help one to understand the gap between ideal and real behavior. Throughout my life as a researcher, I have always looked for the dialogue between church and moral rules and real human behavior as a fruitful method to begin any inquiry into social history.

The study of human sexuality throughout history was in its formative stages in my field in the late 1970s before it developed in full in the 1980s. For reasons similar to those supporting the publication of a collection of essays on women, I edited and co-authored a volume, *Sexuality and Marriage in Latin America*, in 1989, showcasing my expertise and that of several talented colleagues who wrote on several areas of Latin America. We were making a case for the need to address human sexuality as a topic essential to the study of family formation, as well as the physical drive triggering acceptable and non-acceptable forms of behavior in societies under the strict control of religious codes of personal honor. Opening gates is always a satisfactory occupation, especially when one can retrospectively see how far and wide the field became in subsequent years. Those of us involved in that project dealt with heterosexuality. Any other form of sexuality was still a bit on the fringes of our academic horizons. Boundaries have expanded since then, and this is a good thing, as I stated when I was asked in 2015 to write the foreword for a book of essays on sexuality and the unnatural in colonial Latin America, edited by Zeb Tortorici.[1]

The Feminists

While I continued to publish on religious women, and women and sexuality in general in the colonial period, I made an important switch on my research agenda. I developed an "urgent" curiosity to learn when and how "colonial" social and gender mores changed under the increasing pressures of independence and republicanism, urbanization, "class" consciousness, the rise of a new concept of national politics, the emergence of an urban working class, and the expansion of education. By the third quarter of the nineteenth century, women were rapidly becoming educated while at the same time joining the urban working class. Nunneries had lost their relevance as "places" to fulfill a woman's destiny. Women's lives, as I had known them to have been between 1550 and 1800, were "a thing of the past" by the third quarter of the nineteenth century. I was ready to expand my label as a "colonialist" and become, more fully so, a historian of women

---

1. Zeb Tortorici, ed., *Sexuality and the Unnatural in Colonial Latin America* (Oakland, 2016).

in a different chronological period. While the nineteenth century was the laboratory of ideas explaining rapid social changes, I decided that feminism, as an emergent and developing ideology in Latin America between 1890 and 1940, had helped to change women's status significantly, as it had done in a large area of the world.

With the aid of several fellowships through the mid 1970s and the mid 1980s, I was able to sustain my research in that decade. To study feminism I "left" Mexico and turned to three key countries in South America: Argentina, Chile, and Uruguay, commonly known as "Southern Cone" nations. Dates are often not chosen haphazardly. In the last two decades of the nineteenth century, most states in Latin America accepted the fact that their educational systems needed women teachers and that women's education was a key to their own social and economic development. Women writers had already been making a case for this, but until higher education was opened to them, no change would take place. Broadly speaking urban growth and the export sector created a new labor market for women with certain skills to carry out a variety of jobs in local factories. Education and labor demands were the key factors in the process of transformation of the Southern Cone countries between 1880 and 1940. They ushered in a period of essential changes in legal rights for women that set in motion changes on individual and social attitudes about women's role in society.

The Cono Sur nations had a reasonable—albeit not always perfect—political continuity in terms of the constitutional systems: a vigorous press, a strong drive to form labor unions, a substantial input of European immigration bringing "radical" social ideas to their host countries, and an increasing number of women writers and educators that encouraged discussion of issues of civil and political rights, public health, and education. There was also at this time a small but influential number of men open to the thought of revamping the status of women through juridical and legislative actions. Further, these countries had had important political ties among themselves that would make a comparative study possible.

So, I plunged into the study of feminism in full in the mid 1980s and had a lengthy book published in 1995. It remains the only comparative study of feminism in Latin America. As a personal experience, the switch of fields and geographical area was invigorating. Women remained the foundation of my interest, and I saw my switch to a contemporary period as an expansion of my understanding of the changes affecting women and men in real time, since I was part of that transformation. The number of women historians in the US expanded significantly in the 1980s and 1990s, and this change also affected my chosen field. Women were no longer an odd sight at conferences, as it had been the case in the late sixties and early seventies. Research and publication on women had validated the field and gave women full access to academic history. Not all women did women's history, of course, but the momentum gained by women's studies and, more amply, gender studies, meant a vigorous renovation of academic life that was transformational for both women and men. Looking back, I think that having followed a new path was one of the best choices I have made in my career as a historian.

For the study of feminism, I covered the transformation of the labor market as it incorporated women and, just as importantly, began to strengthen labor unions powered by anarchist and socialist ideas that recognized the value of women's work and their role in society. There were also men committed to the introduction, debate, and approval of basic changes in the civil codes and legislation affecting the status of women as wives and mothers. There was discussion of divorce, public health, sexuality and reproduction issues, subjects which had been socially taboo and had never been discussed in the open for hundreds of years. Eventually by the 1930s, suffrage was included in the agenda. I studied these topics comparatively, with information for each country. This broad approach was absolutely necessary to validate the study of feminism in a continent that was "assumed" to have been conservative and Catholic, and that actually remained so until the end of the nineteenth century. It was not an easy task to address these topics across three countries but the effort was worthwhile. The stunning forces of social change experienced in these three countries in this period explain the rapid transformation of Latin American countries from being part of a colonial system until the first decades of the nineteenth century into states aspiring to join global economic and political systems a century and a half later. Women had to be placed in the center of this transformation using the only ideology that seemed to have formulated answers to most of their problems: feminism. It never occurred to me to look at the Church throughout these years, since it remained a bastion of tradition and conservatism. I was not interested in the defense of traditional Catholicism but in change for women.

Researching feminism took me several times on research trips—for months at a time—to the libraries and universities of these three countries. My research on feminism also let me appreciate how important was also the period of transformations taking place in the last quarter of the twentieth century while I was writing on feminism. A second and third generation of Latin American women activists were reaping the fruit of the activities of the first generation of feminists I was studying, but they were also questioning it. As more countries in Latin America attempted to answer the enormous social and economic problems posed by fast-growing populations under often unstable political regimes, the changing roles of women, now fully incorporated into politics, the labor force, and the educational system, raised many questions on the social issues the first-generation "feminism" had not foreseen, let alone solved. After the publication of my book, I wrote several essays on the changing forms of feminism in Latin America up to the late years of the twentieth century, one hundred years after the ideology was first introduced in the continent. They made sense as sequels to my interest in the emergence of feminism. Until the early 2000s, I helped edit international publications on women and Latin American women specifically, and saw my book on feminism translated and read in Spanish America. Feminism and change in the early twentieth century was a fulfilling project that invigorated my career as a historian for two decades.

Returning to the Nuns: Spirituality in the Writings of Cloistered Women

Publishing on feminism was a rewarding experience, but I began to miss my first love: cloistered women. I suppose it was the result of that desire for contrasts and alternative realities that has sustained my interest in history since I became a historian. In 1995 Mexicans observed the three hundredth anniversary of the death of that great seventeenth-century woman of letters, Sor Juana Inés de la Cruz. Conferences and publications on the occasion were only a part of what was developing as a large research field on nuns and convents in the viceroyalty. I returned to my old pastures with the confidence of someone who really never left—as I stated before. While literary analyses of Sor Juana's writings will remain a fixed item in cultural history, historically, there are limitations to anything "new" being discovered on Sor Juana's life owing to institutional and personal boundaries set by her state in life. On the other hand, since the late 1990s history has yielded fascinating information on the "lives and times" of *other* nuns. A new cohort of literary historians and social and feminist historians began to dig into archival sources to reveal a new world of institutional and personal data on nuns' lives, most of them having been ignored throughout history. This new interest was a "continental" happening all throughout Spanish America, which made the field more universally appealing than it was before. Nuns' history was also women's history! By the late 1990s, trends in European church history discussing the role of women in the church since the early Middle Ages through the twentieth century supported and inspired research elsewhere and found an attentive ear in Latin America and Spain. On numerous occasion, I turned to books published on European nuns as intellectual sources. In 1993, before the celebratory observances of Sor Juana's death, and even before the publication of my book on feminism, I published an article on religious life as a feminine experience. Sor Juana would remain a "sun" in Mexican cultural history but I would study other nuns: the planetary system rather than the sun.

My return to the nuns had a demanding objective: to consolidate my research and write the monograph I should have published much earlier on some of the key issues in the history of nuns and nunneries. I returned to church history as a mature historian without regrets. I had achieved my ambition of writing women's history beyond a period and a country. Returning to the cloisters, however, also meant a change in my approach. The in-depth views of financial administration that I had cultivated at the beginning of my career were no longer my focus. With a larger number of practicing historians engaged in the study of nunneries in the key cities of the country, the field had changed significantly. Writers and readers wished to have a deeper look into the intimate scenario inside of the cloisters by focusing on nuns as real women, carrying out daily routines in liturgy, and shaping their personal lives to the rules of their Orders and the demands of their own spiritual goals. There was also a renewed awareness of the reality of the nunnery in its institutional connections with society.

I had new marching orders. No more accounts or investments; rather, I needed more information on personal spiritual development and social issues. I began with the latter, writing an article on the foundation of nunneries for Indian women as a meaningful change in social attitudes, as well as a reckoning of colonial elites and the Church with its own debt towards indigenous peoples. The Indian nunneries encountered some internal problems caused by an insensitive Commissary General, but, in general, society welcomed them and their numbers increased to three nunneries by the end of the colonial period. As for my plans to engage again with nunneries, I found myself more strongly attracted to the spiritual issues in nuns' lives as seen through their writings. My friends in literary studies were very influential in directing me to those sources. Doubtless, Saint Teresa of Avila's writings and their extensive circulation set in motion a great change in women's spiritual literature that encouraged nuns in Spain and elsewhere in Europe to confide their inner life to paper, and to write poetry, theater, and spiritual treatises. Prompted by spiritual advisors, many nuns wrote extensive diaries. This quiet revolution found some echoes in the transatlantic colonies. Apart from the already mentioned Sor Juana, a good number of nuns engaged in writing. They helped to write the histories of their convents, wrote devotional works, some poetry, and about themselves in "diaries" where they poured out their religious doubts and hopes.

In Spanish America and, specifically in Mexico, most of those materials had remained unused by lack of interest or understanding, and also because they were overshadowed by the blinding light of Sor Juana's writings. When I began my own personal re-entry into some of those personal letters and diaries, I understood why I had been unprepared to cope with them when I was younger. One needs life experience to understand the pathos in some nuns' lives and writings. Their struggle to understand and achieve their own spiritual goals was life-consuming and totally disconnected from the engagements of daily life. As a modern reader, I became aware of the distance between contemporary spirituality and that practiced centuries before, when human shortcomings were overemphasized and suffering was regarded as the privileged pathway to grace. Of course, the consolation of devotional life was always at hand to balance the outcome, but the personal struggle was real and revealing. Reading examples of that permanent conflict can be emotionally draining, but it is a necessary exercise for anyone attempting to reconstruct these women's lives.

These documents also convey evidence that "interiority," a mark of male spiritual writers in Spain, was very much part of the Catholic ethos there and elsewhere in the Catholic world, and that, as such, it included women. After Saint Teresa made interiority her own, she passed it on as her heritage to women religious. In Mexico her writings were very popular in the seventeenth and eighteenth centuries, and strongly influenced the output of writing nuns. I began to publish on some of these manuscripts and analyze them as testimonies of the tortured but rich spiritual life of a small group of nuns. Required by their confessors and spiritual directors, writing about their spiritual life took precious moments of their busy life. They were not "literary" pieces but a means of spiritual self-discovery via communication with a spiritual director and, above all, with God. As one of them wrote, writing about her interiority was like writing about the kingdom of God because God was inside herself. Their sometimes-tortured nature doesn't make the reading "easy," but they are of indisputable importance for learning about the meaning of religion and faith for these women.

These writings galvanized my attention and desire to incorporate the literary production either written by religious women or addressed to them as an essential component of their "social" and personal history and the cultural life of the viceroyalty. The writings by nuns absorbed my attention with the same intensity that conventual financial affairs had in my early research. In 2002 and 2006 respectively, and before the publication of *The Brides of Christ*, I coedited two books with my Mexican colleague, Rosalva Loreto-López, on the writings of nuns in Mexico and Spanish America: *Monjas y beatas: La escritura femenina en la espiritualidad barroca novohispana: Siglos XVII y XVIII* (2002), and *Diálogos espirituales: Manuscritos femeninos hispanoamericanos* (2006). The first focused on Mexico and introduced autobiographies, spiritual diaries, and letters in several essays. The second one included extensive excerpts from the writings of nuns in Ecuador, Peru, Chile, Argentina, and Mexico, preceded by introductory comments. This semi-anthological work intended to make such writings accessible to a broad readership and was our best effort to bring together literary and historical attention to a topic that was in need of full international recognition as part of the Spanish American cultural legacy.

My monograph, *Brides of Christ: Conventual in Colonial Mexico*, was published in 2008. It was a fusion of institutional and personal history accessible to students and general readers interested in the unique experience of cloistered women, a way of life that had taken a steep decline from the nineteenth century, but which had possessed relevance as an aspirational way of life for women for centuries. Nuns are still ubiquitous in Latin America as they engage in education and social issues, and their history has become a subject of interest, not only among younger historians, but among a sector of the population educated in traditional values. In my book I attempted to present nuns as real women and not cardboard stereotypes. I followed novices in their decision to take the veil, and the meaning of a choice in religious life. It was then a mark of social elitism. Admission to the convents was only accessible to women of Spanish descent, of legitimate birth, and with a prescribed dowry. The latter could be donated by a patron, and legitimacy was only breached occasionally in favor of daughters born out of "mistakes" by their otherwise acceptable parents. However, racial deviations or lack of "cleanliness" of blood was never tolerated. As a result, nuns were a set of special women and certainly not representative of the lifestyle of the majority of their sex. However, it is the very privilege of their social position that has made it possible to access a sampler of "women's" experiences in a period where most women remained anonymous. As historians, we understand that nuns did not represent all womanhood, but even through the filter of race and class they are a universe of women's experience worth discovering and understanding.

Within the convent, the nuns' individual experiences were pitted against the restrictions of a life structured to meet the sometimes-conflicting objectives of spirituality and the material realities of institutional living. In addition to information on daily life and hierarchical organization, I was keen on including specificity on the spiritual meanings of religious life by focusing on the solemn vows, the love of God, and devotional practices, such as those addressed to Christ, the Virgin Mary, and the Sacred Heart. The vows were the pillars of conventual life, and the devotional universe amplified the foundation of commitment the vows represented. The devotional practices carried out within the convent reflected those outside its walls. In fact, they nourished each other. There was a robust exchange of devotional practices that strengthened the role of convents as magnets of popular religiosity. Despite enclosure, the porosity of the convent resulted in "devotion" to some nuns of known spirituality who, from behind the covered grilles, administered advice to anguished seculars. These themes were counterbalanced by chapters on sickness and death, a reminder of their humanity but also informative about sickness, medical practices, and the spiritual meaning of the end of life.

Another topic included in the book was that of "sexuality" which was not often associated with cloistered women. As Inquisition records show, nuns were the subject of sexual harassment. While this issue had been the subject of historical research in Europe, it had not really been discussed by other historians in my field. This "delicate" topic was yet another form of understanding the humanity of these women and the reaction of their prelates as keepers of their virtue as brides of Christ. "Courting" nuns was a social sport for some men in courtly Spain in the seventeenth century, and while such activities did not take that turn in Mexico, it was imperative to understand the circumstances and outcome of known cases, especially because they cast light beyond the nuns on the transgressing members of the clergy, and on the role of the Inquisition in facing and attempting to solve this challenging situation.

Another outcome of the new research on nuns was a greater focus on the ties between the personal and the institutional. Of special interest to me was a well-known incident of confrontation between nuns and their bishops throughout the 1770s, triggered by the bishops' demands that the nuns return to a "common life" style of living and abandon their use of private cells and servants. I understood this situation as a gender issue, a power struggle between the will of men to redirect women's practices according to their own view and interpretation, and that of the nuns who wished to preserve their traditional form of observance. The roots of this confrontational situation are traceable to the literature on spiritual advice to nuns. Written by men who defined religious women's daily lives and spiritual progress, the small cadre of prelates who decided to reform Mexican nunneries were pitting reformation of observance against their own understanding of a "relaxed" observance. They did not expect a vigorous opposition by a good number of nuns, and while in the end time saw a slow relaxation of the so-called *vida común*, this was an important chapter in the history of nunneries insofar as it saw the expression of direct dissent as an exercise of "free will" against "obedience."

A last chapter on the nuns' writings synthesized what I had learned up to that point from unpublished manuscripts, and enticed me to pursue further inquiries on this topic later on in my research. I am happy to report that I have joined an academic community that has borne witness to a very satisfying growth of studies of cloistered communities in Spain and the Spanish-speaking world in the first two decades of this century. My latest attempt to broaden this field is a manuscript—finished but as yet unpublished—coedited again with my colleague Loreto-López: the transcription and annotation of writings specifically addressed to celebrate, inspire, and entertain religious women within the convents of the Spanish-speaking world. These writings underline the "theatrical nature" of many of those writings, some of which were, in fact, scripts for stage representation inside the convent. In Mexico, we have so far found only one theater script written by a nun, whereas in Spain there were several nun playwrights in the seventeenth century. Mexico was a "colony" where some innovations took time to arrive or were simply repressed by overzealous prelates. Whether or not these writings were written by nuns or not, their ultimate value resides in being written for, being read by, and being performed by women religious. Some examples of a rather "secular" nature of theatre for performance in the convents are already known and they have "surprised" many who are unacquainted with the rich and often contradictory expressions of entertainment in the convents. We chose to highlight those dedicated to celebrate occasions of a religious nature, such as profession, celebration of the nativity, or funeral services. When the nuns got together to celebrate the liturgy, to read poems celebrating a sister's birthday, to sing in the choir in honor of a new professant, or to perform a theatrical composition celebrating a profession or a religious feast, they were celebrating sisterhood as a form of spiritual agape.

A Turn to Men and the Mendicants

The metaphor of searching for new paths and walking on new grounds still applies to my work and to myself as a historian. If serendipity determined my original choice, the determination to find new challenges seems to describe my latter years and my current writing. Exploring the mendicant orders and the lives of men was a new path I decided to follow beginning as early as fifteen years ago. Women in cloisters were in continuous contact with their male ecclesiastical prelates and even secular men, such as administrators, legal advisors, and patrons. I had met those men "governing" and surveying the affairs of nuns as high prelates, confessors, spiritual advisers, and preachers in their churches. Some of them were in almost intimate terms with their advisees, reading their letters and diaries, encouraging or questioning their religious vocation and experiences. The lives of men of the cloth were intertwined with those of nuns, but only in ways that did not impinge on their own chosen path and allowed them to retain their own idiosyncrasy. Men had the freedom to move and travel, write, talk, and emit opinions on all topics, from theology to the juridical system of the land. They could oversee nuns' lives whereas the contrary was never possible. The issue of how biological sex and socially defined gender roles determined people's lives was never quite so starkly delineated for me as when I began to study men.

The incentive of writing something on "men's studies" led me to apply for a Guggenheim Fellowship to study "masculinity" among the "men of God." The grant gave me the initial impulse and seed money to pursue what I began calling "the other side of the moon." For the last ten years I have been reading, writing, and publishing intermittently on personalities and issues of the Franciscan, Augustinian, and Dominican orders in Mexico between 1550 and 1800. I chose three orders to enable me to find their similarities more than their differences and have a meaningful overview of masculinity irrespective of affiliation. Men in these orders shared a general understanding of their position within the Church at large, and their observance had many points in common. In Spanish American history, they shared evangelizing objectives and experienced similar challenges in that task. The three orders dedicated their best men to preach, counsel the lay and the religious, write chronicles and theological and devotional works, teach their own students and even instruct those in higher educational institutions. They also faced similar encounters with secular authorities in their daily interactions, especially as it pertained to their evangelizing mission and indigenous communities.

Turning to men religious, after I reached a certain level of proficiency in women, entailed a steep learning curve. In 2004 I published an essay comparing the concepts of masculinity and femininity implicit in the codes of behavior of members of the religious orders. It was an exploratory piece that allowed me to put my first thoughts in order. But the project had to wait. In 2008, the same year I published *Brides of Christ*, I lost my husband to cancer, an unexpected blow that drained my intellect and my heart for nearly two years. I retired from active teaching and after some struggle succeeded in reshaping my life as an independent scholar by forging into the new research project on mendicants and masculinity, and continued to study nuns' writings. In 2014, I gave a formal public lecture on the new approaches to the study of mendicants from the perspective of masculinity studies at the Mexican Academy of History as my inaugural reception speech as a corresponding member. I have also lectured on the topic at the Pontificia Universidad Católica in Lima, Peru, and the University of San Francisco in Quito as a guest lecturer, as well as a few other presentations at historical meetings in the U.S. These public lectures remind me of the times when I was "breaking arms" (*rompiendo armas*), as we say in Spanish, for women's history. Masculinity Studies are certainly well established in academia by now, but as I have corroborated, in Latin America they are focused on contemporary sociological issues rather than on historical studies. What I am trying to do is to invite the curiosity of my colleagues to the study of masculinity in general in the period prior to 1800. I have chosen men of the cloth because the Church is familiar to me and, frankly, because others in my field have not considered them to be subjects within the realms of "masculinity." Of course, I disagree. The mendicant orders had an extraordinary presence in the sixteenth century as the ushers of conversion among the indigenous peoples, and remained central to the religious care of urban and rural populations for two more centuries. Their robes were seen in the farthest geographical frontiers and their voices were essential to sustain the pulse of living catechesis in the viceroyalty. The secular church could not have maintained its mission without them.

For this project I am focusing on the personal experience of friars as men. I am not interested in institutional history or economic history. Based on what I have written so far, I begin with the assumption that masculinity is a social construct that begins in childhood. I see the potential friar as a child receiving the social and intellectual skills demanded from a boy to be recognized as a "man in progress" in his society, learning how to behave as a man in his society before making a choice to enter a convent as one of the options he had in life. Entering a convent as an adolescent or a young man, the novice apprentice faced the challenges of the novitiate, which was more than a training in religion—it was a training in the social and personal understanding of a special form of manhood required by the Church. The novice renounced some expressions of secular masculinity and embraced others defined as the only ones valid and appropriate for his chosen state. Physical virility was not the test of a friar's masculinity. A man of the cloth found masculinity in, among other variants, the renunciation of the flesh, the observance of duty to his faith, and the commitment to his order and its charisma. He exercised it through preaching and missionary activity, spiritual counseling, and scholarly pursuits in the service of church and faith. As "a man of God," a full-fledged friar would face many challenges, but his authority was based on the special powers he gained as a representative of God before the faithful. In the specific theater of sixteenth century Spanish American society, friars as a group were given special rights they had never before possessed to engage in the conversion of the indigenous population. For at least two centuries, they could also missionize among the general population, acting as confessors, teachers, and authors. They had to engage in many political maneuvers with the secular church and the royal bureaucrats to retain a grip on their role as missionaries and mediators between the laity and God. The engagement of friars with other men of the church, as well as seculars in the social and political arena, created numerous conflicts. There is no end to the story of conflict within and outside of the Church. However, facing secular men, friars, as members of the Church, were fully equipped with a set of spiritual and intellectual arms that placed them in a special niche above most of them. There was no superior over them except God when they officiated before the altar. Theirs was a powerful voice when they advised from the confessional or the pulpit. That was masculine power and theirs was a special form of masculinity that should not be overlooked.

Power, however, was not necessarily what friars had in mind all the time. Even priors and prelates who exercised power within their orders had obligations higher than political pursuits, and had to contend with other duties imposed by their membership in the Church. To capture their experience as men, one must survey what was specific to their special form of manhood. It is a complex task with many possibilities that historians must evaluate carefully in order to draw a reliable picture. I follow the friars in several chosen aspects of their lives after their childhood, as novices, as lay brothers, as transgressors of the vow of chastity, as martyrs, as missionaries in the middle and late years of the viceroyalty, as observers of nature in their frequent travels, and at their deaths. Their experience as men is larger than my chosen topics, but what remains to be done is a task for several historians.

Conclusion

In retrospect, developing a career as a historian was not an easy exercise for me. As I stated, I began on my own as a researcher and a writer. I was a full-time mother and wife in an academic world that was in the "process" of opening doors to women. My strategy was to write and try to publish frequently, to attend national and international conferences, to present papers, to find grants to underwrite my travel to archives, and to accept part-time positions in departments that needed replacements for their mostly male professors on sabbatical. I rephrased the 1960s series "Have gun: will travel" into "Have history: will travel." After traveling to several part-time jobs, I had my first "secure" position at Howard University, close to my husband's workplace, and I stayed as a member of the faculty for nearly two decades, taking several academic absences on scholarship. I learned a lot about teaching there, but my move to Arizona State University in 1995 enabled me to devote all my teaching and research time to my own personal interests and to participate more fully and personally in doctoral programs with graduate students. While there, I also fulfilled one of my ambitions: to host summer programs for history teachers at the secondary and college levels for the National Endowment for the Humanities (NEH). Co-directing with my colleague Lynn Stoner, I hosted two projects: "Converging Cultures: Native America, Europe and the Encounter" in 2000 for high school teachers, and "Hispanic Gendering of the Americas: Beyond Cultural and Geographical Boundaries" in 2002 for college teachers. The latter was the first ever interdisciplinary application dedicated to Latin American women at the NEH, and it surveyed women and feminine issues in literature, cinema, the arts, and history, bringing academic specialists, as well as Latin American women writers and activists, to talk to our grantees. It was one of the most pleasing chapters in my career.

I have written in English and in Spanish, the latter with an eye on my readers in Latin America, and in the final tally of books, chapters in books, and articles in journals both languages come very close in numbers with a slight majority for Spanish. For twenty-five years I was in charge of the section on Mexico for the *Handbook of Latin American Studies*, using the Library of Congress Hispanic Division as my base and in collaboration with my colleague Edith Couturier. The *Handbook* is an annotated bibliography of all major books and articles published on Latin America, and a great professional service to all historians in the field. I became a fixture at the Hispanic Division of the Library of Congress. It had the warmth of a place where staff and other collaborators felt part of a large convivial family. One of the benefits of that service was to get access to the stalls, find books directly, and even borrow some of them. One could keep the copies of all the articles one reviews (not the books, though!). It was a privilege to be a member of the team and one of my fondest memories.

I am a member of the Mexican Academy of History and was elected to the American Academy of Arts and Sciences in 2019. I also received the Distinguished Service Award from the Conference on Latin American History in 2009, and the Distinguished Scholarship Award from the American Historical Association in 2015. In 2016 The Rocky Mountain Council on Latin American Studies established the annual Bandelier-Lavrin Prize for the best published work on Colonial Latin American History to honor pioneering efforts in the field of history. I am deeply humbled and honored by these awards, especially when I remember how my face muscles ached when I first had to speak English all day long! I think that my main contribution to history has been to write extensively in Spanish and English on women in general and women in the Church in particular, for a continental body of female readers who were ready to learn about their own history and begin writing on it. It has been a fulfilling journey, even though it started with a good dosage of serendipity.

Chalk and Cheese:
Moving between Historical Cultures

Hugh McLeod*

I was born in 1944. My parents came from Leeds, but my mother, who had been an English teacher, stopped when she had children, and was living in High Wycombe, and my father was with the Royal Marines in Belgium. His first job after the war was in London and we lived there until 1952, when he got a job in a research laboratory of the Plessey electronics company. This was in Cobham, and we moved to a Surrey village, where my parents continued to live until after I had left home. From there I would travel into Guildford, where from 1955 to 1962 I attended the Royal Grammar School.

I was fortunate to grow up in a home with lots of books. My mother had the classics of English literature, as well as modern novels. My father had books on politics, religion and history. I think there were four formative moments in my childhood. The first was the discovery of history. From as early as when I was seven years old, there is a photograph of me reading *A Child's History of England*. This history focused heavily on the medieval period and the author liked a good story. The book was arranged so that the story was on one side and an illustration on the other; I can still remember the pictures of the White Ship sailing to its doom and Ranulf Flambard escaping from the Tower of London. A second important moment concerns my father's enthusiasm for sports and games of all kinds, especially cricket and chess. By the age of nine I was a cricket fanatic, and though it took longer to become equally keen on chess, the passion lasted longer because I was a better chess player than cricketer. The third was my interest in politics, which I can date to a specific event, namely Suez. I became a supporter of the Labour Party, which I have remained. The fourth, which developed more gradually, was my growing interest in Christianity from about the age of fifteen. My parents were regular churchgoers, and at various times we went to Congregationalist, Presbyterian, and Anglican churches, though they eventually settled on the Church of Eng-

* Hugh McLeod is emeritus professor of church history in the Department of History of the University of Birmingham. His email address is: D.H.MCLEOD@bham.ac.uk.

land, partly because of the inspiring preaching of the rector of the village church. One thing that strengthened my own interest was studying the Reformation at school and wanting to learn more about the specific teachings of the various churches and the differences among them. Another was the teaching of Mr. Malleson, the senior English teacher, who also taught Religious Education, and who awakened my interest in the Bible, as well as pointing me to such books as William James's *Varieties of Religious Experience*. As a student at Cambridge, I attended the college chapel, as well as sometimes going to the evening services at Great St Mary's, where there were often visiting celebrity preachers. I can remember queuing for a service where John Robinson was due to preach, only to be turned away because the church was already full. In the 1970s I started attending Quaker meetings and I became a member of the Society of Friends in 1978. I have remained active in local meetings, first in Birmingham and more recently in Derby.

At school, History was always my favourite subject and I never doubted that I wanted to study it at university. I was encouraged by the senior History teacher, the sardonic Douglas Mark Sturley, and his enthusiastic assistant, Dr. B. Gordon Blackwood. Sturley had a mission to suppress any signs of naïve idealism in his pupils. I remember an essay on the Enlightened Despots where he had crossed out the word "ruthless," replacing it with "realistic," and had changed "he had no scruples" to "he had no illusions."

Before I went to Trinity Hall, Cambridge, in 1963, I spent several months in France and Switzerland. My parents paid for me to do a language course in Paris, for which I shall always be grateful, as French historians have had a big influence on my work. In Switzerland I worked on a small farm, together with two generations of the farming family and a Spanish worker, Luis. This did little for my Swiss German, as we were working too hard to do much chatting, but it was an interesting insight into an older way of life. There was little mechanization and hours of work were long, though with frequent breaks for meals or snacks. During breakfast the patriarch read a passage from the Bible.

Trinity Hall was best known as a nursery of lawyers, but there was a strong group of History students, including John Pollard, the historian of the papacy. Two of the tutors, Nick Richardson and John Nurser, had a significant influence on me. Both were individualists who would not have been at home in the contemporary world of regular "assessments" of teaching, "reviews" of research and counting of publications. I found Nick, an historian of modern French politics, an inspiring teacher. He made me

Hugh McLeod

want to be a professional historian and he was the first person to suggest that I could be one. John, who was also an Anglican priest and whose major book was on the religious background to the Universal Declaration of Human Rights,[1] probably had more influence than anyone else on the direction my research would take. He recommended books more because they were interesting than because they would help us to pass the exams, and one in particular was important for me, *Churches and the Working Classes* by Inglis.[2] Inglis had valuable things to say about "the churches," but much less about "the working classes." John was also interested in the emerging sub-discipline of the sociology of religion. He invited me to seminars in which some of the leading figures in the field took part, and he also recommended the work of Gabriel Le Bras and other pioneers of French *sociologie religieuse*.

After graduating in 1966 I was determined to register for a PhD if I could find a supervisor. I wanted to work on some aspect of English religion in the eighteenth or nineteenth century. I spoke to several possible

---

1. John Nurser, *For All People and All Nations: Christian Churches and Human Rights* (Geneva, 2005).
2. Kenneth Stanley Inglis, *Churches and the Working Classes in Victorian England* (London, 1963).

supervisors before being accepted by George Kitson Clark who was then close to retirement but had long been the leading historian of Victorian England at Cambridge. He lived in a suite of rooms above the Great Gate at Trinity College, in one of which his research seminar was held every Wednesday evening. Many of his students had worked on aspects of Victorian religion and Cambridge was probably the leading centre for this growing field of research. My contemporaries were Sheridan Gilley and Stuart Mews, and a little before me had been David Thompson, Ted Royle, Edward Norman and Clyde Binfield. So I was fortunate to be part of a large group of students working in related areas, as well as having access through the seminar to work on many aspects of nineteenth and early twentieth century Britain and Ireland. There was then no formal training of historians at Cambridge and no requirement to take a Master's before going on to a doctorate. The training came through one-to-one meetings with the supervisor and through participation in the weekly seminar, where, as well as papers by research students, there were frequent visiting speakers, most often from the USA. Kitson Clark had a "sink or swim" approach to supervision. His job was to show students when they were on the wrong path, but it was the student's job to find the right path. In my own case I almost despaired of receiving the green light from him. When it finally came, I think it was because he recognized that I had found my own voice.

My doctoral thesis was entitled "Membership and Influence of the Churches in Metropolitan London 1885–1914." I had two key sources: the Religious Census of London in 1903-4 which attempted to count attendance by men, women and children at every church or synagogue in the metropolis,[3] and the notebooks compiled by Charles Booth and his assistants while preparing his monumental *Life and Labour of the People in London*.[4] I also used every autobiography I could find by those living in London at the time. The main theme was the influence of class on the very different patterns of religious practice found in the various districts of the city.

My studies started with difficulty, as I failed to win a scholarship in my first year. I had to piece together income from a variety of sources, mainly various kinds of teaching, which inevitably impinged on the time available for research. I must nonetheless have received a favourable report from my supervisor, as I gained funding at the start of my second year.

---

3. Richard Mudie-Smith, ed., *The Religious Life of London* (London, 1904).

4. Charles Booth, *Life and Labour of the People in London*, 17 vols. [Ser. III: "Religious Influences"] (London, 1902–3).

Kitson came from a dynasty of Leeds industrialists. Like many such, they had been Unitarians and Liberals in the nineteenth century and moved to being Anglican and Conservative in the twentieth. Kitson was staunchly Anglican and one of his major books was focused on the involvement of Victorian clergy in social reforming movements.[5] He gave short shrift to the sniping at the clergy which was commonly practised by graduate students, and even by some distinguished historians, at the time. He once accused me, probably rightly, of Nonconformist bias. The agenda for my thesis came from Inglis's book and the aim of showing not only what the churches were doing, but what the working classes were doing and how this compared with what those in other classes were doing. History from the bottom up was the contemporary fashion, and it was one which I aspired to follow. There were various influences on the ways in which I approached this task. From Kitson Clark there was a broadly sympathetic understanding of the clergy of all denominations—which did not preclude criticism of the class perspective of many Anglicans. I attended the *Past & Present* conference on "Popular Religion" held in July 1966, just as I was thinking about my field of research. There I saw in action many of the key figures in the social history of religion and in social history more generally, and I was particularly inspired by John Kent's paper on revivalism.[6] I was also fascinated by the geographical patterns of religious practice revealed by students of Britain's 1851 Religious Census. And, like most historians of religion in the later '60s, I was interested in the causes of secularization and the debates between British sociologists of religion, notably Bryan Wilson, arch-exponent of the Secularization Thesis, and David Martin, who at that time was pleading for the "elimination" of the concept of secularization.[7] David was to be the external examiner for my thesis and remained both a friend and my initial contact with the world of sociology.

My career as a university historian was made possible by three strokes of good fortune. The first was an appointment as an Arts Faculty Research Fellow (what would now be called a Post-Doc) in the University of Birmingham. It was based in the Department of Modern History,

---

5. George Kitson Clark, *Churchmen and the Condition of England, 1832–1885* (London, 1973).

6. Which later fed into John Kent, *Holding the Fort: Studies in Victorian Revivalism* (London, 1978).

7. Bryan R. Wilson, *Religion in Secular Society* (London 1966); David Martin, "Towards Eliminating the Concept of Secularisation," in: Julius Gould, ed., *Penguin Survey of the Social Sciences* (Harmondsworth, 1965), 169–82.

and in January 1970 I came to meet my new head of department, a diplomatic historian. He asked about my research, and I explained that I was working on the relationship between religion and social class in Victorian cities. He listened patiently, and then said that this was very interesting, but he could not see its historical significance. If he had waited a few years, he would have discovered that this apparently recherché theme had become almost fashionable. Between 1974 and 1976 there was a flood of publications on this and related themes.[8] The second stroke of good fortune was the acceptance of a revised version of my thesis for publication, with the title *Class and Religion in the late Victorian City*.[9] It came from a relatively new publisher, Croom Helm, and was one of the earliest books in their social history series. The title was suggested by the publisher, who said that "Every word in that title will sell." At the time, anything to do with Victorian Britain was likely to be popular—though the vogue was for books which included some scandal, aimed at challenging the upright and uptight Victorian stereotype. But all aspects of social history were thriving, and urban and religious history were among the most flourishing branches.

For me the most important aspect of Birmingham was the Social History Seminar, started by Dorothy Thompson, the historian of Chartism, and Richard Johnson, then best known for his work on the history of education. When Richard's interests moved elsewhere, I became the co-convenor. Dorothy had a talented school of graduate students, many of them working on Birmingham history. The seminar offered a lively programme both of home-grown and visiting speakers and many of my own papers started there. In view of Dorothy's combative temperament, it was a venue which some speakers wished they had avoided. The orthodoxy of the time tended to be that religion was all about "social control," so I had to get used to responding to that line of argument.

When I think of the schools of historical writing which influenced my first book, I would mention the drive, very influential in Britain at the time, to count anything that can possibly be counted, including church membership and attendance, and their correlates. I have never in later books included so many statistical tables. Three very different historians also influenced my work. First, there was John Foster, whose work was hotly

---

8. Among the most notable being Robert Moore, *Pit-men, Preachers and Politics* (Cambridge, 1974); James Obelkevich, *Religion and Rural Society: South Lindsey, 1825–75* (Oxford 1976); Stephen Yeo, *Religion and Voluntary Organisations in Crisis* (London, 1976).

9. (London, 1974).

debated in Birmingham's Social History Seminar.[10] I was fascinated by his account of working-class radicalism in early nineteenth-century Oldham, but what influenced me more directly was his use of marriage registers as a historical source. Foster's interest was in how far the choice of partner reflected the emergence of a clearly defined working class; mine was in the geographical distance between those marrying. I argued that this reflected three kinds of community in London, one "neighborhood-based," one "district-based" and one "national and international," with each being related to different patterns of religious practice. Second, there was Clyde Binfield, whose doctoral thesis was the most entertaining I had ever read. I was particularly struck by a series of articles he published in the later '60s on the internal life of Nonconformist chapels in the later nineteenth century, and especially the tensions arising from the liberalizing of theology. These had an important influence on my account of the Victorian "crisis of faith."[11] Third was the French historian Christiane Marcilhacy and her books on the diocese of Orléans in the mid-nineteenth century, in which she tried to construct a "collective mentality" of the various sections of the population.[12] I tried to do the same for London. I can see in retrospect that this "mentality" is too rigidly defined and pays insufficient attention to the diversity of thinking and behaving within a particular milieu, in spite of much that is shared.

Around 1900, most London Catholics were working class and most were Irish-born or (more often) of Irish descent. My main discussion of Catholics was in a chapter on "Working-Class London." Catholics were more concentrated than members of any other denomination, except for the Jews, the major parishes being in areas close to the river Thames and the docks. My main claim was that Catholicism "was the only form of religion that integrated its adherents into a working-class environment, instead of making them stand out from it." I can see now that this claim was too blunt, but it makes the point that although attendance at Mass was much lower than in Ireland, and lower too than in New York or, probably, Liverpool, it was higher than the rate of church-going among working

---

10. John Foster, "Capitalism and Class Consciousness in Earlier Nineteenth-Century Oldham" (PhD thesis, University of Cambridge, 1967); id., *Class Struggle in the Industrial Revolution* (London, 1974).

11. Clyde Binfield, "Nonconformity in the Eastern Counties, 1840–1885" (PhD thesis, University of Cambridge PhD, 1965); id., "The Thread of Disruption," *Transactions of the Congregational Historical Society*, 20, no. 5 (1967), 156–66; id., "Chapels in Crisis," *Transactions of the Congregational Historical Society*, 20, no. 9 (1968), 237–54.

12. Christiane Marcilhacy, *Le diocèse d'Orléans sous l'épiscopat de Mgr Dupanloup* (Paris, 1963); id., *Le diocèse d'Orléans au milieu du XIXe siècle* (Paris, 1964).

class Protestants and, in particular, many non-practising Catholics retained a strong Catholic identity and a strong respect for the clergy. So a large part of this (relatively brief) discussion focused on the relationship between priests and people.

Reflecting the publisher's view that the book would chime with contemporary concerns, it was more widely reviewed than any book I have written since, and the tenor of the reviews also varied more widely. I appreciated the positive reviews by expert critics, such as that by Peter Marsh in the *American Historical Review*, but there were also more negative evaluations, such as that by Robert Currie in the *English Historical Review*. I enjoyed recently rereading the book, though there are parts which I would write differently if I were doing it now. My style of writing has evolved in the years following—partly in response to the critics, especially those who were friendly critics. My later books have been more disciplined and sharply focused—though possibly less fun. I cut out most of the jokes, as well as the long footnotes. I was attentive to Clyde Binfield's comment that I had stereotyped the Baptists, and I recognized a tendency to stereotype Evangelicals more generally. In subsequent work, I have seen it as part of my job as an historian to present all religious groups—and indeed political groups—in terms which they themselves could have recognized and to avoid loaded language.

After a year in which I had a Temporary Lectureship in the Department of History at Warwick University, a third stroke of good fortune came in 1973. I was appointed to a Lectureship in Church History in Birmingham's Department of Theology. The competition was strong and the appointing committee was divided, but I had the support of John Gordon Davies, the formidable head of department. He was good at getting his way. This was a turning-point for me in three ways. It meant that I had secure employment. It also meant that I would continue in religious history, whereas if I had stayed in the History Department it is possible that my research might have taken new directions. And it also meant that my historical interests broadened chronologically and geographically. I taught a course on the Reformation, and also lectured and gave seminars on a wide range of nineteenth and twentieth century themes, including slavery, apartheid and religious persecution in the USSR. It also broadened my knowledge of contemporary religion. Students taking a degree in Theology or taking Theology courses came from a wide variety of religious backgrounds, including not only all the familiar forms of religion and irreligion, but others which I had not encountered before, notably Pentecostalists and, in later years, many Muslims, as well as at least one Pagan and one Satanist.

My first article was strongly influenced by French *sociologie religieuse*[13] and arose from my fascination with geographical patterns of religious observance.[14] Basing myself partly on the British Religious Census of 1851 and partly on various local censuses of attendance conducted by newspapers in 1880s and '90s, I showed that urban church-going reflected patterns of church-going in the surrounding countryside—not perhaps surprising, but it ran contrary to the then current assumption that church-going was low in larger towns and high in smaller towns. I also broke down larger towns into smaller areas, showing the expected class differences, but also that some denominations, such as the Primitive Methodists, which had a relatively small national membership, nevertheless had a significant presence in working class districts of some cities. I showed a draft to my colleague, Dorothy Thompson, who said that the paper was "convincing but not very interesting." But her husband, Edward Thompson, was more encouraging. He was interested in my findings on working class districts of cities, and said the paper was "promising."

The most helpful suggestion by reviewers of *Class and Religion* was that oral history might offer the best way of approaching some of the questions I had tried to answer in the book. Several of my subsequent publications have drawn on oral history, the first being my contribution to a volume on the lower middle class of Victorian and Edwardian Britain.[15] I made considerable use here of the transcripts of interviews conducted in two major oral history projects, one led by Elizabeth Roberts and focusing on the working class in North Lancashire between 1890 and 1930, and the other a more ambitious project being conducted by a large team, led by Paul Thompson and Thea Vigne. It focused on the Edwardian period and it covered all social classes and most regions of Britain. The former project benefited from Roberts's in-depth knowledge of the region and her ability to empathise with interviewees; the quality of interviewing in the latter project was more uneven, but its strength lay in its broader scope and the possibilities for comparison between regions. Later, in preparing a short book for the Economic History Society,[16] I read transcripts of all of the

---

13. Especially Fernand Boulard and Jean Rémy, *Pratique religieuse urbaine et régions culturelles* (Paris, 1968).
14. Hugh McLeod, "Class, Community and Region: The Religious Geography of Nineteenth-Century England," in: Michael Hill, ed., *Sociological Yearbook of Religion in Britain*, 6 (London, 1973), 29–72.
15. Hugh McLeod, "White-Collar Values and the Role of Religion," in: Geoffrey Crossick, ed., *The Lower Middle Class in Britain* (London, 1977), 61–84.
16. Hugh McLeod, *Religion and the Working Class in Nineteenth-Century Britain* (Basingstoke, 1984).

interviews with those who had grown up in working-class families in the cities and industrial regions of Britain. Doing this persuaded me that the church-going minority in the Victorian and Edwardian working class was larger than I (or indeed most historians—Elizabeth Roberts[17] being a notable exception) had realized, and that there were also considerable regional differences. For example, church-going was considerably higher in the textile towns of Lancashire and West Yorkshire (as well of course in South Wales) than in, for instance, London or the North-East of England. The interviews also permitted a more nuanced view of the varieties of belief and unbelief among non-church-goers and differences between men and women. I explained these findings in a paper at a History Workshop in 1982, which was later published.[18] In the '80s and '90s, other historians took these lines of argument considerably further than I had done.[19]

My teaching at Birmingham provided the basis for my second book, *Religion and the People of Western Europe 1789–1970*,[20] Which was commissioned by Oxford University Press as a follow-up to John Bossy's *Christianity in the West 1400–1700*. Beginning with the French Revolution and ending with the 1960s, I looked at the countryside, the urban middle class and the working class. So class was still central, though I also looked at the popularity in the nineteenth century of Evangelicalism and Ultramontanism, the emergence of Religions of Humanity, and differences between the religion of women and men, which was a relatively new theme at the time. The book was important for me in making my work known in other parts of Europe. In 1997 I published a revised version, which took the story up to 1989.[21]

Whereas in my first book the section on Catholics was relatively brief, here they took centre-stage. I began with the conflict between the French Revolution and the Catholic Church, and the grass-roots revival in the later 1790s. I argued that in the early decades of the nineteenth century there was a resurgence of 'enthusiastic' forms of religion among both Catholics and Protestants. But while this led to the splintering of Protes-

---

17. Elizabeth Roberts, *Working Class Barrow and Lancaster, 1890–1930* (Lancaster, 1976).

18. Hugh McLeod, "New Perspectives on Victorian Working-Class Religion," *Oral History Journal*, 14 (1986), 31–49.

19. See, for example, Mark Smith, *Religion in Industrial Society: Oldham and Saddleworth, 1740–1865* (Oxford, 1995); Sarah C. Williams, *Religious Belief and Popular Culture in Southwark, 1880–1939* (Oxford 1999).

20. (Oxford, 1981).

21. Hugh McLeod, *Religion and the People of Western Europe, 1789–1989* (Oxford, 1997).

tantism and a multiplication of 'sects' outside the State Churches, the spread of Ultramontane forms of piety greatly strengthened the Catholic Church, especially in the countryside and to a lesser extent in cities too. Older pilgrimages revived and in the middle and later years of the century many new pilgrimages began, initially in the face of some scepticism on the part of many bishops, but eventually with their active support. The later years of the century also saw the emergence of what came to be called the 'Catholic ghetto.' I argued that this was only the most striking example of a wider phenomenon in later nineteenth-century Europe, as religious and political (notably Socialist) sub-cultures formed with the purpose of strengthening a religious or political identity and insulating the faithful from hostile influences—most often that of the Liberal bourgeoisie.[22] Across several generations, from about the 1870s to the 1960s, the Church succeeded in many countries in building a Catholic world, underpinned by numerous organisations, sometimes including political parties.

Meanwhile I was working on my biggest project, which, after many years of research and of publishing delays appeared with the title *Piety and Poverty: Working Class Religion in Berlin, London and New York 1870–1914*.[23] If, as I have said, I moved between my first and my second book towards a more focused and disciplined style of writing, between my second and third major publications, I came increasingly to highlight complexity and nuance, rather than the crispness and clarity I aimed for in *Religion and the People*. *Piety and Poverty* is a favourite of mine, partly because of the memories it brings back and the amount of work that went into it, but it has had less impact than some of my other books. This may be because it was conceived in the '70s and published in the '90s, by which time the themes handled in the book were no longer fashionable. For example, I put a lot of effort into obtaining data on the social class of church-goers, which had been a hot topic in the '70s, but no longer aroused so much interest. Nonetheless I think the book successfully combined answers to broad questions about urban and working-class religion—questioning, for example some influential views of the relationship between religion and the experience of poverty, including Marx's claim that religion acted as "the opium of the people"; local detail about the three cities; and, in the chapters headed "Male and Female" and "Religion in a Half-Secular Society," examination of the religious lives of individuals.

---

22. See also Hugh McLeod, "Building the 'Catholic Ghetto': Catholic Organisations, c. 1870–1914," in: William J. Sheils and Diana Wood, eds., *Voluntary Religion* (Oxford 1986), 411–44.

23. (New York, 1996).

In comparing the three cities, I was struck by the wide differences between them, most clearly reflected in the church-going statistics. According to my estimates, 38% of non-Jewish adults attended a church in Manhattan borough on the day of a census in 1902, as against 22% in London and about 6% in Berlin at around the same time. The interesting point is that Protestant church-going was only slightly higher in New York than in London: the difference is explained by the fact that Catholics were both more numerous and more observant in New York. According to my estimates, 50% of adult Catholics were counted at a service and the figure for the Irish may have been even higher, since there is evidence to suggest that Catholics from the other major ethnic groups in the city, notably the Italians, were less regular in attendance. As in Britain, Irish Catholic identity was strengthened by memories of Ireland, by support for the Nationalist cause, and by the experience of or memory of discrimination in their new home, embodied in the notorious message that "No Irish need apply." The difference between America and Europe was that by 1900 the Irish in New York, as in other American cities, though still predominantly working class, enjoyed considerable power through their leading role in the city's Democratic Party as well as in the Archdiocese, reinforced by the frequent links between clergy and politicians. In districts like the Middle West Side of Manhattan with dense communities of immigrants from Ireland and descendants of immigrants, the clergy enjoyed immense status and influence, supported by parish organisations of every kind and a public opinion which was loyal to the Church. Women tended to be more devout than men, and took a more active role in maintaining a Catholic atmosphere in the home, but there was also a male piety sustained by the Holy Name societies, as well as the numerous Catholic sporting organisations.

I remained at Birmingham until my retirement in 2010, after which I continued to supervise my doctoral students until the successful completion of their theses. In 2004, following some internal reorganization within the School of Historical Studies, of which Theology and Religion (as it had become) was then a part, I moved back to where I had started: the Department of Modern History. I was twice short-listed for posts elsewhere, at Edinburgh, where Jay Brown was appointed, and at Harvard, where Bob Scribner was appointed. But I am happy to have spent so long at Birmingham—not least because of the History of Religion Seminar, which began in the early '90s in the Prince of Wales pub in Moseley, where I met with John Edwards, a historian of late medieval Spain and of the Reformation era, and Mike Snape, now best known for his work on religion and war. Our original idea was that the seminar would cover all aspects and periods of religious history. Birmingham at the time did have great strength in the history of Christianity and was increasingly strong in the History of Islam too, and we heard papers from colleagues on pre-historic and Roman religion, as well as medieval Islam. But although we had a hard core of regulars, including, as well as ourselves, Graeme Murdock and Werner Ustorf, we found that many people would only come to papers which were directly relevant to their own research, so the original idea tended to get lost. We met in the evenings in one another's homes and a glass of wine or juice was served before we started. The seminar was notable for the friendly spirit that is often lacking in more formal seminars, and it continued until Mike left to take up a chair of Anglican Studies at Durham in 2015.

In the later 1990s I was working on two works of synthesis, both commissioned by editors of series. The first was *Religion and Society in England 1850–1914*.[24] Among other things, it gave me an opportunity to return to the 'crisis of faith' in the later Victorian years. I had given this extended, but perhaps one-sided treatment in *Class and Religion*, focusing on how the 'crisis' was experienced, rather than on the broader social processes at work. Here I tried to redress the balance. It also marked the beginning of my interest in the relationship between religion and sport to which I shall return later.

The second was *Secularisation in Western Europe, 1848–1914*,[25] commissioned by my colleague John Breuilly for a series which he edited. John rightly suggested that starting in 1848 made more sense than starting in 1870, as I had intended. The revolutions of 1848 were clearly crucially important in Germany and France, though less so in England, the third country to be discussed in the book. My aim was to produce a social-historical counterpart to the history of ideas offered by Owen Chadwick in his well-known book on secularization in Europe.[26] I think I succeeded in this, but the book was not widely reviewed, and probably remains less read than Chadwick's book—though a translation into Czech suggests that the readership is not confined to the UK. My main point was that, whereas historians and especially sociologists often think of a unified secularizing process, the extent of secularization at any time has varied not only between neighbouring countries but between different areas of life. In the second half of the nineteenth century, the secularization of individual belief and practice had already made considerable progress, especially in

---

24. [Social History in Perspective] (Basingstoke, 1996).
25. [European Studies Series] [(Basingstoke, 2000).
26. Owen Chadwick, *The Secularization of the European Mind in the Nineteenth Century* (Cambridge 1975).

France, but the role of religion in politics remained considerable; religion was an important component not only of national identities, but also of the individual identities of many people who were far from devout, and religion was deeply embedded in popular culture, especially in traditionally Catholic countries. Until the 1960s there was a balance between the secularizing tendencies and the continuing strength of religion in many areas of society and of individual lives.

Conferences have played a large part in my academic life, both because many of my publications began as conference papers,[27] and probably would not have been written but for this invitation, and because most of my academic collaborations began with meetings at a conference. As examples of the latter, I met Jeff Cox for the first time at the History Workshop on Religion and Society held at Friends' House London in 1983, which was probably the largest gathering ever held of those interested in the social history of religion, and I also had a meeting there with Bob Scribner. This led to my collaboration with him in a series on "Christianity and Society in the Modern World," which included many notable books on the period from the Reformation to now.[28] The most widely read, no doubt, was Callum Brown's *The Death of Christian Britain*,[29] to which I shall return later. I had first met Callum at the Social History Conference in 1981, and I first met David Hempton, with whom I would also later work, at a conference of the Ecclesiastical History Society in the later '80s. While there are good reasons why academics might reduce their travel to distant parts of the world, the requirement to meet online has severely reduced the value of the conferences held during the covid pandemic. One, based in the Netherlands, in which I took part, was a disaster because of technical prob-

---

27. For example, Hugh McLeod, "Religion in the British and German Labour Movements: A Comparison," *Bulletin of the Society for the Study of Labour History*, 50 (1986), 25–36; id., "Weibliche Frömmigkeit und männlicher Unglaube?" in: *Bürgerinnen und Bürger*, Ute Frevert, ed. (Göttingen, 1988), 134–56; id., "Protestantism and British National Identity, 1815–1945," in: Peter van der Veer and Hartmut Lehmann, eds., *Nation and Religion* (Princeton, NJ, 1999), 44–70; id., "Varieties of Anti-Clericalism in Later Victorian and Edwardian England," in: Nigel Aston and Matthew Cragoe, eds., *Anticlericalism in Britain, c.1500–1914* (Stroud, 2000), 198–220; id., "Religion and the Organisation of British Workers, c.1840–1960," in Lex Herma van Voss, Patrick Pasture and Jan De Maeyer, eds., *Between Cross and Class: Comparative Histories of Christian Labour in Europe, 1840–2000* (Bern 2006), 285–304.

28. The series published initially by Methuen and later by Routledge began with Callum Brown, *A Social History of Religion in Scotland since 1730* (London, 1987), and ended with John Pollard, *Catholicism in Modern Italy: Religion, Society and Politics since 1860* (Abingdon, 2008).

29. (Abingdon, 2001); 2nd edition (Abingdon, 2009).

lems. The other such events went smoothly so far as the technology was concerned but they largely excluded the informal discussions and the new contacts which are essential parts of face to face academic meetings.

In 2002 I was elected president of the Ecclesiastical History Society, the main organization of historians of Christianity in the UK. It also regularly includes speakers and participants from other countries. The president chooses the theme for that year's conferences. I chose "Retribution, Repentance and Reconciliation," and invited speakers ranging from Christine Trevett on forgiveness and reconciliation in the early Church to John de Gruchy on the Truth and Reconciliation Commission in South Africa. I chose as the theme for my presidential address "Christianity and Capital Punishment."[30] This reflected a longstanding interest in the theme, since at sixteen I had won a public speaking competition for the youth of Guildford with a speech calling for abolition. As well as referring to the usual statistical arguments and the probability that those who had been hanged in our country in recent years included some who were innocent, I also made use of religious arguments concerning the sanctity of life. I was therefore very interested to see that Richard Evans, in his brilliant history of capital punishment in Germany, argued that the declining support for the death penalty was an aspect of secularization.[31] I was also interested in a book by a former Anglican prison chaplain, Harry Potter, who argued that the continuing support from the Church of England and especially the bishops was crucial to the continuation of hanging into the 1950s and that the withdrawal of this support from the later part of that decade was a key factor in the suspension and then abolition of the death penalty in the '60s.[32] Excellent as both books were, I was not convinced by these central arguments. I suggested that rational arguments for or against the death penalty were less significant than its symbolic significance and that this changed frequently— not least when a former opponent of the punishment, such as Robespierre, found himself in power. Starting with the Catholic Enlightenment and the abolitions in Tuscany and the Austrian Empire in the later eighteenth century and concluding with the current debates in the USA, I argued that the most consistent opponents of the death penalty have been Socialists and

---

30. Hugh McLeod, "God and the Gallows: Christianity and Capital Punishment in the Nineteenth and Twentieth Centuries," in: *Retribution, Repentance and Reconciliation*, eds. Kate Cooper and Jeremy Gregory (Woodbridge, 2004), 330–56.

31. Richard J. Evans, *Rituals of Retribution: Capital Punishment in Germany, 1600–1987*, 2nd ed. (London, 1997).

32. Harry Potter, *Hanging in Judgment: Religion and the Death Penalty in England* (New York, 1993).

dissenting Christian minorities, but that those in political power or positions of privilege have shown a reluctance to relinquish this part of their armoury, even if they had a history of earlier opposition.

The historical organization in which I have been most actively involved is the "Commission Internationale d'Histoire et d'Études du Christianisme" (CIHEC), the international organization of historians of Christianity, affiliated to the International Historical Congress. It arose out of the 1950 Congress in a spirit of post-war reconciliation, bringing together historians mainly from France, Belgium and West Germany, and also Catholic and Protestant historians, at a time when they tended to be organized separately. In time, historians from other parts of Europe as well as the U.S. got involved, including some from Poland and Romania, and more recently from other parts of the former Eastern Bloc. My involvement began when I was asked to organize a panel on urban religion in the nineteenth and twentieth centuries as part of a series of sessions organized by CIHEC at the International Historical Congress in Madrid in 1990. In subsequent years I gave papers or organized sessions at many CIHEC conferences, large and small, including those at every International Historical Congress up to Jinan in 2015. I was a committee member from 1995, and then president from 2005 to 2010. Whereas in its early days French influences were dominant, I would say that now its role is most important in countries, particularly in eastern Europe, where research on Christian history was formerly discouraged, and where international contacts are thus especially needed.

The Madrid conference was important for me not only because it was my first experience of organizing an international panel, but because it laid the basis for my first edited volume.[33] Since then I have edited several volumes, either individually or working with two or three colleagues. The first was a Religious History of Britain as part of a British-French collaboration for a French series. I was brought in by Stuart Mews and we worked with the French historian of Victorian Britain, Christiane d'Haussy.[34] Then I was part of a team organizing a conference in Paris on the decline of Chris-

---

33. Hugh McLeod, ed., *European Religion in the Age of Great Cities, 1830–1930* (Abingdon, 1995).

34. Christiane d'Haussy, Stuart Mews and Hugh McLeod, eds., *Histoire religieuse de la Grande-Bretagne, XIXe et XXe siècles* (Paris 1997); Hugh McLeod and Werner Ustorf, eds., *The Decline of Christendom in Western Europe, 1750–2000* (Cambridge, 2003); Todd Weir and Hugh McLeod, eds., *Defending the Faith: Global Histories of Apologetics and Politics in the Twentieth Century* (Oxford, 2020).

tendom as part of a historical project funded by the World Council of Churches. For this I was brought in by my colleague, Werner Ustorf, and after considerable delays it led to another book. More recently I assisted Todd Weir and Benjamin Ziemann in organizing a conference at the British Academy with the title "Defending the Faith." This focused on "Apologetics" (Christian, Hindu, Jewish, Muslim, Secularist), showing how in the multi-confessional world of the twentieth century religious and anti-religious bodies of all kinds defended their own beliefs and refuted the attacks from outside, while strengthening the morale and trying to ensure the orthodoxy of those inside. Todd and I edited the resulting volume.

My biggest editorial task was to be responsible for the twentieth-century volume of the Cambridge History of Christianity.[35] This was limited to the "Western" forms of Christianity, with "Eastern" being the subject of a separate volume. Three volumes in the nine-volume series had a single editor while the others had two or even three editors. Like many editors, I drew quite heavily on people whom I knew and who I was confident would deliver. I do not think that, as one American critic claimed, the volume weas Eurocentric, but because of the lack of money for translations the contributors were either native English-speakers or had very good English. I divided the volume into three sections: "Institutions and Movements," which looked at those with a global reach, including for example the Papacy and Pentecostalism; "Narratives of Change," in which the chapters focused on regions of the world, often divided between before after 1945; and "Social and Cultural Impact," which was the most potentially difficult part to manage in a balanced way. Authors were asked to look globally at a particular theme, but inevitably their expertise was limited to particular parts of the globe, and they sometimes struggled to deal with issues which were very important in some other countries, but not at all in those which they knew most about. The volume received a negative review in *Church History* and, while I would question many of the reviewer's criticisms, one was, I think, valid and important, namely that we gave too little attention to popular culture, including the impact of radio, television, gospel music, country and western music, rock music, novels about the Rapture or Nigerian exorcism videos.

My first book had been fortunate in its time of publication and the same was true of *The Religious Crisis of the 1960s*.[36] Interest in the 1960s was

---

35. Hugh McLeod, ed., *The Cambridge History of Christianity*, 9 vols. (Cambridge, 2006–2008, here 2006), Volume 9: *World Christianities c.1914–2000*.

36. (Oxford, 2007).

strong and the book's international perspectives attracted a readership beyond the UK. Moreover, Callum Brown's *Death of Christian Britain* had stirred up interest in religion in the '60s, as well as provoking controversy. So the time was ripe for a book which covered some of the same ground in a different way.

My interest in the '60s arose in the first instance from having lived through the decade. The earlier histories of religion in the '60s were written by people who remembered those years. Their histories were inevitably influenced by their own memories and indeed by their emotional relationship with that decade—strongly positive in Callum's case, mainly negative in some other cases, such as that of Gérard Cholvy and Yves-Marie Hilaire, who regarded the later '60s and early '70s as a tragedy.[37] My own memories influenced my writing in that I saw the '60s not only as a time of religious crisis, but also of religious ferment. Both aspects, in my opinion, are essential to an understanding of the decade. So far as my relationship with the '60s is concerned, it was mainly positive, but with some reservations. I appreciated the greater informality and the loosening of conformist pressures which the decade brought. In particular, I valued the democratic and egalitarian ideals of the time, and I regret their subsequent decline. However, I deplored the romanticization of political violence which became fashionable in the later part of the decade.

The 1960s played a significant part in *Religion and the People*, where I saw these years as marking the end of an era in Europe's religious history. My interest in the '60s was renewed by hearing Callum speak at a conference in Paris in 1997 and by his subsequent book. Then I was invited to give a paper on the historiography of Christianity in the twentieth century at a session organized by CIHEC in the International Historical Congress in Oslo in 2000. I gave a review of the literature, by then quite extensive, on religion in the '60s.[38] I made the claim, repeated in my book, that future historians would see the 1960s as marking a break in Europe's religious history as decisive as that brought about by the Reformation. In 2004 I was invited to give the Vonhoff Lectures at the University of Groningen which gave me the opportunity to give my own ideas of the period more shape. My approach was distinctive in three ways. First, I recognized that "the Sixties" were an international phenomenon: while the principal focus in my

---

37. See Gérard Cholvy and Yves-Marie Hilaire, *Histoire religieuse de la France contemporaine*, 3 vols. (Toulouse, 1985–88).

38. Hugh McLeod, "Writing the Religious History of a Crucial Decade," *Kirchliche Zeitgeschichte*, 14 (2001), 36–48.

book was on England, I also gave attention to other countries, most notably France and the USA. Second, my focus was on the way that "ordinary people" experienced the '60s, rather than the bishops and the politicians, or the activists and the celebrities. This led to my extensive use of oral history. Third, I rejected the chronologies both of those like Callum Brown, who saw a radical change of direction in the '60s, and those like Alan Gilbert,[39] who saw the 60s as merely the culmination of a long-term evolutionary process of secularization. I argued that the causes of change had to be seen on at three levels: long-term pre-conditions, such as the critiques of Christianity and Judaism, going back to the eighteenth century; medium-term catalysts, most notably the onset of affluence after World War II; and the impact of specific events, most notably the US Civil Rights Movement, The Vietnam War and Vatican II. "The Sixties" arose from the interaction of these three kinds of factors.

I attempted to look very broadly at religious change in the "Long Sixties" which I defined as 1958–74, laying special emphasis on the impact of affluence in weakening community, thus permitting more individualistic life-styles. I also looked at changes in the churches, noting both the strong reforming impulses in the mid-'60s and the increasing polarization between progressives and conservatives in the later part of the decade; at "1968" and the political radicalization of the time; at the counter-culture and its "alternative spiritualities"; at sex, gender and the family; and at the sweeping legislative changes with regard to homosexuality, divorce and abortion.

In 2011 the sociologist Hans Joas organized a conference in Erfurt where historians from several countries responded to my book from the point of view of their own country. I do not think that any of them presented a picture of change in the '60s which was incompatible with mine, but taking account of what they said would have enabled me to have presented a more nuanced picture. In the meantime Callum Brown, who had been invited to the conference but was unable to be there, had published a more thorough-going critique,[40] so when I published my response to points made by speakers at the conference, I included a response to Brown.[41] The

---

39. Alan D. Gilbert, *The Making of Post-Christian Britain* (London 1980).
40. Callum G. Brown, "What Was the Religious Crisis of the 1960s?" *Journal of Religious History*, 34, no. 4 (2010), 468–79.
41. "Review Symposium on Hugh McLeod, *The Religious Crisis of the 1960s*," *Journal of Religion in Europe*, 5, no. 4 (2012), 425–520. Guillaume Cuchet, a leading authority on modern French Catholicism, has provided an excellent commentary on our debate in "La 'crise religieuse des années 1960': Autour d'un débat récent dans l'historiographie britannique," *Revue Historique*, 679 (2016), 629–44. He and Géraldine Vaughan were later instrumental in

basic difference between us was that he sees one big central story of "The Sixties," namely a mass revolt by the younger generation, especially young women, against the churches and against the puritanical restrictions which many blamed on the churches. Besides this central story, everything else, according to Brown, was a sideshow. My view was that this was *one* of the stories of "The Sixties," but that it stood alongside other equally important stories, including the political radicalization of the later '60s, the impact of Vatican II, and the social changes associated with rising prosperity, to mention only three of the most significant.

The "Long Sixties" could be traumatic for Catholics, because up to that time they had been generally more successful than the Protestants in resisting the secularizing trends. In 1960 there were still parts of rural Europe, for example in Brittany, where 90% of the population were practising Catholics. But in a few years between 1965 and 1975, these figures often fell by a half or more. In both Protestant and Catholic Churches the mid-'60s had seen demands for radical reforms in Church and society, and rising hopes that rapid changes were possible, even likely. Because Vatican II had raised hopes for change so high, the disappointment was all the greater when changes were limited and came slowly. Most denominations saw a decline in the numbers of their clergy, both because of fewer vocations and because of those leaving the priesthood, but the Catholic losses were much more severe. Research in France suggests that most of those who left had gone through a longer period of disillusionment with the set-apartness of the clergy and the hierarchical nature of the Church.[42]

While the political and religious dramas of the decade, as well as the sexual revolution, made the headlines, some of the social changes were much more subtle and imperceptible. One of the advantages of oral history is that it can pick up some of the less dramatic but equally significant changes. I was struck by an interview with a woman who recalled that she and her husband had regularly attended the Methodist church until the time of their marriage, but then they increasingly came to spend Sunday, their only free day together, going out on their motor bike—with the result that they 'floated away' from the church.

I faced the question of how far changes in that decade followed a common pattern and how far there were distinctive national trajectories. I

---

making possible a French translation of my book: Hugh McLeod, *Le déclin de la chrétienté en Occident: Autour de la crise religieuse des années 1960*, trans. Élise Trogrlic (Geneva, 2021).

42. Martine Sevegrand, *Vers une Église sans prêtres* (Rennes, 2004).

think in retrospect that I may have placed insufficient emphasis on national differences. One national difference which I did discuss, however, was the growing gap opening up in the '70s between a more religious USA and an increasingly secular Europe. I argued that in the '60s churches in both Europe and the USA had suffered serious losses. But the situation in the USA began to stabilize around 1972, while the trend in Europe continued to be downward. In 2010 I had the chance to explore this theme more fully. I was given a Fellowship at the Swedish Collegium of Advanced Studies in Uppsala as part of a small group interested in longer term patterns of religious change. Also in the group were Hans Joas, one of the Collegium's permanent fellows, and two historians from the USA, David Sorkin and Jeff Cox. I rejected the view that there was a fundamental divide between a "religious" United States and a "secular" Europe, arguing that up to the 1970s Europe was not "less religious" than the United States but "differently religious." Moreover, there were big differences between European countries and between American regions. From the perspective of the early twenty-first century when, especially during the presidency of George W. Bush, many Europeans were concerned at the political influence of the Religious Right in the USA, and many Americans were concerned at the growth of secularism in Europe and also at the rising importance of Islam, it appeared that there were deep-rooted historic differences which might explain the current situation. I argued, however, that the real divergence took place in the 1970s. I subsequently discussed the question with David Hempton and we planned two conferences at Radcliffe and Harvard, papers from which eventually fed into a collective volume.[43] Our idea was to pick nine issues where it might be argued that there were significant European/American differences and then to invite two authors, one mainly expert on the USA and one mainly expert on one or more European countries, to debate the issue. David and I, while agreed on quite a lot, also had some significant differences, so we wrote two concluding chapters. David's theme was the accumulation of small differences which led Europe and America in what were ultimately different directions. My theme was change over time in the nature and extent of the differences. In the nineteenth century, American religious history was very different from that of France, for example, but the religious similarities between the USA and Great Britain were far greater than the differences. From the early twentieth century onwards, Britain and the USA diverged as secularization, though apparent in both countries, advanced more rapidly in Britain. But the presence especially of the

---

43. Ed. David Hempton and Hugh McLeod, *Secularization and Religious Innovation in the North Atlantic World* (Oxford, 2017).

Catholic Church in many parts of Europe and its roots in popular culture remained strong up to the 1960s, in spite of the greater role of secularism in European than in American politics.

My most recent project, leading to a book on *Religion and the Rise of Sport in England*, now in the process of publication,[44] has developed over many years. My interest in the subject began with my book on *Religion and Society 1850–1914*. I was struck by the fact that the decline in church-going from about 1890 coincided with the Victorian sports boom, and I wondered if there was a connection. To complicate the question, I was well aware that the churches had often contributed to the boom by forming cricket and football clubs or providing gymnasia. When Sturt Mews was elected president of the Ecclesiastical History Society in 1999 and selected as his theme "Work, Rest and Play" (a reference to the advertising slogan "A Mars Bar a Day Helps you Work, Rest and Play"), I took the opportunity to return to the theme with a short paper. I presented the relationship between Victorian Churches and sports in the form of a modified version of Jane Austen's *Pride and Prejudice* in which this relationship moved through successive phases of repulsion, attraction and ultimately (diverging here from Austen) a friendly separation. I then developed the theme in the following years, usually in response to invitations to contribute to conferences or collective volumes. The first was a paper on "Nonconformity and Sport" for a Festschrift in honour of Clyde Binfield.[45] For a Festschrift in honour of Keith Robbins, I took a more international approach, examining the relationship between religion, sport and politics in several European politics, highlighting the difference between England and the many European countries, including France, Germany and Ireland, where sport was more strongly politicized.[46]

An invitation to deliver the Hulsean lectures in Cambridge in 2008 gave me the opportunity to tie my thoughts on the Victorian period more fully together. But as one questioner asked, "What happened before and what happened after?" In the book which I finally completed in 2021 I tried to answer those questions, bringing the story up to the present day. The peculiar circumstances of 2020 and 2021 influenced the shape of my later

---

44. Forthcoming from Oxford University Press.
45. Hugh McLeod, "'Thews and Sinews': Nonconformity and Sport," in: David Bebbington and Timothy Larsen, eds., *Modern Christianity and Cultural Aspirations* (Sheffield, 2003), 28–46.
46. Hugh McLeod, "Religion, Politics and Sport, c. 1870–1939," in: Stewart J. Brown, Frances Knight and John Morgan-Guy, eds., *Religion, Identity and Conflict in Britain: From the Restoration to the Twentieth Century* (Farnham, 2013), 195–212.

research. Access to archives was cut off for long periods, and I had to make much greater use of sources available through the internet. While the relationship between religion and sport in the nineteenth century is well-documented and there are some (though not many) major studies by historians,[47] very little research has been done on the twentieth century. So in discussing the nineteenth century I was in dialogue with other historians, including some for whom religion was secondary to their main concerns, but in writing about the twentieth century I was to a large extent on my own, apart from Jack Williams, a leading historian of cricket, who was the first to point to the importance of the churches in sport in the inter-war years.[48]

My research showed that many of the sports clubs and facilities established by churches in the Victorian years continued into the 1960s and only went into rapid decline in the '70s and '80s. It was precisely then that Evangelical churches began to come to the fore in church-based sport and large numbers of new clubs and leagues were formed. I suggested that the history of the relationship between religion and sport encapsulates the various stages of English religious history since the later eighteenth century. It begins with the "unreformed" Church of England and its connections with "traditional" sports. Then in the early nineteenth century, the rise of Evangelicalism brought growing tensions as Christian preachers attacked many of the then-popular sports because of their cruelty or brutality, and all of them because of their associations with gambling. Some Evangelicals simply regarded all sports as a waste of precious time. However, the growing liberalization of theology in the later part of the nineteenth century was associated with a friendlier view of sport—or at least of "good" sports such as football and cricket. The first half of the twentieth century was the era of what some historians have called "diffusive Christianity": church-going was in decline but the churches remained familiar and respected institutions, not least because of the huge range of recreational activities which they provided, especially for the young, but for many adults too. The later twentieth century saw growing secularization and the decline of church-based sports. But by the end of that century and the beginning of the twenty-first, there was not only a changed religious world but a changed relationship between religion and sport. In spite of continuing secularization, there was a large growth of sports chaplaincy, involving, for example, the majority of major soccer clubs; the impact of immigration and the

---

47. Notably Dominic Erdozain, *The Problem of Pleasure: Sport, Recreation and the Crisis of Victorian Religion* (Oxford, 2010).
48. Jack Williams, *Cricket and England: A Cultural and Social History of the Inter-War Years* (London, 1999).

globalization of sport meant that star athletes came from a wide variety of religious backgrounds, including many Muslims; and the Evangelicals who had once condemned sport were now its most enthusiastic advocates.

When I retired in 2010, Callum Brown and Mike Snape organized a small conference and presented me with a Festschrift with contributions from historians and sociologists from a number of countries.[49] I am immensely grateful to Callum and Mike, as well as to all the other contributors, for their work in making this fine volume possible. I also appreciated the diversity of the contributors, including scholars with opposing views on major historical or sociological issues. So far as my historical work is concerned, I have tried to avoid joining a party, and have valued having friends with very different approaches and belonging to organisations with different cultures. Introducing me before a lecture in Sheffield some years ago, Clyde Binfield made the perceptive comment that he had heard me speak both at the Ecclesiastical History Society and at a History Workshop and "they are as different as chalk and cheese." My historical roots lie in the social history of the 1960s and '70s, and in spite of the various learning experiences which I have described here, my approach to history has not changed fundamentally since then. The theme of my work has continued to be the interaction between religion and society, but I have explored this theme by focusing on many different areas, including, for example, the labour movement, national identity, the role of religion in legislative changes, anti-clericalism and everyday life. My interest in comparative history has led me to spread my net widely, and I think this has both advantages and disadvantages. In my recent work on the history of sport I have been aware that I do not have the in-depth knowledge of any one sport which most specialists in the field have. And, indeed, I do not have the kind of in-depth knowledge of the history of any religious denomination, including my own, which any denominational historian has. My corresponding strength, I hope, lies in a readiness to enter sympathetically into very different religious worlds.

---

49. Callum G. Brown and Michel Snape, eds., *Secularisation in the Christian World* (Farnham, 2010).

A Story of Gifts:
Becoming a Historian of American Catholicism

Leslie Woodcock Tentler*

Not long after Christmas, I was seated next to Nelson Minnich, editor of this publication, at a Washington dinner party. "How's the essay coming?" was practically the first thing he said to me. Now, it's true that I'd missed several deadlines for this particular assignment, although my excuses were impeccable, given that I was finishing a book manuscript and preparing it for publication. But Nelson had correctly intuited that my heart wasn't in this particular assignment. "It's rather like writing your own obituary," I pointed out. "One can view it that way," he responded. "But I prefer to think of it as an opportunity to express gratitude for the gifts one receives over the course of a long career." Duly chastened, I agreed to meet the upcoming deadline. That I managed to do so is largely due to Nelson's reframing of the project, the valedictory aspects of which were indeed inhibiting me. So I thank him for his typically gracious counsel. Mine has in fact been a story of gifts, and it has been good to acknowledge it. This is perhaps especially true with regard to the gifts that arrived oddly packaged.

I came to the University of Michigan in the fall of 1963 as an exceedingly green but eager freshman. I had no firm ideas about a major, although I opted with genuine excitement for Sociology 100 as my lone first-semester elective. The subject had not been taught at my excellent suburban high school, which was probably part of its attraction. It was also something of a natural for someone with parents like mine—both of them veterans of the labor movement and long-time political activists. All such electives, however, required the approval of the honors program's director, then a formidable professor of German literature. "Oh no, my dear," he said as he drew a thick line through "Sociology 100" on my course election card. "You belong in History 101"—which in those days was the first half of Western Civ. Although I would be community organizing with a radical student group by the following summer and acquiring fluency in rights-talk, I was capable in the moment of nothing but meek assent. History 101

---

* Dr. Tentler is professor emerita of the Catholic University of America. Her email address is Tentler@cua.edu.

it was. I quickly fell in love with the subject and, after an appropriately lengthy interval, also with the instructor, a brand-new assistant professor by the name of Thomas Tentler.

My passion for the history of late medieval and early modern Europe quickened in subsequent semesters. So did my taste for political activism. I remember a hurried journey south in the spring of my sophomore year to participate in civil rights demonstrations in Montgomery, Alabama, then at the epicenter of the struggle over voting rights. I heard Lyndon Johnson propose the 1965 Voting Rights Act in a speech before a joint session of Congress while sitting with fellow marchers on a darkened Montgomery street that had troopers on horseback at both ends. They too were listening via transistor radio, and when Johnson said "we shall overcome" in his inimitable Texas drawl, those hitherto terrifying troopers sagged visibly in their saddles. The experience, still vivid in memory, helped to shape the historian I became, not just in terms of my interpretive biases but in a more immediate sense, as well. Shortly after my return, I enrolled for the following semester in a section of the junior honors seminar devoted to the Renaissance. The class, as it happened, was oversubscribed, which prompted the presiding professor to query each student as to his or her extracurricular activities. Upon hearing my account, in which the Montgomery experience figured, he promptly ejected me from the class and assigned me to an inexplicably under-enrolled section on the U.S. Civil War.

My assent to this second instance of professorial high-handedness was something less than meek. But as in the case of the earlier instance, this one proved to be a gift. It was in Professor William Freehling's splendid class that I both conceived a passion for American history and learned to engage historical texts in a genuinely critical way. Revisionist scholarship was already transforming the study of slavery and the Reconstruction era, and, fueled by my political passions, I entered into the debate with a life-transforming zeal. It was also in Freehling's seminar that I quite literally found my voice. In previous classes, even in discussion sections, I rarely spoke, conditioned at least in part by cultural assumptions that equated loquaciousness in females with foolishness—or worse, aggression. But I was so talkative, indeed so combative, in Freehling's seminar that I was often sick to my stomach after class was over, fearful that I had talked too much or been less than acceptably deferential to my male fellow students. Throughout my college years, I should note, I experienced nothing but respect and support from the Michigan history faculty, all but one of whom were men. For me, the enemy lay within and the Freehling seminar marked the outset of a long internal struggle.

Leslie Woodcock Tentler

Michigan history honors students, then as now, devote their senior year to researching and writing a senior thesis. Thoroughly committed by this time to politically relevant scholarship, I chose as my subject the racial dimensions of the United Auto Workers' campaign to organize the enormous Ford Rouge complex in 1940 and 1941. Roughly 10 percent of Rouge workers were African-American, all of whom had ample reason to distrust the labor movement when it came to protecting workers like them. How, then, did the union strive to ensure that, in the event of a strike, black workers would honor the picket line? The thesis introduced me to archival research, by which I was immediately entranced, and also to its frustrations—given that the archives in question consisted of the mostly unorganized papers of the UAW's local 600, which happened to be voluminous. Still, I was supremely happy rifling through those documents at local 600's headquarters—happy enough to ensure that I would follow through on my still-tentative plans to apply to history graduate programs and aim for an academic career. That my completed thesis won a prize seemed to validate aspirations that I still could not help but regard as audacious.

Against all advice, I decided to stay at Michigan for my graduate studies. I was romantically involved with someone already enrolled in a Michigan graduate program, which helps to explain this almost certainly unwise decision. But my choice had more fundamentally to do with an almost crippling lack of self-confidence, a problem with which I was wrestling but had far from overcome. And yet even this unwise decision brought major gifts in its wake. The first, in order of time, was my introduction to the field of urban history in the person of Sam Bass Warner, Jr., a recent addition to the Michigan faculty. I can still remember my excitement at learning in Warner's seminar about new—to me—sources of evidence like city directories and manuscript census schedules, and their applicability to research into the history of everyday life. A second gift, received primarily from my fellow graduate students, was exposure to the then-radical notion that gender should be a critical variable in our reconstruction of the past. Michigan's climate was hardly unique in this regard. But the university's tradition of student activism meant that interest in women's history and related gender issues was unusually strong in my graduate school cohort. The best gift of all was eventual marriage to fellow historian Tom Tentler, most unlikely to have come about had I left Ann Arbor.

The next several years were so eventful that even in memory they retain something of a frenetic quality. Between 1973 and 1979, I finished my degree, took my first academic job, gave birth to three children, and published my first book. I also became a Catholic, which partly explains a subsequent reorientation of my research agenda. Coming of professional age in the mid-1970s, I was something of a pioneer in terms of the academy: my generation of female PhDs was the first to seek university teaching jobs in significant numbers. Many of us did not survive professionally—hence the dearth, until quite recently, of senior female faculty in a great many fields. My own experience suggests why this was so. Marriage to a fellow academic, especially one with tenure, radically limited my employment prospects. I was supremely fortunate to find a tenure-track job within commuting distance of Ann Arbor. Had I been consigned to adjuncting, as might easily have happened, I would almost certainly have gone into another line of work. The demands of child-care were often overwhelming. I remember years of chronic exhaustion, accompanied by deep anxiety about my children's well-being. Convinced that I had to be home for dinner every single night, I refused in those early years to attend any conference that would have taken me away from Ann Arbor. Bad for my professional prospects, to say the least. But I will concede—this is meant as encouragement for today's young scholars—that having children did teach me to work with laser-like concentration. Prior to the birth of my first child, I hadn't realized how leisurely the rhythms of my graduate-school existence had been.

Despite the innumerable obstacles, I managed to publish my revised dissertation, which appeared in 1979 as *Wage-Earning Women: Industrial Work and Family Life in the United States, 1900–1930*.[1] Born of my interests in labor history and the nascent field of women's history, the book analyzed women's employment in the broader context of working-class life. What did employment—I looked specifically at factory and retail work—mean for women's understanding of the possibilities open to their sex, given a sex-segregated labor market, persistently low female wages, and the fantasizing about romance and marriage that typically dominated workroom life? It was quite possible, I concluded, for paid employment to be both a transformative experience for a young woman, causing her to seek and achieve a far greater independence in her social life than her mother had enjoyed, and one that prompted her to see her natural destiny as marriage and non-employed motherhood. It was time, in short, to reassess the persistent notion that paid employment was an unambiguous force for women's emancipation. The book sold surprisingly well—it was controversial in its argument, which made it a natural for teaching, and fed a growing hunger for texts on American women's history. Indeed, it has to date outsold any of my subsequent offerings in American Catholic history.

I made scant mention of religion in *Wage-Earning Women*, although probably a majority of my subjects were Catholic, given that my sources dealt mainly with New York, Boston, Philadelphia, and Chicago, and a significant minority were Jewish. Nothing in my graduate training had prepared me to think of religion as a significant category of analysis, much less a subject of interest in its own right. But by 1979 I had converted to the Catholicism with which I had flirted in adolescence, and that development—let me be frank—made it easier for me to grasp religion's salience for the kind of history I wished to do. I had hoped in *Wage-Earning Women* to probe the nature of family and community life in the urban working-class—to write "labor" history in the broadest and most generous sense. My sources, however, rich though they were, mostly told me about life on the job. How might I construct a fuller picture of the contexts in which my subjects lived and made their choices? Religion was obviously a piece of the puzzle, given that I was dealing with the United States, where religious institutions have historically played a central role in many working-class communities. This was evident on my frequent forays into Detroit, about which I was then teaching a course along with several col-

---

1. Published in New York by Oxford University Press.

leagues. The city was still a bastion of organized labor, but its churches and synagogues vastly outnumbered its union halls.

It was in conjunction with one of those Detroit forays that I stumbled onto my next research project, which led in turn to what can only be called a reorientation of my career. Visiting a magnificent, if gently decaying, Polish church near the city center, I was engaged by its historically-informed pastor in a long conversation about the church's origins. (Since the church in question was located just two blocks from another enormous Polish church, I was already curious. Could this now-mostly-empty piece of urban wilderness have ever been so densely populated as to have supported two Catholic churches in such close proximity?) The church I was visiting, as I learned, had been born in schism in the 1880s, the result of a bitter dispute in the neighboring congregation over a priest who had been summarily dismissed—for ample cause, in all likelihood—by the local bishop. The ensuing conflict had been episodically violent: a young man was fatally shot, two priests were assaulted by female parishioners and forcibly prevented from saying Mass, and women were prominent too in confrontations with the police. Knowing almost nothing at this juncture about the history of American Catholicism, I was both stunned—could Catholics really be capable of such behavior?—and hungry to learn more.

A bit of digging confirmed the pastor's account and prompted me to a fuller investigation, during which I began to explore the existing literature on American Catholic history. I soon discovered that the conflict which had drawn my interest was anything but an aberration. Catholics were in fact capable of extreme behavior when it came to defending what they typically described as their rights in the church. Those putative rights nearly always centered on two issues: the ownership of parish properties and the hiring and dismissal of parish clergy. (My schismatic Detroit congregation vested ownership of its church and school in an elected board of lay trustees, who at least in theory both hired the pastor and defined the reach of his authority.) No bishop, needless to say, was willing to cede either "right" to the laity—hence the bitter and protracted nature of the conflicts that sometimes resulted. Earlier generations of Catholic historians had had little to say about such conflicts. It was otherwise with my contemporaries in the field, who were frequently partisans of the "new" social history. Eager to understand lay experience and perspectives, they saw in such breaches of the usual order a means of exploring communal values and the assumptions that undergirded life in the immigrant enclaves. Since little work had yet been done on parish rebellions among the Poles, my research made a modest contribution to this particular mode of reassessing the Catholic past.

It was in the course of my "Polish" research that I first visited the archives of the Archdiocese of Detroit, which were then in what might charitably be called a primitive state. The archives were open only one day a week, tended by a devoted but decidedly part-time archivist, and had space for a single researcher. I could reserve that single seat in advance, but in the event of a priest's needing to use the archives, I would have to surrender it. (Would a woman religious have similarly outranked me? I never did find out.) The archivist, Father—later Bishop—Leonard Blair, was kindness itself on the days we shared his miniscule workroom, and he clearly hoped to persuade his superiors to take the archives more seriously. But research under these conditions was exceedingly difficult and I was grateful that my project was of limited duration. Did historians of American Catholicism regularly confront such obstacles, I wondered. And what about the linguistic demands of the field? It had not been difficult to cope with the relatively few Polish-language documents relevant to my project, given that I had studied Russian in high school and college; a semester's worth of Polish classes brought me up to speed. But researching the polyglot Catholic past would presumably require a greater linguistic facility than I thought I possessed.

My "Polish" research was hampered by more than limits on archival access. I had three young children at home—a daughter and twin sons—and a heavy teaching load. Finding time for research was hard and I was experiencing symptoms of acute emotional exhaustion. My socially-conservative department chair proved in this instance to be a gift, if an ironic one. Open about his conviction that the mothers of young children should not be employed, he readily agreed to my teaching a reduced load after the birth of the twins and was willing to grant me an unpaid leave for a subsequent academic year, when my husband's sabbatical took us to England. We were poor as proverbial church mice during that sabbatical year, but it was a life-saver. London is where I took Polish classes and turned my mass of "Polish" research into a journal article.[2] It was also where our family life re-gained a measure of serenity. I include these domestic details for a reason, although some may object to their presence in what is supposed to be a form of intellectual biography. To ignore them would be to collude with a powerful bias in our national culture, which is faithfully reflected in the various professions—that parenthood is a private choice, the consequences of which should be borne by the choosers alone. No need, then,

---

2. Leslie Woodcock Tentler, "Who is the Church? Conflict in a Polish Immigrant Parish in Late Nineteenth-Century Detroit," *Comparative Studies in Society and History* 25:2 (April 1983).

for the various professions to accommodate parents at the outset of their careers by modifying expectations as to productivity or extending time to tenure. The University of Michigan, at a branch of which I was then teaching, did eventually embrace the latter reform some twenty years after my children were born.

I returned from the year abroad with new energy, although my research agenda appeared to have run aground. My "Polish" research had indeed provided new insight into the life of a working-class population that mainstream labor historians had tended to neglect, if only because relatively few Polish-Americans in the past have been prominent labor activists. But, for the reasons cited above, further research on American Catholicism seemed impractical. Then I received an unexpected phone call. The caller was Father Blair, late of the archdiocesan archives and now secretary to the archbishop, who conveyed surprising news. The archdiocese had hired a full-time professional archivist and space had been designated at the chancery for a commodious reading room, which would be open to researchers a full five days a week. The archbishop, moreover, wanted to commission a professionally-researched history of the archdiocese to commemorate its upcoming sesquicentennial. The writer of this history would have full access to the archives, Father Blair assured me, and be free of ecclesiastical vetting—there would be a "no censorship" clause in the contract and the completed manuscript was to be published by a university press rather than the archdiocese itself. Would I be interested in applying for the job?

Of course I said yes. But in retrospect, there were good career-linked reasons not to. At least among Americanists, diocesan history was—then, as now—barely recognized as an acceptable professional genre. As for ecclesiastical sponsorship in any form, it was and is definitely beyond the bounds of professional propriety. By committing myself to the Detroit project, moreover, I risked being permanently identified as a historian of American Catholicism rather than a labor historian or a historian of immigration—never mind that I would still be dealing with many of the same human subjects—and American Catholic history at that juncture was hardly describable as a genuine sub-field. It boasted no prestigious journals, its practitioners seldom featured at major professional conferences, and the jobs available to specialists were—save at certain Catholic colleges—close to non-existent. At this point in my career, however, my connections to the profession were sufficiently tenuous that all I could see in Father Blair's offer was intellectual salvation—three whole years away from teaching, an archive within commuting distance, the chance to write a second book. I did not expect to move from my current academic job, where my superiors were in fact supportive of the project, less because of the Catholic angle than its Detroit connections, which were thought to be good for public relations.

Thus began three of the happiest years of my entire professional life. Save for the antebellum decades, the Detroit archives were wonderfully rich, as were those of its principal teaching order. At least some of the missing documents from the diocese's early years, moreover, had been long ago rescued by an enterprising archivist at Notre Dame, and I had the funds to travel there. True, the archdiocesan archives had been organized according to episcopal priorities, which are not necessarily those of the researcher. But I had sufficient time in the archives to satisfy my own priorities and to accumulate—slowly, painstakingly—a fair amount of information about both the laity and the local clergy, in addition to seemingly endless details about what is best described as ecclesiastical housekeeping. In the end, I read almost everything. I compiled a collective biography of the diocese's priests between the mid-nineteenth and the mid-twentieth centuries, which revealed important changes over time, especially when it came to career patterns. Thanks to mandatory parish reports, I learned a good deal about changing sacramental practice and trends in devotional offerings. The diocesan newspaper, with which I spent untold purgatorial hours, provided generous insight into parish social life, as I had rather expected it would; it was also an unanticipated source of information about changing funeral customs and the place of death in Catholic consciousness. I had not expected to find much about sexual discipline and its contestation in either the archives or the paper, but by the end of my research I had uncovered a surprising amount of provocative data, some of which would have eluded a more hurried researcher. Trudging through a particularly dreary cache of letters from and to a late-nineteenth century bishop, I encountered one from an itinerant mission preacher detailing the startlingly large number of abortions—"actual or intended"—that had been confessed to him at a recent mission in Kalamazoo. Nothing in the missive suggested surprise on the part of the writer.

The diocesan archives were much less rich when it came to such "secular" topics as politics and social movements, save where explicitly Catholic issues were directly at stake. (This is much less true of the records that date from the 1960s and after, but at the time these were closed even to me.) Supplementary collections elsewhere sometimes helped to fill the gap, as with the papers of the Detroit Association of Catholic Trade Unionists, housed at Wayne State University, where the papers of a prominent labor priest were also to be found. Serendipity led me to the privately-held papers of another priest known for his social activism and broad local contacts and to what remained of the archives of the local Catholic Worker, which had close ties to the labor movement. (The founder's widow was a fellow parishioner.) But as my research progressed, it gradually dawned on me that I was in fact compiling evidence that was "secular" in its implications despite its apparent "churchiness"—evidence that spoke directly to such matters as the course of Detroit's development, directly affected for a number of years by the Chancery's decisions about where to plant new parishes. Detroit was a city that shouldn't have worked, given its ethnic heterogeneity, explosive growth, and the brutality of its industrial regime. That it more or less did was attributable in part to the social glue provided by the Catholic Church with its network of parishes, schools, colleges, hospitals, social service, and cultural organizations. I did not doubt, by the time my book was published, that I had things to say to my colleagues in urban, labor, and immigrant history.[3]

My erstwhile colleagues evidently disagreed: despite positive reviews, *Seasons of Grace* sold anemically. Nor did I help my cause by turning almost immediately to a research focus that smacked of the ecclesiastical—to wit, the Catholic diocesan clergy in the United States. I had been surprised, in the course of my previous research, at how little attention this decidedly interesting population had received from historians of American Catholicism. Understanding the clergy—their training, modes of life, self-understanding, and self-presentation—seemed to me essential to a full reconstruction of the Catholic sub-culture at the various stages of its evolution. Given that priests were often communal as well as religious leaders, moreover, studying the clergy also seemed key to a fuller understanding of the Church's role as a mediating institution. I did intuit that, for many of my colleagues, the clergy represented an outmoded way of doing Catholic history—one that focused on clerical elites rather than the laity. And I knew from experience that studying the clergy meant serious problems with sources, which were apt to be thin and, all too often, hard to access. If Catholic priests in the past kept diaries or wrote personal letters, as some must have done, few diocesan archives have bothered to collect them. I was lucky in Detroit: two successive bishops had required regular letters from seminarians studying in Europe and from chaplains serving in the Second World War, and those letters—some of them surprisingly candid—were archived. Other than that, however, priests' correspondence in the archives dealt mostly with grievances of various sorts, many of them petty, and with the occasional scandal—useful up to a point but hardly providing a balanced picture of clerical life. A good deal of relevant information about Detroit's

---

3. Leslie Woodcock Tentler, *Seasons of Grace: A History of the Catholic Archdiocese of Detroit* (Detroit: Wayne State University Press, 1990).

priests, moreover, was filed in collections that I strongly suspected were off-limits to research. (I knew better than to ask.) With free access to the archives' vault, I could access that material. Most researchers could not.

Nevertheless, I persisted, focusing initially on the French-speaking clergy so prominent in the Great Lakes region in the early decades of the nineteenth century. Happily for me, they proved to be letter-writers, and some of their letters had been rescued by the aforementioned archivist at Notre Dame, to whom I continue to be grateful. I also had useful scraps from my Detroit research, most notably a rich collection of documents from an experiment in rural ministry in the Michigan Thumb in the 1920s. Several articles resulted.[4] I knew, of course, that I would eventually have to broaden the geographic scope of my research. Ideally, I would compile a collective biography of the priests in three additional dioceses, to supplement what I had found in Detroit. I would certainly need a generous grant, given the time away from home such an endeavor would require. But would I ever again enjoy the kind of access I'd had in Detroit, without which such a project might not be possible? Doubts nagged at me in my vulnerable moments. With a sabbatical on the horizon, however, I continued to think in terms of a book-length study. Surely there were dioceses whose leaders would grasp the importance of a project like mine and agree to cooperate.

Although priests were my principal preoccupation over the course of the 1990s, the most significant article that I published then—significant, at least, in terms of its readership—had little to do with the priesthood. Titled "On the Margins: the State of American Catholic History," this article challenged the assumptions that undergirded what I saw as the persistent marginalization among American historians of scholarship on Catholicism.[5] Why, for example, were labor historians so dismissive of the communal achievements embodied in Catholic parish founding and working-class support of parochial schools? Did such achievements have nothing to do with the gradual development of class consciousness? Why were my colleagues in women's history so indifferent to women's religious

---

4. Leslie Woodcock Tentler, "'A Model Rural Parish: Priests and People in the Michigan Thumb," *Catholic Historical Review* 78:3 (July 1992); Leslie Woodcock Tentler, "'How I Would Save Them All:' Priests on the Michigan Frontier," *U.S. Catholic Historian* 12:4 (Fall 1994); Leslie Woodcock Tentler, "Reluctant Pluralists: Catholic and Reformed Clergy in Ante-Bellum Michigan," *U.S. Catholic Historian* 15:2 (Spring 1997); Leslie Woodcock Tentler, "'God's Representative in Our Midst:' Toward a History of the Catholic Diocesan Clergy in the United States," *Church History* 67:2 (June 1998).

5. Leslie Woodcock Tentler, "On the Margins: the State of American Catholic History," *American Quarterly* 45:1 (March 1993).

orders, given their significance as a socially-sanctioned alternative to marriage and motherhood and the professional attainment they made possible for their members? Why did even those historians of ethnicity who emphasized the role of Catholicism in the immigrant community tend to ignore it as they dealt with more assimilated ethnic populations in the decades after the First World War? Historians of American Catholicism, I think, were grateful for such questions. Most of us knew the sense of marginality on which the article was premised. A "state of the field" article, moreover, is almost bound to attract a larger-than-usual readership, if only because none of us can keep up with current scholarly output.

The 1990s also brought a deeper involvement on my part with the Cushwa Center for the Study of American Catholicism at Notre Dame—a gift indeed for someone whose research interests were not shared by her immediate colleagues. Through Cushwa conferences and seminars, I met other historians of American Catholicism and was encouraged to think in bolder ways about my research agenda. Of particular significance was the "Twentieth Century Project," generously funded by the Lilly Foundation, which aimed to spur research on American Catholicism between the earliest days of the century and the turmoil that followed Vatican II. Surprisingly little had been published on this period. Was the church in the immediate pre-conciliar decades too centralized administratively, too aggressive when it came to sexual discipline, too reflexively patriotic, and too complacent intellectually to appeal to a cohort of historians who had valorized the variety and rambunctiousness of the immigrant church? I rather suspect that this was the case. Too many of us, whether we acknowledged it or not, were deeply invested in providing a kind of scholarly imprimatur to post-conciliar American Catholicism. The "Twentieth Century Project," which spawned a number of excellent monographs, resulted in a more nuanced understanding of the decades under study and a new appreciation of the Council's complex roots.

Although I participated in the Twentieth Century Project, I did not use the opportunity to produce a history—or, chronologically speaking, a partial history—of the American diocesan clergy. But priests still figured, given that my project entailed a history of Catholic pastoral practice with regard to marital contraception and the variety of lay responses to this particular mode of sexual discipline. What accounts for the sudden shift in my research focus? I think, in retrospect, that I was exceedingly anxious about the problem of archival access were I to embark on a book-length study of the clergy. How many bishops were likely to grant me the freedom I had enjoyed in Detroit? Better, perhaps, to defer the problem—to assume that it could be resolved at some point in the conveniently hazy future. But it's also true that I'd long been fascinated by the birth control question, which had occasionally surfaced in the course of my earlier research. I was particularly intrigued by its link to the recent history of confession—to the rapid spread of frequent confession in the middle decades of the twentieth century and the near-collapse of the sacrament in the decades following Vatican II. That near-collapse signaled a radical shift in lay understanding of ecclesial authority and I strongly suspected that birth control played a major role in this regard. Given my long-standing interest in the Catholic politics of gender, moreover, the subject was a natural. Then, too, I could remember a time in the not-terribly-distant past when Catholics themselves seemed obsessed with the subject. Growing up in a heavily Catholic neighborhood, I knew that Catholics couldn't practice birth control even before I knew precisely what birth control was.

Having found a congenial subject did not solve my source problems. I knew that plentiful sources existed for the 1950s and '60s, when birth control was increasingly a topic of public policy debates and, ultimately, of intra-Catholic contention. But how many of these sources addressed the specifics of pastoral practice, especially in the confessional? I had no idea. Nor did I know whether much was available, by way of relevant documents, for earlier decades in the twentieth century. Indeed, I began my research assuming that the resulting narrative might well begin in 1945. But I was in for a happy surprise—or, perhaps more accurately, a series of happy surprises. Sources proved to be abundant, albeit somewhat less so for the earliest years of the century. Pastoral literature was particularly informative, even for the late nineteenth century. My earliest document was a set of teaching notes produced in 1875 by a Passionist missioner, who was tasked with instructing his neophyte confreres on how to preach about sex. Catholic couples resorted to birth control "more commonly than many suspect," he informed them, although the subject had of necessity to be "HINTED AT PRUDENTLY," lest ignorant members of the congregation be schooled in sinful behavior.[6] Few of the mission sermons I found, whether printed or in manuscript form, deviated from this counsel prior to the First World War. Only the Redemptorists regularly preached on the subject with clarity and vigor.

Mission sermons were among the richest of my archival sources. (I was graciously welcomed and assisted at the archives of the Passionist Fathers,

---

6. Fr. Gaudentius Rossi, C.P., "Some Instructions about the Sermons, Meditations, and Catechisms Delivered by Our Fathers, in Our Missions," April 1875. Passionist Provincial Archives, Holy Cross Province, Chicago.

the Paulists, and the Redemptorists.) But other sources surfaced, too. By the 1920s, with the advent of a vociferous movement to promote birth control for the married, relevant documents appeared in the papers of the National Catholic Welfare Conference and at each of the six diocesan archives that I visited. With the promulgation in 1930 of *Casti Connubii*, effectively the first papal encyclical to denounced contraception as a grievous sin, the documentary flood-gates were opened. *Casti Connubii* had summoned priests to abandon their hitherto reticent ways and be proactive as confessors when it came to marital birth control. But how to do so in the context of a world-shattering depression? Both printed and archival sources wrestled with this question, and particularly with the problems posed by the advent of a physiologically-plausible mode of family limitation based on periodic abstinence. Under what circumstances was the use of "rhythm" licit? Sources grew even richer following the Second World War, with the rise of family life ministries and a more positive theology of marital sex. The early 1960s brought a veritable explosion, with sources now marked by a new frankness and, increasingly, a lay perspective.

Although sources proved to be gratifyingly numerous, I decided early on to incorporate oral history into the project—specifically interviews with priests. The decision raised eyebrows among a fair number of my colleagues. Why priests, they wanted to know, rather than lay men or, especially, women? The answer was easy: because priests played such critical roles as apologists for and enforcers of church teaching, most notably as confessors. But if I was sure about priests as my subject, I was deeply uneasy about oral evidence, being old enough by then to understand the fallibility of memory. I had serious doubts, moreover, about whether my interviewees would speak frankly or, indeed, whether I would find many interviewees at all. I did, in fact, find a goodly number of willing subjects—56 priests, nearly all of whom spoke with remarkable candor. (Casting the interviews as life histories helped to jog the memories of the many men who initially professed not to remember much about what was now the distant past; by the time my respondent had told me about his family, childhood parish, seminary experience, and preparation as a confessor, he was typically off and running.) I used the resulting evidence cautiously. But it did assist me toward a more nuanced view of my documentary sources and a more sympathetic orientation to the sometimes reluctant enforcers of a sexual discipline that most Catholics came to reject. My book[7] was the

---

7. *Catholics and Contraception: An American History* (Ithaca, NY: Cornell University Press, 2004).

richer for those interviews and so was I. Nearly every man with whom I spoke was thoughtful, gracious, and intelligent; most evinced a pastoral sensitivity that lent them a kind of radiance. Their testimony was a gift; so were their persons.

Catholics and Contraception was published in 2004, at the height of the sex abuse crisis. Like other Catholics, I responded to that crisis with shock and dismay; indeed, I came close to leaving the church. My scholarly self was thrown off-balance, too. How, in the present circumstances, could I possibly continue my research on priests? More than access to sources was at issue, although such access had obviously become much more difficult. Blindsided as I was by the scandals, I lost confidence in my ability to understand my subjects. How to account for the apparent extent of the scandals and the willingness of both bishops and the perpetrators' fellow priests to look the other way? I simply did not know. Read through the lens of the escalating scandals, moreover, even seemingly innocuous evidence came to seem suspect. Michigan's priests, for example, had for many decades been permitted to house teen-aged boys at their rectories either as domestic workers—unattached older women were often in short supply in rural districts in the nineteenth century—or when an aspiring seminarian needed tutoring in Latin, a subject that many rural schools did not teach prior to the 1920s. Such arrangements, I'd initially thought, probably worked to lessen the distance between priest and people, permitting the priest to be seen as a quasi-paterfamilias. Should I now regard them as inherently sinister? And what did such arrangements suggest about the dominant Catholic mentality with regard to the nature and incidence of homosexuality?[8]

Paralyzed by doubt and residual anger, I decided to abandon my long-deferred "priests" project. I did manage one additional article, this one based on archival sources too rich to ignore, but otherwise put my notes in storage, where they remain to this day.[9] For roughly the next decade, I devoted my scholarly energies to the years surrounding the Second Vatican Council and the radical changes in Catholic thought and practice that emerged in this turbulent time. Issues of sex and gender loomed large—a natural outgrowth of my work on contraception.[10] I grew curious about the

---

8. I explore the subject in greater detail in "Evidence and Historical Confidence," a contribution to "Forum: Writing Catholic History After the Sex Abuse Crisis," *American Catholic Studies*, 127:2 (Summer 2016).

9. Leslie Woodcock Tentler, "'To Work in the Fields of the Lord': Roots of the Crisis in Priestly Identity," *U.S. Catholic Historian* 29:4 (Fall 2011).

10. Representative publications include Leslie Woodcock Tentler, "Souls and Bodies: The Birth Control Controversy and the Collapse of Confession," in Michael J. Lacey and

shape of such conflicts in other western nations, most notably those where Catholic practice pre-Council had been robust. Funding from the Lilly Foundation underwrote a conference I organized at Catholic University, to which institution I had moved at the end of the 1990s, which in turn gave rise to an edited book: *The Church Confronts Modernity: Catholicism Since 1950 in the United States, the Republic of Ireland, and Quebec.*[11] Although I could hardly call myself a comparativist, that book resulted in several invitations to participate in similar projects, where scholars from various countries contributed expertise to a larger conversation about religious change.[12] My graduate teaching at Catholic University began to incorporate a comparativist dimension, too—something that proved surprisingly energizing. Reading about the recent religious history of locales as disparate as Sweden and Italy, I felt like a student again.

Interest in comparative history was also flourishing at the Cushwa Center, with which I remained closely involved. It was under Cushwa's auspices that in 2012 I returned to Detroit to immerse myself in newly-opened archival records from the episcopate of Archbishop, later Cardinal, John Dearden (1959–80). My work in Detroit was part of an ambitious comparative project which examined the implementation of Vatican II reforms in a number of dioceses around the world—in Europe, Mexico, Latin America, and India as well as Canada and the United States.[13] As one would anticipate, the post-conciliar story varied—sometimes quite dramatically—depending on local circumstances. In Detroit, the immediate post-Council years were marked by rising racial tensions, which culminated in 1967 in what was then the worst urban rioting in the American

---

Francis Oakley, eds., *The Crisis of Authority in Catholic Modernity* (New York: Oxford University Press, 2011) and Leslie Woodcock Tentler, "Breaking the Silence: Sex, Gender and the Parameters of Catholic Intellectual Life," in James L. Heft, SM and Una M. Cadegan, eds., *In the Logos of Love: Promise and Predicament in Catholic Intellectual Life* (New York: Oxford University Press, 2015).

11. Published in 2007 by the Catholic University of America Press, Washington, DC. I was the editor and also wrote the introduction.

12. See, for example: Leslie Woodcock Tentler, "Sex and Sub-Culture: American Catholicism Since 1945," in Nancy Christie and Michael Gauvreau, eds., *The Sixties and Beyond: Dechristianization in North America and Western Europe, 1945–2000* (Toronto: University of Toronto Press, 2013) and "How Exceptional? U.S. Catholics Since 1945," in David Hempton and Hugh McLeod, eds., *Secularization and Religious Innovation in the North Atlantic World* (New York: Oxford University Press, 2017).

13. Leslie Woodcock Tentler, "Through the Prism of Race: The Archdiocese of Detroit," in Kathleen Sprows Cummings, Timothy Matovina and Robert A. Orsi, eds., *Catholics in the Vatican II Era: Local Histories of a Global Event* (Cambridge, UK: Cambridge University Press, 2018).

twentieth century. Local Catholic leaders, most notably Archbishop Dearden, worked in unprecedented fashion to facilitate integration of Catholic schools and heavily Catholic neighborhoods—efforts that many Catholics admired but that others deeply resented. Polarization was the result—something that at least some Catholics attributed to the Council's reforms. Others lamented what they saw as a failure of post-conciliar nerve—a reluctance on the part of Catholic leaders to preach social justice with sufficient vigor or embrace what these critics saw as the Council's mandate of continual reform.

Detroit was approaching bankruptcy as I returned to do research and the Catholic Church in the city is fairly described as being by then in a moribund state. Three draconian rounds of church closings since the late 1980s had seen to that. The archdiocesan archives, housed now at the seminary, were located in what had been in my youth an upper middle-class neighborhood. Much had changed, and not for the better. Abandoned houses dotted nearby streets; lost souls drifted through vacant lots; a once-thriving parish church stood empty—window gaping, fixtures stripped, saplings sprouting from the roof. To drive these mean streets and then to read the excited plans of Council-era Catholic activists was almost unbearably painful. (Among the most energetic of these activists, many of whom were clergy, was the former pastor of the abandoned church just mentioned.) They had so much hope for the city they loved, so much faith in the Church as an agent of racial healing. On certain days in the archives, those documents almost reduced me to tears. This level of emotional engagement was, I suppose, a gift of sorts; the heart has a place in our scholarly work, although its promptings must be thoughtfully monitored. Working on so recent a time period, moreover, was a kind of return to Sociology 100—that freshman-year elective so abruptly snatched from my plate. I even found survey data among my abundant sources.

I was still at work on the Cushwa project when I retired from teaching. That involvement did much to ease the transition, which seemed at the time like embarking on an extended research leave. But soon enough the question loomed: what would I do with my retirement? Ever my activist parents' daughter, I had moments when continued scholarly work seemed a self-indulgent option. With the country in so parlous a state, surely it would be better to devote my energies to politics or advocacy? Material considerations also entered in: travel to archives costs money and I was growing weary of the super-economy lodging and meals such travel invariably entailed. (Low-cost quarters at a duck farm on a partially-deserted street in Detroit proved to be good fun, although the neighborhood was daunting.) Then came a wholly unlooked-for query from Yale University Press: might I be interested in submitting a proposal to write a new survey of American Catholic history? The prospect was irresistible. Depending as I would have to do on the scholarly work of others, I would be able to work from home. I would also be able to use at least some of the archival leftovers that were cluttering my study. And after years of work on American Catholic history, how difficult could such a project be? Not one to look a gift-horse in the mouth, I said yes immediately.

Five years later, as I write, the resulting book is on the verge of publication.[14] Writing it was the hardest thing I've ever done, at least in a scholarly sense. I discovered huge gaps in my putatively vast knowledge of the American Catholic past. I had been aware of how little I knew about the colonial centuries in North America, especially the work of French and Spanish missionaries. I expected to have to read extensively on this period and assumed—correctly, as it happened—that this would prove to be a gift. I had not expected, however, to have to read extensively on the years of American nationhood and certainly not on the Catholic history of the period since the Civil War. But extensive reading was definitely called for, given how little I actually knew about the specifics of the Catholic past, especially those many specifics with which my previous research had not dealt. Even more vexing were interpretive questions—what to include, what to omit, what meaning to impose on a narrative that ultimately spanned close to five hundred years. Even matters of style were a challenge, since I assumed an audience primarily made up of non-academics who nonetheless merited a serious scholarly offering. Small wonder that the book went slowly, despite my freedom in retirement to plug away at it daily.

For all these reasons, I had some black times as the book proceeded. Had I not signed a contract with the publisher, I would almost certainly have abandoned the project mid-stream. But as I slowly came to realize, even this time of scholarly trial was also a time of gifts. There was the satisfaction of seeing a coherent narrative emerge from the welter of evidence I had accumulated—a narrative that came to possess a plausible degree of thematic coherence. There was the always-renewable joy of learning new things. Best of all was my growing appreciation for the collective nature of historical scholarship. I had to read widely for this project, including older books and articles of the sort often dismissed as dated or scorned as excessively pious and lacking in imagination. Rather to my surprise, I learned a

---

14. Leslie Woodcock Tentler, *American Catholics: A History* (New Haven: Yale University Press, 2020).

lot from such sources. Even dated or unimaginative scholarship, after all, can rest on scrupulous research. I would venture to guess, moreover, that many of our scholarly predecessors, perhaps especially the priests among them, were more formidable linguists than most students of American Catholicism today. Not many of us, alas, can do research in multiple languages. (I confess to knowing only enough Latin to flag a relevant source, which I then convey to my medievalist spouse for translation; I do the same with sources in German.) Humility is a gift, or so it is said, and my reading induced good stores of humility. But most of all, it made me grateful. Our scholarly labors, my reading reminded me, are part of something larger, no matter how dated or unimaginative our own publications may eventually come to seem.

Nearing the end of my career, I have long since come to regard myself as a historian of American Catholicism, although much of my undergraduate teaching was devoted to courses in urban, labor, immigrant, and women's history. Perhaps I simply gave up on the notion that historians of labor or immigration would accept work like mine as relevant to their pursuits. Positive developments, however, have played the major role. The field of American Catholic history has grown and matured, with bright young scholars bringing new energy and long-time practitioners producing work of admirable breadth and sophistication. Who would not be pleased to regard such a lively community as one's own? I don't much like the balkanization so evident among historians of the American past and sometimes fear that presenting myself as a historian of American Catholicism simply contributes to the problem. I am grateful, after all, for my years of teaching courses on subjects other than religion, which helped me to situate my research in broad historical context. But most of us need a scholarly community and participation in such a community almost invariably bestows identity. The trick is to keep that identity from limiting our vision, even as we remain grateful for the many gifts it brings.

www.ingramcontent.com/pod-product-compliance
Lightning Source LLC
Chambersburg PA
CBHW042343300426
44109CB00049B/2773